Approaches to Teaching British Women Poets of the Romantic Period

Edited by

Stephen C. Behrendt

and

Harriet Kramer Linkin

*A gift from the Sonia Raiziss Giop
Charitable Foundation helped
make publication of this book possible.*

The Modern Language Association of America
New York   1997

©1997 by The Modern Language Association of America
All rights reserved. Printed in the United States of America

For information about obtaining permission to reprint material from
MLA book publications, send your request by mail (see address below),
e-mail (permissions@mla.org), or fax (212 533-0680).

Library of Congress Cataloging-in-Publication Data

Approaches to teaching British women poets of the romantic period /
edited by Stephen C. Behrendt and Harriet Kramer Linkin.
p.   cm. — (Approaches to teaching world literature ; 60)
Includes bibliographical references and index.
ISBN 0-87352-743-7 (cloth). — ISBN 0-87352-744-5 (paper)
1. English poetry—Women authors—Study and teaching. 2. English
poetry—Women authors—History and criticism—Theory, etc.
3. English poetry—19th century—History and criticism—Theory, etc.
4. English poetry—18th century—History and criticism—Theory, etc.
5. Women and literature—Great Britain—Study and teaching.
6. English poetry—19th century—Study and teaching. 7. English
poetry—18th century—Study and teaching. 8. Romanticism—Great
Britain—Study and teaching. I. Behrendt, Stephen C., 1947–   .
II. Linkin, Harriet Kramer, 1956–   . III. Series.
PR585.W6A66   1997
821'.709287—dc21   97-34319

ISSN 1059-1133

Cover illustration for the paperback edition: *On Some Rude
Fragment of the Rocky Shore*, engraving from
Elegiac Sonnets and Other Poems, by Charlotte Turner Smith,
7th ed., 1795. Courtesy of the University of Nebraska Libraries.

Set in Caledonia and Bodoni. Printed on recycled paper

Published by The Modern Language Association of America
10 Astor Place, New York, New York 10003-6981

CONTENTS

Preface to the Series   ix

Preface to the Volume   xi

Introduction: An Overview of the Survey *Stephen C. Behrendt*   1

PART ONE: MATERIALS *Harriet Kramer Linkin*

Editions   9
The Instructor's Library   11
    Reference Works   11
    Critical Works   13
Recommended Reading for Students   19

PART TWO: APPROACHES

Introduction *Stephen C. Behrendt*   23

General Issues: Approaching the Texts

Something Evermore About to Be: Teaching and Textbases   25
    Stuart Curran

How Their Audiences Knew Them: Forgotten Media
    and the Circulation of Poetry by Women   32
    Paula R. Feldman

"The Choicest Gifts of Genius": Working with and
    Teaching the Kohler Collection   40
    Jane King and Kari Lokke

"In Tangled Mazes Wrought": Hypertext and Teaching
    Romantic Women Poets   45
    Joel Haefner

Teaching Alien Aesthetics: The Difficulty of Difference
    in the Classroom   51
    Scott Simpkins

Strategies for Replacing the Six-Poet Course   58
    Judith Pascoe

Literature and History: Critical and Theoretical Perspectives

Distinguishing the Poetess from the Female Poet   63
  Anne K. Mellor

Romantic Women's Poetry as Social Movement   69
  Mary A. Favret

Women Poets and Colonial Discourse: Teaching More
  and Yearsley on the Slave Trade   75
  Alan Richardson

Understanding Cultural Contexts: The Politics of Needlework
  in Taylor, Barbauld, Lamb, and Wordsworth   80
  Carol Shiner Wilson

Transatlantic Cultures of Sensibility: Teaching Gender
  and Aesthetics through the Prospect   85
  Julie Ellison

Staging History: Teaching Romantic Intersections of
  Drama, History, and Gender   89
  Greg Kucich

The Aesthetics of Loss: Charlotte Smith's
  The Emigrants and *Beachy Head*   97
  Kay K. Cook

Hemans's "The Widow of Crescentius": Beauty,
  Sublimity, and the Woman Hero   101
  Nanora Sweet

Teaching the Poetry of Mary Tighe: *Psyche,*
  Beauty, and the Romantic Object   106
  Harriet Kramer Linkin

Teaching Individual Poets

Men, Women, and "Fame": Teaching Felicia Hemans   110
  Susan J. Wolfson

Charlotte Smith's Lessons   121
  Sarah M. Zimmerman

Anna Seward, the Swan of Lichfield: Reading *Louisa*   129
  Elizabeth Fay

Joanna Baillie's Poetic Aesthetic: Passion and
  "the Plain Order of Things"   135
  Catherine B. Burroughs

The Milkmaid's Voice: Ann Yearsley and the
  Romantic Notion of the Poet   141
  Madeleine Kahn

Specific Course Contexts and Strategies

Teaching with Annotated Editions   148
    Stephen C. Behrendt

Introducing Felicia Hemans in the First-Year Course   153
    Deborah Kennedy

The Appeal of the Domestic in the First-Year Course:
    Susanna Blamire   157
    Becky Lewis

Gendering Subjectivity: Women Romantics in a
    Poetry Survey Course   161
    Donelle R. Ruwe

Justification Strategies in the Writings of Joanna Southcott:
    Teaching Radical Women Poets in Conservative Institutions   165
    Kevin Binfield

Sight, Sound, and Sense: L. E. L.'s Multimedia Productions   170
    Glenn T. Dibert-Himes

Notes on Contributors   175

Survey Participants   179

Works Cited   181

Index   203

PREFACE TO THE SERIES

In *The Art of Teaching* Gilbert Highet wrote, "Bad teaching wastes a great deal of effort, and spoils many lives which might have been full of energy and happiness." All too many teachers have failed in their work, Highet argued, simply "because they have not thought about it." We hope that the Approaches to Teaching World Literature series, sponsored by the Modern Language Association's Publications Committee, will not only improve the craft—as well as the art—of teaching but also encourage serious and continuing discussion of the aims and methods of teaching literature.

The principal objective of the series is to collect within each volume different points of view on teaching a specific literary work, a literary tradition, or a writer widely taught at the undergraduate level. The preparation of each volume begins with a wide-ranging survey of instructors, thus enabling us to include in the volume the philosophies and approaches, thoughts and methods of scores of experienced teachers. The result is a sourcebook of material, information, and ideas on teaching the subject of the volume to undergraduates.

The series is intended to serve nonspecialists as well as specialists, inexperienced as well as experienced teachers, graduate students who wish to learn effective ways of teaching as well as senior professors who wish to compare their own approaches with the approaches of colleagues in other schools. Of course, no volume in the series can ever substitute for erudition, intelligence, creativity, and sensitivity in teaching. We hope merely that each book will point readers in useful directions; at most each will offer only a first step in the long journey to successful teaching.

Joseph Gibaldi
Series Editor

PREFACE TO THE VOLUME

One of the most exciting developments in literary and cultural studies is the dramatic reevaluation of the British Romantic scene. That scene, we are learning anew, included women far more prominently—and their presence and their influence were acknowledged by their male contemporaries far more generally—than has been appreciated for the last century. Previously marginalized women poets like Helen Maria Williams, Charlotte Turner Smith, Mary Darby Robinson, Mary Tighe, Letitia Elizabeth Landon (L. E. L.), and even Felicia Hemans are today being returned to the Romantic literary landscape from which the post-Romantic culture excised them. Their recovery has itself prompted important investigations of how and why the ostensible custodians of culture in the literary, literary-critical, and publishing establishments engineered their removal. On both sides of the Atlantic teacher-scholars and their students are earnestly participating in this project of rediscovery. The most profound consequence of their efforts will be a thorough redrawing of the literary and cultural landscape. For it is immediately apparent that the British Romantic movement as many of us have long known it is in fact a historically and culturally inaccurate construct.

Recent years have witnessed new and serious attention to the prose of Romantic women writers. But literary history has, under the guise of objective scholarly criticism, continued to mask a significant part of the period's dynamic literary scene by excluding the visible and influential contributions of women poets to the period's literary culture. The principal result has been the evolution and ossification of a narrow and often masculinist ideological paradigm of Romantic poetry, one that profoundly misrepresents historical and cultural reality by minimizing or entirely ignoring the striking diversity of the period's poetry. Although feminist and new-historicist criticism in particular have recently helped deconstruct prevailing notions about the Romantic ideology, the current flourishing of interest in women writers of the period was necessary to accelerate the process in earnest.

The liberating and invigorating task of redrawing the landscape of Romantic poetry still faces serious obstacles. First, the traditional gendered notions about the Romantic period—and about Romantic poetry in particular—are so deeply entrenched both in culture and in the academic curricula that many of us have until fairly recently been virtually blind to what has been left out of our classrooms, our textbooks and anthologies, and scholarly inquiry in general. Second, typical courses in Romantic poetry are generally stuffed to the bursting point already with just the work of the major canonical male poets; adding the women, one may rationalize, risks rendering one's courses impossibly unwieldy on the one hand or, on the other, possibly diluted. This anxiety arises, though, from a long-standing, unthinking adherence on the part of many of us to the entrenched Romantic canon and to our assumptions about it. Further, many of us may have resisted radical change in the canon because it necessarily jeopardizes both the overall structure of and the assumptions behind courses in which we have invested time, effort, and ideological capital.

Perhaps our main challenge, therefore, lies in exploring new ways of thinking about the value of the poetry women produced during the Romantic period. The burgeoning discussion of this subject, at conferences and in print, reveals both how strong and widespread are the winds of change and how irresistible and sweeping will be the changes that are already becoming apparent. The highly visible rush to revise existing anthologies and to generate new ones in order to accommodate rediscovered women poets tells us something important about the current direction of scholarship and teaching in Romantics studies. All this activity points to the very real appetite for the work of these neglected writers and to the profound effect their inclusion is certain to have on our conception of British Romanticism.

The first section of this book, "Materials," makes some preliminary observations about issues involved in teaching the women poets of the Romantic period and recommends relevant primary and secondary materials and resources that experienced instructors have found useful. In preparation for the essays that follow, this section also reports on the replies to our survey questionnaire, passing along the good advice our colleagues offered and summarizing the types of information they said they would like to see in this volume.

In the "Approaches" section instructors discuss classroom strategies for teaching the women poets. While these essays reflect a considerable diversity of critical, theoretical, and methodological perspectives, each contributor directly or indirectly emphasizes pedagogy, as is usual in the Approaches series. This section also includes several essays treating particular textual, archival, and technological resources. Since the availability of adequate texts is likely to remain a problem for years, many instructors will find particular value in these essays, which describe such matters as electronic textbases and computer-assisted teaching, highlighting ways in which instructors can—indeed already do—prepare alternative, supplementary texts designed for their individual needs.

We want to acknowledge first Joseph Gibaldi, general editor of this series, for his initial interest in the project and for his encouragement from the start. Likewise Sonia Kane, who has provided valuable editorial assistance and sage advice throughout the process leading to print. We wish to thank too our colleagues in the classroom, who responded to our project with great generosity of intellect and of spirit; the preliminary survey elicited a remarkable amount of information and insight, together with far more excellent essay proposals than we could accommodate. Most striking of all have been the enthusiasm and urgency that have permeated all our exchanges with our respondents and contributors—actual and potential. It has been a particular pleasure to read and consider this abundance of creative suggestions, insightful material, and ingenious and innovative plans for teaching. To be able to share even a portion of this wealth of wisdom is most gratifying to us. We are all familiar with the overwork that plagues many of our colleagues, and yet we have received, time and again, lengthy, thoughtful, and stimulating communications—whether e-mail notes, formal letters, or finished essays—that reveal the vitality of intellect that informs our profession and that point to the inventive and thoroughly committed teaching at institutions of every sort, involving students at all levels of interest and expertise. We thank especially the colleagues who contributed the essays included here, all of whom responded promptly and courteously—and patiently—to our requests for revisions, editorial adjustments, and plain tinkering.

We also want to thank our institutions, the University of Nebraska and New Mexico State University, for supporting us in this project.

Stephen C. Behrendt

Harriet Kramer Linkin

Introduction: An Overview of the Survey

Several things became apparent immediately from the responses to the preliminary survey of instructors that informs the present volume. First, the enormous surge of interest in the women poets of the Romantic period is accompanied by an urgent need for good modern, scholarly editions of the primary texts. The first such work, Stuart Curran's edition of Charlotte Smith's poetry, is already widely used in a variety of classroom situations; indeed, the edition's availability undoubtedly contributes to the central presence of Smith on so many syllabi. A second, William McCarthy and Elizabeth Kraft's edition of Anna Letitia Barbauld's poetry, is also reliable, though its expensive hardbound-only format largely precludes its adoption for the classroom. When it comes to anthologies and other multiauthor collections, the situation is vexed. As of this writing, no anthology entirely satisfies most survey respondents, although several promising ones are imminent and two others have recently appeared (see "Editions," in part 1, "Materials"). The Everyman (Dent) anthology edited by Jennifer Breen is widely used, mainly because it is relatively inexpensive and widely available, but most respondents are dissatisfied with its scanty selections and its inclusion of principally short, sentimental, lyric verse rather than a more broad selection of types, genres, and subject-matter concerns that would better represent women's poetry of the period. As one respondent put it, "Women poets need to be seen as the authors of long works, not just of short ones." In particular the long narrative poetry has been overlooked, and explicitly political poetry has received especially slight attention. Now that Andrew Ashfield's anthology is at last widely available in America, it will almost certainly become the paperback text of choice for many instructors, at least for the moment. Well-annotated and featuring a more extensive selection of poems than any earlier anthology of this kind, this anthology does for the Romantic period to some extent what Roger Lonsdale's well-regarded anthology of women poets did for the eighteenth century. While some colleagues criticize Ashfield for excerpting poems like Barbauld's *Eighteen Hundred and Eleven* and Smith's *The Emigrants* and others lament the poor selection of poems from Felicia Hemans and Letitia Elizabeth Landon in particular, the anthology is nevertheless valuable.

Happily, publishers are responding to the need for anthologies that take a more inclusive view of the poetry of the Romantic period. Jerome J. McGann's *New Oxford Book of Romantic Period Verse* and Duncan Wu's *Romanticism: An Anthology* take a step in this direction, although the integration of the poets represented, women and men, major and minor, is not as seamless as many respondents appear to have desired; in response Wu is preparing a substantially revised edition. Further, a CD-ROM version of the anthology, produced by David Miall, contains all the texts, supplemented with additional poems, critical materials, and multimedia enhancements. However, women's writing still accounts, disappointingly, for less than ten percent of the much-anticipated new edition of David Perkins's *English Romantic Writers*. Several new anthologies by scholars directly involved in the recovery of marginalized writers dramatically increase the range and scope of materials available to teachers. Since Paula R. Feldman set out deliberately to avoid duplicating in her anthology poetry that is already widely accessible, she expands still further the corpus of primary texts. The determinedly alternative anthology edited by Anne K. Mellor and Richard Matlak, *British Literature, 1780–1830*, addresses this complicated matter in ways that many instructors are likely to find helpful and productive, since it provides not just primary literary texts but also a fine selection of illuminating historical, critical, scientific, and otherwise contextual materials.

Secondary materials are comparably scarce. Several groundbreaking studies (most prominently those of Stuart Curran, Margaret Homans, Anne Mellor, Marlon Ross, and Glennis Stephenson) have opened up scholarly discourse, but clearly a great deal remains to be done on individual women poets, on the poets as variously configured groups (or constellations), and on the poets in relation to their male literary and cultural contemporaries. This work is going forward in earnest, but its full effect will not be apparent for some years. Meanwhile, much additional research and publication is needed simply to recover the lives, the histories, the circumstances, and the sociopolitical and cultural contexts of the women poets, about many of whom we know surprisingly little. Ostensibly scholarly studies on many are old and outdated and are informed by assumptions about the place of the woman writer—assumptions that modern scholarship and sensibilities reject.

And despite the genuine interest and enthusiasm many instructors have brought to teaching these poets, both in Romantic period courses and in broader offerings, most respondents are anxious to learn how others are approaching the poets. As when any noncanonical writers are introduced into the curriculum, instructors feel an inevitable insecurity teaching writers with whom they may have had no prior classroom experience. These anxieties are necessarily magnified tenfold when the works by the array of writers in question have been marginalized, ignored, or erased for at least a century and when the authors' place and identity have likewise been misrepresented or erased—as happened with these women poets after the creation of the Romantic ideology. This ideology, characterized by its stereotypical image of the aloof, visionary, male poet of grand idealisms and bardic bearing, finds no place for the woman poet. Nevertheless, twentieth-century views of British Romanticism have been dominated by this ideology and by its inaccurate and reductive image of both Romanticism and its poets. Instructors now wrestle with the exciting but daunting project of catching up—of revisioning what we understand by Romanticism—in order to recover a vast number of heretofore largely invisible texts. Many respondents greatly desired a forum for sharing with others their experiences teaching this new body of material. For example, one respondent wished for an arena for exchange of strategies for developing a conception of Romanticism that pays greater attention to women's poetry.

Finally, to our query about the most important requirement for successful classroom teaching of these poets, one colleague gave perhaps the most telling response: "A longer semester!" Most instructors, constrained by the one-term survey of Romantic poetry that is standard in many departments, are already hard-pressed to cover the traditional big six canonical male poets (Blake, Wordsworth, Coleridge, Byron, Shelley, Keats). Given the riches that are emerging from the recovery of the women poets and given too the reevaluation of marginalized *male* poets of the period, instructors are understandably concerned about accommodating everything and everyone necessary to the revisioning of British Romanticism and its poets. This concern, we believe, extends beyond poetry alone; that is, in reconceptualizing Romanticism, scholars should consider genre as well as gender. The Romantic dramatic literature designed for stage production (Baillie's *DeMonfort*, for instance, as opposed to strictly metaphysical dramas like Shelley's *Prometheus Unbound*) remains insufficiently studied, and the influence of this considerable body of material on Romantic poetry and fiction has never been adequately examined. There is room too for the popular media—sensational fiction, the periodical press, and the caricature print— all of which likewise helped shape Romantic poetry by women and men alike. The dilemma that instructors confront at every turn becomes readily apparent when one considers not just authors (female and male) but also literary genres (drama, memoirs, letters, history, popular fiction and poetry, and protest literature of many sorts) that have been marginalized or expunged from the curriculum—and hence, for many of us and our students, from the literary scene—by the constraints imposed by the duration of academic terms in our institutions.

In other words, how are we to fit everyone in without hopelessly diluting our courses or creating an unproductive superficiality and seeming lack of focus? Voicing the concerns of many and epitomizing the challenge facing scholars, teachers, and students at this time, one respondent remarked that the essays would be most useful "if they dealt with the correlation of women poets to male poets or to the larger poetic tradition, and if they engaged the issue of how reading women poets challenges conventional notions of the Romantic period." For the foreseeable future, courses in Romantic poetry are likely to be far more concerned than they have been in the past with remapping the literary landscape and in the process redefining Romanticism in more historically accurate, and more ideologically generous, terms than has traditionally been the case. At the same time, teachers whose primary course emphases are not specifically in Romanticism but who choose to include women poets of the Romantic period will need to explore with their students these same issues. That exploration, recovery, and redefinition cannot but be healthy for all concerned (including the authors), however much anxiety and uncertainty it may at first seem to produce. These needs supply part of the impetus for the present volume.

The British women poets of the Romantic period are taught, in varying combinations, in courses ranging from general studies and introductory literature courses for nonmajors to advanced graduate courses in specific authors, themes, and topics. In addition, these poets are beginning to appear in the readings for entry-level writing courses, as well as in courses in women's studies at all levels. One common element in these courses is the enthusiastic response among the students—particularly, but not exclusively, the women—to their discovery of a group of writers who speak to the interests and experiences of modern women. That such writers existed, and indeed flourished, in a literary period whose reputation and received ideology is overwhelmingly masculinist comes as a pleasant and generally instructive surprise to students of both sexes. One respondent observed, "My female students are thirsty for literature that places them, as women, in a historical literary context." Moreover, the excitement that many students experience in participating themselves in this process of literary recovery is often heightened by the ways in which the work of these poets both contributes to and diverges from the traditional rubric of Romanticism. One respondent put it this way: "Students are interested in the fact that while many of these poets were extraordinarily popular during the Romantic period, the students themselves have usually not heard of the women they are reading. As a result, they delight in what seems to them a special 'discovery.' They like it when they recognize subjects, themes, and ideas shared by both female and male Romantic poets." Especially in courses that specifically focus on the Romantic context, though, a new critical and cultural awareness begins to emerge as "students start to see differences, first between female and male visions and then among male visions; in other words, they begin to see all the poets more as individuals than as examples of a particular ideology." Moreover, working inside and outside the classroom with these writers better attunes students to the often very different aesthetic assumptions that inform these women's poetry. This work also helps students interrogate the criteria of intrinsic worth and aesthetic value that have often been invoked to shape literary canons by privileging one sort of writing and excluding others whose assumptions, procedures, and products do not conform to the privileged model.

Whether the poets are taught in combination with their male contemporaries, which is by far the most common approach, or on their own, most colleagues pay particular attention to the authors' literary, sociopolitical, and cultural contexts. Thus it is hardly surprising that while feminist theory and feminist methodologies inform the research and teaching of most respondents, new-historicist and cultural studies approaches rank high on the list of corollary orientations, as do more familiar historicist approaches. Somewhat less frequent, but still numerous, were mentions of groundings in aesthetic and rhetorical theory. Still less common were approaches building on reception theory and reader-response criticism, biographical (including psychobiographical) criticism, psychosocial theory (Carol Gilligan's work on female psychology was expressly singled out), and psycholinguistics. Few respondents even mentioned the debate over essentialism and social construction or seem to have regarded it as particularly relevant. Perhaps more surprising was the absence among responses of Marxist theory, which may indicate the extent to which issues of gender appear to take priority over the issues of class with which they are often connected; this despite Donna Landry's well-known study of eighteenth-century working-class women's poetry.

Indeed, while economic issues are clearly of interest to those whose perspectives include new historicism and cultural studies, few instructors appear to treat very extensively in their classes the pragmatic issues of economics affecting these women, many of whom wrote for a living during the later eighteenth century and the first half of the nineteenth. It is therefore significant that few people mentioned the fertile relation between poetry and other forms of writing by women—the novel in particular; here the work of scholars like Cheryl Turner, Dale Spender, Terry Lovell, Kathleen Hickok, and Gaye Tuchman, who specifically emphasize economic considerations in the writing and marketing of fiction, holds important potential for teachers of poetry. The responses point up the critical need for further study of the demographics of authorship, readerships, and publication—who published what, where, at what price, in how many copies, and for whom?—as they relate to women poets and their male counterparts alike.

Who gets taught, then? Not surprisingly, the answer reflects the availability of texts and the inclusion of authors in mass-market anthologies. Most often taught, to about the same extent, are Charlotte Smith, Mary Robinson, Dorothy Wordsworth, and Felicia Hemans; Anna Letitia Barbauld, Letitia Elizabeth Landon (L. E. L.), Helen Maria Williams, and Anna Seward, also taught in roughly the same frequency, form a second echelon. As is clear from many of the essays in this collection, instructors are most characteristically guided in their choices by the practical necessities of the aim and scope statements that govern their courses. Surveys have to *survey* the scene, thematic courses have to stay on track, and so on. But the creativity of instructors working with this exciting new body of material is matched only by the richness of the material itself.

It is perhaps appropriate here to say a word or two about the implications for Romantics studies generally of the explosion of interest in the women poets (and indeed in women writers in all the genres) during the period. One consequence will surely be a new interest in looking at texts themselves. While there is little likelihood of a return to the sort of narrowly defined formalism of movements like New Criticism, we are likely to see readers and scholars concentrating more on the recovered works themselves than they have on more familiar canonical works. Simply getting acquainted with this extraordinary body of material will occupy us for some time.

Of course, this reading will inevitably be informed by the whole range of contemporary critical and theoretical approaches. A large part of the task, after all, involves contextualizing this poetry and situating it both within its contemporary cultural milieu as best as we can reconstruct it and within our contemporary critical and intellectual consciousness of the vast otherness of that material and those times. Accomplishing these tasks will necessarily mean reassessing as well virtually every other received opinion about Romanticism: its parameters, its preoccupations, its ideals, its literary forms, and its authors and its canon. The danger, which is endemic to all literary and cultural studies subject to the time and space constraints of academic terms, is that we may replace old canons with new, old familiarities with new, and old carelessnesses about issues of gender, class, and race with new (perhaps more fashionable) carelessnesses. Many respondents to our survey worry about this ossification, whether openly or only implicitly. And with good reason. For as literary history reminds us at every turn, structures tend to solidify as soon as we cease tinkering with them. Even concrete, after all, does dry eventually, and one can carve initials into its surface only for so long. Our challenge is to keep the structures—and the intellectual and pedagogical assumptions that underlie and inform them—fluid, while striving to make greater sense of their components for ourselves, our colleagues, and our students. In this respect the current effort to recover, assess, and teach the poetry written by British women during the Romantic period is not just historically and pedagogically worthwhile, it is also intellectually and professionally healthy.

The twenty-first century is certain to witness the exciting (albeit anxious) processes of sifting and winnowing textual and contextual materials, of reassessing and reorienting the crucial aspects of our conception of Romanticism, and of reformulating ourselves both as scholars and as teachers who will help shape the next generations of scholars and teachers.

Part One

MATERIALS

Editions

The greatest obstacle to teaching the women poets of the Romantic period has been the absence of good, reasonably priced scholarly editions and anthologies. As one respondent put it, "The most important need for successful classroom teaching of these poets is a first-rate textbook." Happily, by the time this collection appears instructors should have a number of choices. Two important comprehensive Romantic anthologies published in 1994 intersperse good if limited selections of women's poetry among the more extensive selections from the men: Duncan Wu's *Romanticism: An Anthology* and the second, revised edition of David Perkins's *English Romantic Writers* (however, representation of women in the latter is still lamentably meager, both in the texts and in the updated bibliography). The American publication of Andrew Ashfield's *Women Romantic Poets, 1770–1838* occurred in 1995 after much delay. And in 1996 and 1997 superior anthologies appeared: Anne K. Mellor and Richard Matlak's *British Literature, 1780–1830*, Wu's *Romantic Women Poets*, and Paula R. Feldman's *British Women Poets of the Romantic Era*. Several earlier anthologies will likely remain available, although many respondents expressed reservations about them, including Jennifer Breen's *Women Romantic Poets: 1785–1832* (partially corrected and reprinted in 1994) and Jerome J. McGann's *The New Oxford Book of Romantic Period Verse*. Roger Lonsdale's *Eighteenth-Century Women Poets* overlaps the beginning of the Romantic period, as do Robert W. Uphaus and Gretchen M. Foster's *The Other Eighteenth Century* and Katharine M. Rogers and William McCarthy's *The Meridian Anthology of Early Women Writers*. Sandra M. Gilbert and Susan Gubar's *Norton Anthology of Literature by Women* and Ann Stanford's *The Women Poets in English* provide useful long historical perspectives, even if their selections of Romantic poetry are disappointingly short. Instructors might also turn to more specialized anthologies for additional materials, including Betty T. Bennett's thematic *British War Poetry in the Age of Romanticism: 1793–1815* and Moira Ferguson's *First Feminists: British Women Writers, 1578–1799*.

Modern scholarly editions of individual writers are beginning to appear; William McCarthy and Elizabeth Kraft's *The Poems of Anna Letitia Barbauld* is a welcome addition to Stuart Curran's *The Poems of Charlotte Smith*, which surely sets the standard for classroom editions. Volumes forthcoming or under contract include Judith Pascoe's *The Poems of Mary Robinson*, Mitzi Myers's *The Poems of Jane Taylor*, Gary Kelly and Susan Wolfson's *Felicia Hemans: Selected Poems*, and Feldman's *The Poems of Felicia Hemans*. The appendix to Susan Levin's *Dorothy Wordsworth and Romanticism* contains a fairly complete collection of that poet's work. Woodstock and Garland publish important reprint series that make available rare or out-of-print books, though editions in both series are priced well beyond classroom budgets. Nevertheless the Woodstock series of facsimile reprints, chosen and introduced by Jonathan

Wordsworth, provides editions of Susanna Blamire, Isabella Lickbarrow, Anna Seward, Helen Maria Williams, Ann Yearsley, Joanna Baillie, Mary Robinson, Felicia Hemans, Anna Letitia Barbauld, Caroline Bowles, Letitia Elizabeth Landon, Charlotte Smith, and Mary Tighe. The Garland series, edited by Donald Reiman, makes available Joanna Baillie, Mary Betham, Charlotte Dacre, Felicia Hemans, Amelia Opie, and Mary Tighe, among others. And a new twelve-volume set edited by Caroline Franklin for Routledge, *The Romantics: Women Poets of the Romantic Period, 1770–1830*, provides still other texts.

Nevertheless, teachers will certainly need to continue to rely—though less heavily than in the past—on materials they have gathered themselves. Currently, many instructors assemble and photocopy their own handouts and readers or course packs from materials that they own or have secured through libraries or personal research. An invaluable although occasionally cumbersome resource is the electronic-text database of early women writers at Brown University's Women Writers Project. It provides a considerable selection of women's poetry and prose published before 1830; all of it is available in photocopies for teaching or research purposes, and there are plans to make much of it available electronically (some of the Renaissance materials are already available in this form). McGann promises to make available a larger text database for online access through "British Poetry, 1780–1910: A Hypertext Archive of Scholarly Editions" (with David Seaman), based at the University of Virginia (http://etext.lib .virginia.edu/britpo.html). Those with computer acumen might also use such tools as Veronica to find e-text sources. Other Internet sites are sure to have appeared by the time this volume is published. Two particularly active and useful sites are "The Voice of the Shuttle: Web Page for Humanities Research," at the University of California, Santa Barbara (http://humanitas.ucsb.edu), and PEAL, a text archive at the University of Pennsylvania (gopher://dept.english .upenn.edu:70/11/E-Text/PEAL). Finally, "Romantic Chronology," an evolving Web project spearheaded by Laura Mandell and Alan Liu (http://humanitas .ucsb.edu/projects/pack/rom-chrono/chrono.htm), offers an expanding textual and historical archive that should make the World Wide Web an active and productive place indeed for Romanticists.

A number of instructors make profitable use of early anthologies like Alexander Dyce's *Specimens of British Poetesses* (1827), George Bethune's *The Female Poets: With Biographical and Critical Notices* (1848), Frederic Rowton's *The Female Poets of Great Britain* (1850), Robert Chambers's *Cyclopaedia of English Literature* (1853), and Sarah Josepha Hale's *Woman's Record; or, Sketches of All Distinguished Women, from Creation to AD 1854* (1855) to duplicate materials for the classroom that situate women's poetry in a larger historical context. The differing qualities and widely ranging sensibilities that inform these anthologies can provide dramatic lessons in the dynamics of canon formation in the course of offering access to women's poetry.

The Instructor's Library

The following review of secondary materials available to the instructor is by no means comprehensive. Many of the secondary materials we and our survey respondents regard as important are not exclusively or specifically about the women poets whose works are the focus of this collection. But these materials are important to an instructor who wishes to get a better sense of the historical and cultural contexts for those poets, as well as of emerging modern critical and theoretical responses to them and to women writers generally. A number of the materials recommended, then, point—directly or indirectly—toward the broader contexts in which women's poetry of the Romantic period is being taught, just as they help reestablish the contexts in which it was written.

Reference Works

Bibliographic resources necessarily begin with J. R. de J. Jackson's remarkably extensive *Romantic Poetry by Women: A Bibliography, 1770–1835*. This work is helpfully supplemented by Gwenn Davis and Beverly A. Joyce's *Poetry by Women to 1900: A Bibliography of American and British Writers* (companion volumes cover drama and fiction), R. C. Alston's *A Checklist of Women Writers, 1801–1900: Fiction, Verse, Drama*, Marilyn Williamson's annotations to the facsimile edition of Rowton's *Female Poets*, and Ferguson's *First Feminists*. Jackson's *Annals of English Verse, 1770–1835: A Preliminary Survey of the Volumes Published* indicates the place of women's poetry in the period generally, cataloging poetry publications year by year and revealing the vastness of the corpus of formally published Romantic verse. It is still difficult to trace poems that appeared in periodicals, although new definitive scholarly editions of individual poets will help establish much of what the writers published there under their own names or under pseudonyms. Two useful resources for such tracing include Andrew Boyle's *An Index to the Annuals* and Frederick W. Faxon's *Literary Annuals and Gift Books: A Bibliography, 1823–1903*.

We still lack modern collections or editions that gather or discuss contemporary reviews of women's poetry, such as J. G. Lockhart's "Modern English Poetesses," though several such projects are under way. Consequently, instructors must track down this material, usually available on microform, for themselves. William S. Ward's four-volume set *Literary Reviews in British Periodicals: A Bibliography* is particularly helpful; it covers 1789–1826 and offers excellent guidance to published reviews of women's and men's writing (in all genres) from the period. The brief essays in the four volumes of *British Literary Magazines*, prepared under the general editorship of Alvin Sullivan, trace periodicals' intellectual and—often more important—political orientations and their publication policies; thus the volumes provide scholars great help in assessing original reviews. Additional resources that identify or usefully contextualize materials from periodicals include John Clive's *Scotch Reviewers: The Edinburgh Review, 1802–1815*, John O. Hayden's *The Romantic Reviewers, 1802–1824*, James M. Kuist's *The Nichols File of the Gentleman's Magazine: Attributions of Authorship and Other Documentation in Editorial Papers at the Folger Library*, Benjamin Christie Nangle's *The* Monthly Review, *Second Series, 1790–1818: Indexes of Contributors and Articles*, Frank Riga and Claude A. Prance's *Index to the* London Magazine, and Alan Strout's *A Bibliography of Articles in* Blackwood's Magazine, *Volumes I through XVIII, 1817–1825*.

Biographical materials are distressingly scarce and generally brief. The principal sources are Janet Todd's *Dictionary of British and American Women Writers, 1660–1800* and her *Dictionary of Women Writers*. Lonsdale's *Eighteenth-Century Women Poets: An Oxford Anthology* contains brief sketches of the earlier writers, as do the invaluable *The Feminist Companion to Literature in English: Women Writers from the Middle Ages to the Present*, edited by Virginia Blain, Patricia Clements, and Isobel Grundy; Claire Buck's *The Bloomsbury Guide to Women's Literature*; Joanne Shattock's *The Oxford Guide to British Women Writers*; Laura Dabundo's *Encyclopedia of Romanticism: Culture in Britain, 1780s–1830s*; and Margaret Drabble's *The Oxford Companion to English Literature*. Although many entries in the *Dictionary of National Biography* are outdated, it remains an important resource, as does the *Dictionary of Literary Biography*. For biographies of individual women poets, respondents recommend such classic but older works as Margaret S. Carhart's *The Life and Work of Joanna Baillie* and Florence Hilbish's *Charlotte Smith, Poet and Novelist (1749–1806)*.

Like older anthologies, earlier biographical resources not only provide a wealth of primary and secondary materials but also foreground cultural and historical perspectives in important ways. Among these works are Mary Matilda Betham's *A Biographical Dictionary of the Celebrated Women of Every Age and Country* (1804), Mary Hays's *Female Biography; or, Memoirs of Illustrious and Celebrated Women of All Ages and Countries* (1803), and Anne Katharine Elwood's *Memoirs of the Literary Ladies of England, from the Commencement of the Last Century* (1843). While information presented must be treated with caution (erroneous citations are repeated from one resource to another), pertinent and often provocative entries on women poets of the Romantic period are located in Anna Maria Lee's *Memoirs of Eminent Female Writers* (1827), Samuel L. Knapp's *Female Biography: Containing Notices of Distinguished Women, in Different Nations and Ages* (1834), Bethune's *Female Poets* (1848), Hale's *Woman's Record* (1855), Jane Williams's *The Literary Women of England* (1861), Eric S. Robertson's *English Poetesses: A Series of Critical Biographies, with Illustrative Extracts* (1883), and Janet E. Courtney's *The Adventurous Thirties: A Chapter in the Women's Movement* (1933). Not to be overlooked is John Boyer Nichols's nine-volume set *Literary Anecdotes of the Eighteenth Century* (1812–15) and his eight-volume *Illustrations of the Literary History of the Eighteenth Century: Consisting of Authentic Memoirs and Original Letters of Eminent Persons* (1817–58).

Critical Works

Given the rich variety of theoretical perspectives from which instructors approach the writings of women poets, the scope of critical works recommended by survey respondents for teachers coming to these poets for the first time ranges widely. Some of the secondary studies identified as important extend beyond the boundaries delineated by genre, period, nationality, and even gender. Many respondents pointed to the need to reconsider aesthetic assumptions and to expand awareness of various political and social pressures; as one person remarked, "I had to retrain myself as a reader to particularly engage these writers: the internalized codes of culture had to be read, not metaphysical truths." The studies recommended by survey respondents tend to focus as often on the cultural production of texts as on the poets.

Among works specifically treating women poets of the British Romantic period, those most frequently cited as indispensable include Curran's groundbreaking essay "Romantic Poetry: The 'I' Altered," Marlon B. Ross's *The Contours of Masculine Desire: Romanticism and the Rise of Women's Poetry*, and Mellor's *Romanticism and Gender*. Mellor's collection *Romanticism and Feminism* is also repeatedly recommended, as is Curran's *Cambridge Companion to British Romanticism*, particularly for the two essays Curran contributes to the volume, "Women Readers, Women Writers" and "Romantic Poetry: Why and Wherefore?," as well as his valuable if brief introduction to *The Poems of Charlotte Smith*. McGann's "Poetry, 1785–1832" in *The Columbia History of British Poetry*, edited by Carl Woodring, provides an important dialogical overview of a Romantic period that includes women poets; McGann's frequently recommended "Literary History, Romanticism, and Felicia Hemans" (published under the names Anne Mack, J. J. Rome, and Georg Mannejc) offers a more localized example of inclusion, as does Joel Haefner's "(De)Forming the Romantic Canon: The Case of Women Writers." Respondents cite Irene Tayler and Gina Luria's "Gender and Genre: Women in British Romantic Literature" as an early essay that continues to raise fundamental questions about the place of women poets in Romanticism.

Several recent collections offer immediately useful essays that focus on women poets, notably Mary Favret and Nicola Watson's *At the Limits of Romanticism: Essays in Cultural, Feminist, and Materialist Criticism*, which includes Lucinda Cole and Richard G. Swartz's "'Why Should I Wish for Words?': Literacy, Articulation, and the Borders of Literary Culture" and Nanora Sweet's "History, Imperialism, and the Aesthetics of the Beautiful: Hemans and the Post-Napoleonic Moment"; Carol Shiner Wilson and Haefner's *Re-visioning Romanticism: British Women Writers, 1776–1837*, with Curran's

"Mary Robinson's *Lyrical Tales* in Context," Ross's "Configurations of Feminine Reform: The Woman Writer and the Tradition of Dissent," Jane Aaron's "The Way above the World: Religion and Gender in Welsh and Anglo-Welsh Women's Writing, 1780–1830," Susan J. Wolfson's "'Domestic Affections' and 'the Spear of Minerva': Felicia Hemans and the Dilemma of Gender," Carol Shiner Wilson's "Lost Needles, Tangled Threads: Stitchery, Domesticity, and the Artistic Enterprise in Barbauld, Edgeworth, Taylor, and Lamb," Pascoe's "Female Botanists and the Poetry of Charlotte Smith," Julie Ellison's "The Politics of Fancy in the Age of Sensibility," and Haefner's "The Romantic Scene(s) of Writing"; Feldman and Theresa M. Kelley's *Romantic Women Writers: Voices and Countervoices*, which includes Isobel Armstrong's "The Gush of the Feminine: How Can We Read Women's Poetry of the Romantic Period?," Wolfson's "Gendering the Soul," McCarthy's "'We Hoped the *Woman* Was Going to Appear': Repression, Desire, and Gender in Anna Letitia Barbauld's Early Poems," Anthony John Harding's "Felicia Hemans and the Effacement of Woman," and Pascoe's "Mary Robinson and the Literary Marketplace"; and Alan Richardson and Sonia Hofkosh's *Romanticism, Race, and Imperial Culture, 1780–1834*, with essays including Nancy Moore Goslee's "Hemans's 'Red Indians': Reading Stereotypes," Richardson's "Epic Ambivalence: Imperial Politics and Romantic Deflection in Williams' *Peru* and Landor's *Gebir*," and Mellor's "'Am I Not a Woman, and a Sister?': Slavery, Romanticism, and Gender."

Additional articles published in collections or journals that provide important critical work on individual women poets include John Anderson's "'The First Fire': Barbauld Rewrites the Greater Romantic Lyric," Curran's "Charlotte Smith and British Romanticism," Moira Ferguson's "Resistance and Power in the Life and Writings of Ann Yearsley," Germaine Greer's "The Tulsa Center for the Study of Women's Literature: What We Are Doing and Why We Are Doing It" (which takes Landon as a case in point), Deborah Kennedy's "Storms of Sorrow: The Poetry of Helen Maria Williams" and "Thorns and Roses: The Sonnets of Charlotte Smith," Harriet Kramer Linkin's "Romanticism and Mary Tighe's *Psyche*: Peering at the Hem of Her Blue Stockings," Tricia Lootens's "Hemans and Home: Victorianism, Feminine 'Internal Enemies,' and the Domestication of National Identity," Pascoe's "'The Spectacular Flaneuse': Mary Robinson and the City of London," Daniel Robinson's "Reviving the Sonnet: Women Romantic Poets and the Sonnet Claim," Glennis Stephenson's "Poet Construction: Mrs. Hemans, L. E. L., and the Image of the Nineteenth-Century Woman Poet" and "Letitia Landon and the Victorian Improvisatrice: The Construction of L. E. L." (both of which inform her full-length study *Letitia Landon: The Woman behind L. E. L.*), and Mary Waldron's "Ann Yearsley and the Clifton Records."

Highly recommended studies that at times move beyond the strict parameters of women's poetry of the British Romantic period include Jane Aaron's *A Double Singleness: Gender and the Writings of Charles and Mary Lamb*, Meena Alexander's *Women in Romanticism: Mary Wollstonecraft, Dorothy*

Wordsworth, and Mary Shelley, Isobel Armstrong's *Victorian Poetry: Poetry, Poetics, and Politics*, Norma Clarke's *Ambitious Heights: Writing, Friendship, Love: The Jewsbury Sisters, Felicia Hemans, and Jane Welsh Carlyle*, George Dekker's *Coleridge and the Literature of Sensibility*, Lillian Faderman's *Surpassing the Love of Men: Romantic Friendship and Love between Women from the Renaissance to the Present*, Moira Ferguson's *Subject to Others: British Women Writers and Colonial Slavery, 1670–1834* and her *Eighteenth-Century Women Poets: Nation, Class, and Gender*, Kathleen Hickok's *Representations of Women: Nineteenth-Century British Women's Poetry*, Margaret Homans's *Women Writers and Poetic Identity* and *Bearing the Word: Language and Female Experience in Nineteenth-Century Women's Writing*, Donna Landry's *The Muses of Resistance: Laboring-Class Women's Poetry in Britain, 1739–1796*, Angela Leighton's *Victorian Women Poets: Writing against the Heart*, Levin's *Dorothy Wordsworth and Romanticism*, Sylvia Haverstock Myers's *The Bluestocking Circle: Women, Friendship, and the Life of the Mind in Eighteenth-Century England*, and Irene Tayler's *Holy Ghosts: The Male Muses of Emily and Charlotte Brontë*.

To this list of works that focus at least in part on the topic at hand, we add the respondents' recommendations of critical studies whose subjects certainly fall outside the expected parameters but that are nevertheless important, insofar as they establish a broader sphere of women's writings and thus contextualize the contributions of these women poets to or through the writing culture of their times.

The many full-scale studies that are useful to the instructor, though they examine women primarily as writers of prose, include classic works of feminist criticism from the 1960s and 1970s, namely, Patricia Meyer Spacks's *The Female Imagination*, Ellen Moers's *Literary Women: The Great Writers*, Elaine Showalter's *A Literature of Their Own: British Women Novelists from Brontë to Lessing*, and Gilbert and Gubar's *The Madwoman in the Attic: The Woman Writer and the Nineteenth-Century Literary Imagination*. Similarly focused feminist critiques from the 1980s include Judith Lowder Newton's *Women, Power, and Subversion: Social Strategies in British Fiction, 1778–1860*, Mary Poovey's *The Proper Lady and the Woman Writer: Ideology as Style in the Works of Mary Wollstonecraft, Mary Shelley, and Jane Austen*, Leslie Rabine's *Reading the Romantic Heroine: Text, History, and Ideology*, Jane Spencer's *The Rise of the Woman Novelist from Aphra Behn to Jane Austen*, Nina Auerbach's *Romantic Imprisonment: Women and Other Glorified Outcasts* and *Communities of Women: An Idea in Fiction*, Nancy Armstrong's *Desire and Domestic Fiction: A Political History of the Novel*, and Patricia Yaeger's *Honey-Mad Women: Emancipatory Strategies in Women's Writing*. Among the more recent studies, respondents recommend Laurie Langbauer's *Women and Romance: The Consolations of Gender in the English Novel*, Todd's *The Sign of Angellica: Women, Writing, and Fiction, 1660–1800*, Gary Kelly's *Women, Writing, and Revolution, 1790–1827*, Eleanor Ty's *Unsex'd Revolutionaries:*

Five Women Novelists of the 1790s, Favret's *Romantic Correspondence: Women, Politics, and the Fiction of Letters*, and Cheryl Turner's *Living by the Pen: Women Writers in the Eighteenth Century*. Also recommended is Elizabeth Kowaleski-Wallace's *Their Fathers' Daughters: Hannah More, Maria Edgeworth, and Patriarchal Complicity*, which offers an interesting consideration of the issue of female complicity that extends the early and decidedly polemical argument of Lynne Agress's *The Feminine Irony: Women on Women in Early Nineteenth-Century English Literature*. One might also include Marilyn Butler's excellent *Maria Edgeworth: A Literary Biography* for Edgeworth's literary relations with other women writers such as Barbauld, Baillie, and Seward.

Of the numerous articles and essays on women's prose of the Romantic period, a small selection of relevant studies might include Aaron's "'On Needlework': Protest and Contradiction in Mary Lamb's Essay"; Alexander's "Dorothy Wordsworth: The Grounds of Writing"; Stephen C. Behrendt's "Questioning the Romantic Novel" and "Mary Shelley, *Frankenstein*, and the Woman Writer's Fate"; Favret's "Spectatrice as Spectacle: Helen Maria Williams at Home in the Revolution" and "Telling Tales about Genre: Poetry in the Romantic Novel"; Harriet Guest's "The Wanton Muse: Politics and Gender in Gothic Theory after 1760"; Sonia Hofkosh's "A Woman's Profession: Sexual Difference and the Romance of Authorship"; Chris Jones's "Helen Maria Williams and Radical Sensibility"; Vivien Jones's "Women Writing Revolution: Narratives of History and Sexuality in Wollstonecraft and Williams"; Levin's "Romantic Prose and Feminine Romanticism"; Mellor's "Why Women Didn't Like Romanticism: The Views of Jane Austen and Mary Shelley" and "A Criticism of Their Own: Romantic Women Literary Critics"; Mitzi Myers's several important essays "Little Girls Lost: Rewriting Romantic Childhood, Righting Gender and Genre," "Hannah More's Tracts for the Times: Social Fiction and Female Ideology," "Sensibility and the 'Walk of Reason': Mary Wollstonecraft's Literary Reviews as Cultural Critique," and "Reform or Ruin: 'A Revolution in Female Manners'"; and Judith Scheffler's "Romantic Women Writing on Imprisonment and Prison Reform." Quite a few essays make challenging connections between texts written by men and those written by women, such as Kurt Heinzelman's "The Cult of Domesticity: Dorothy and William Wordsworth at Grasmere," Hofkosh's "Sexual Politics and Literary History: William Hazlitt's Keswick Escapade and Sarah Hazlitt's *Journal*," Homans's "Keats Reading Women, Women Reading Keats," Kennedy's "Revolutionary Tales: Helen Maria Williams's *Letters from France* and William Wordsworth's 'Vaudracour and Julia,'" Susan Luther's "A Stranger Minstrel: Coleridge's Mrs. Robinson," Jane Moore's "Plagiarism with a Difference: Subjectivity in 'Kubla Khan' and *Letters Written during a Short Residence in Sweden, Norway, and Denmark*," and Wolfson's "Individual in Community: Dorothy Wordsworth in Conversation with William."

Perhaps too fine a line must be drawn to differentiate works that examine the writing culture women inhabit from those that center on the culture itself, as Moira Ferguson argues in her introduction to *First Feminists*. A number of studies cross that line to shed important light on the role of contemporary periodicals as a venue for women's writings while contemplating how the periodical culture shapes reading. Among these works are Alison Adburgham's *Women in Print: Writing Women and Women's Magazines from the Restoration to the Accession of Victoria*, Ina Ferris's *The Achievement of Literary Authority: Gender, History, and the Waverly Novels*, and Barbara Charlesworth Gelpi's *Shelley's Goddess: Maternity, Language, Subjectivity*. Kathryn Shevelow's *Women and Print Culture: The Construction of Femininity in the Early Periodical* focuses primarily on the shaping of periodical culture from 1691 to 1712, but her discussion provides an important framework for comprehending later developments, as do many of the essays collected in Isabel Rivers's *Books and Their Readers in Eighteenth-Century England*. While Richard Altick's *The English Common Reader: A Social History of the Mass Reading Public, 1800–1900* and Jon Klancher's *The Making of English Reading Audiences, 1789–1832* do not focus on women writers and readers, both social histories provide important views of contemporary audiences. Richardson's more recent *Literature, Education, and Romanticism: Reading as Social Practice, 1780–1832* is significant because it actually attends to the gender and class issues that inform the intersection of literature and education.

To introduce these last three works on social history is to move somewhat beyond the matter of writing culture exclusively to studies that examine culture itself in ways that not only enable consideration of historical issues that inform reading but also often invoke the writings produced by women poets of the Romantic period. One such study is Leonore Davidoff and Catherine Hall's exemplary *Family Fortunes: Men and Women of the English Middle Class, 1780–1850*, which offers an essential overview of cultural concerns that includes important biographical material on the extended Taylor family as well as pertinent literary criticism on Jane and Ann Taylor; Lawrence Stone's *The Family, Sex, and Marriage in England, 1500–1800* also includes useful discussion of a number of women writers as well as of the cultural conditions that affected the production and reception of Romantic literature. While G. J. Barker-Benfield's *The Culture of Sensibility: Sex and Society in Eighteenth-Century Britain* draws primarily on the novel, his expansive study certainly illuminates cultural matters relevant to the production of women's poetry, as do Todd's *Sensibility: An Introduction* and McGann's study *The Poetics of Sensibility*. A fairly comprehensive overview of numerous backgrounds can be located in Marilyn Gaull's excellent *English Romanticism: The Human Context*. For studies that pursue a socioeconomic perspective, instructors should see the portions of Gaye Tuchman's *Edging Women Out: Victorian Novelists, Publishers, and Social Change* (with Nina Fortin) that identify literary production in the early portion of the nineteenth century; Judith Phillips Stanton's "Statistical Profile of Women Writing in English from 1660–1800" provides additional data, as does Jan Fergus and Janice Farrar Thaddeus's "Women, Publishers, and Money, 1790–1820." The essays collected in Mary Prior's *Women in English Society, 1500–1800* provide important material on women's lives, as does the richly detailed work of M. Dorothy George in *London Life in the Eighteenth Century.*

A number of the works cited as particularly useful concern the formation and institution of the canon or the making of women's literary history. The larger arguments and overviews found in such works as Marilyn Butler's *Romantics, Rebels, and Reactionaries: English Literature and Its Background*, McGann's *The Romantic Ideology: A Critical Investigation*, Gerald Graff's *Professing Literature: An Institutional History*, Jonathan Arac's *Critical Genealogies: Historical Situations for Postmodern Literary Studies*, David Perkins's *Is Literary History Possible?*, Ann Rosalind Jones's *The Currency of Eros: Women's Love Lyric in Europe, 1540–1620*, and Margaret J. M. Ezell's *Writing Women's Literary History* raise issues that continue to provoke reexamination of Romanticism as well as of current approaches to recuperating women's literary history. Also recommended for articulating perspectives on canonicity and circumstance are Behrendt's "Anthologizing British Women Poets of the Romantic Period: The Scene Today"; Paul Cantor's "Stoning the Romance: The Ideological Critique of Nineteenth-Century Literature"; Wolfson's "Questioning 'the Romantic Ideology': Wordsworth"; Linkin's "Women and Romanticism: Reformulating Canons in the Classroom," "The Current Canon in British Romantics Studies," and "Taking Stock of the British Romantics Marketplace: Teaching New Canons through New Editions?"; Gilbert and Gubar's "'But Oh! That Deep Romantic Chasm': The Engendering of Periodization"; Mary V. Davidson's "What We've Missed: Female Romantic Poets and the American Nature Writing Tradition"; Frances Ferguson's "On the Numbers of Romanticisms"; McGann's "Rethinking Romanticism"; and John Rieder's "Wordsworth and Romanticism in the Academy." The introductions to several recent collections and editions offer especially helpful essays on canonicity, including Lonsdale's *Eighteenth-Century Women Poets*, Laura Claridge and Elizabeth Langland's *Out of Bounds: Male Writers and Gender(ed) Criticism*, Stephen Copley and John Whale's *Beyond Romanticism: New Approaches to Texts and Contexts, 1780–1832*, and Favret and Watson's *At the Limits of Romanticism*. In connection with canonicity and revaluation, many instructors cite the importance of major feminist discussions of psychology, sociology, anthropology, and philosophy, such as Nancy Chodorow's *The Reproduction of Mothering: Psychoanalysis and the Sociology of Gender*; Carol Gilligan's *In a Different Voice: Psychological Theory and Women's Development*; Julia Kristeva's *Revolution in Poetic Language*; Gayle Rubin's "The Traffic in Women: Notes on the 'Political Economy' of Sex"; Mary Field Belenky, Blythe McVicker Clinchy, Nancy Rule Goldberger, and Jill Mattuck Tarule's *Women's Ways of Knowing: The Development of Self, Voice, and Mind*; and Ellison's important and often-cited *Delicate Subjects: Romanticism, Gender, and the Ethics of Understanding.* Also recommended are works that focus primarily on canonical male writers to establish the parameters of what Mellor terms masculine Romanticism, such as Diane Long Hoeveler's *Romantic Androgyny: The Women Within*, Ross's "Romantic Quest and Conquest: Troping Masculine Power in the Crisis of Poetic Identity," Richardson's "Romanticism and the Colonization of the Feminine," Judith Page's *Wordsworth and the Cultivation of Women*, and Julie Carlson's *In the Theatre of Romanticism: Coleridge, Nationalism, Women*, which provide useful ways of considering the gendered contexts within which women poets of the Romantic period wrote. Additional materials of importance to the instructor's library may be discerned from the individual essays that follow.

Recommended Reading for Students

Almost all the readings recommended for students are cited and described above; the works specifically identified as useful for undergraduate and graduate students similarly establish historical, cultural, and feminist contexts for the study of women's poetry. Many instructors direct students to works whose topics extend beyond the strict parameters of women's poetry of the Romantic period; as one respondent notes, the most beneficial criticism is often that by scholars writing on women and the novel, historians writing on culture and society, and theorists writing on feminist issues.

For undergraduate students, the most frequently assigned secondary materials concerned directly with Romantic women poets include Curran's "Romantic Poetry: The 'I' Altered" as well as selections from Ross's *The Contours of Masculine Desire*, and Mellor's *Romanticism and Feminism* and *Romanticism and Gender*. Instructors send students to the *Dictionary of Literary Biography*, the *Dictionary of National Biography*, and *The Feminist Companion to Literature in English* (Blain, Clements, and Grundy) for biographical materials; for larger critical background on the culture of the Romantic period, instructors recommend Marilyn Butler's *Romantics, Rebels, and Reactionaries*, Gaull's *English Romanticism*, Curran's *Poetic Form and British Romanticism*, Lonsdale's introduction to *Eighteenth-Century Women Poets*, and the classic formulations of Romanticism located in Meyer H. Abrams's "English Romanticism: The Spirit of the Age" and René Wellek's "The Concept of Romanticism in Literary History." Students also acquire detailed information on the cultural and literary positions of women in Romanticism from such assigned readings as Poovey's *The Proper Lady and the Woman Writer*, Mellor's "Why Women Didn't Like Romanticism," Levin's "Romantic Prose and Feminine Romanticism," Spencer's *The Rise of the Woman Novelist from Aphra Behn to Jane Austen*, Rabine's *Reading the Romantic Heroine*, Hoeveler's *Romantic Androgyny*, and Ellison's *Delicate Subjects*. Graduate students read not only works among those listed in this section—particularly those by Mellor, Ross, Curran, Poovey, Ellison,

Lonsdale, and Gaull—but also Tayler and Luria's "Gender and Genre," Showalter's *A Literature of Their Own*, Homans's *Bearing the Word*, Gilbert and Gubar's *Madwoman in the Attic*, Nancy Armstrong's *Desire and Domestic Fiction*, Langbauer's *Women and Romance*, Hickok's *Representations of Women*, Dekker's *Coleridge and the Literature of Sensibility*, Page's *Wordsworth and the Cultivation of Women*, and Davidoff and Hall's *Family Fortunes*, as well as many of the works recommended for instructors. Additionally, graduate students frequently read excerpts from Romantic-era writings that provide important historical and cultural context, including reviews of women poets by their contemporaries or references to them in the letters and journals of their contemporaries, such as Leigh Hunt's "Specimens of British Poetesses" and William Hazlitt's *Lectures on the English Poets*, as well as the usefully historicized introductory and biographical prefaces to extant nineteenth-century editions of their works (such as those edited by Henry Chorley, Laman Blanchard, and William Michael Rossetti).

Part Two

APPROACHES

Introduction

The essays that follow, developed from suggestions offered by colleagues who responded to our survey, reflect a wide range of approaches. We begin the section with essays that take up broad issues of texts, textuality, and technology, as well as several that focus on history or methodology, curricular packaging of courses in Romanticism, and aesthetics. The next group of essays examines ways of placing women poets into broader social, political, historical, intellectual, and artistic contexts. These essays, most of which discuss multiple authors, examine the teaching of their works in a variety of individual courses at institutions whose missions vary considerably. The third set of essays moves to discussions of single poets and how they are taught, again, in a broad variety of institutions and curricula. Finally, the essays in the last section focus on still more particularized courses and teaching strategies, for instance, the first-year writing course or the community college course in general literature. These shorter essays are in some respects microapproaches whose insights and suggestions hold real potential for instructors working with different and often more specialized curricula.

In assembling these essays we strove to make this collection broadly representative of the considerable diversity that characterizes the teaching of Romantic literature. Contributions by well-known scholars stand side by side with those from colleagues whose names and work are perhaps less immediately recognizable. We likewise sought to include contributions by women and men from a variety of geographic areas and types of institutions. Hence the essays present approaches to teaching the women poets in advanced graduate courses and introductory courses for undergraduate nonmajors and at institutions ranging from PhD-granting research universities to community colleges. Not all the courses represented here are traditional English classes, nor are the methodologies and technological enhancements described unique to courses in traditional literary studies. The essays reflect the diversity of every aspect of Romantics studies at this remarkable historical moment in which the landscape of British Romanticism is being remapped by scholars at all stages of their careers, many of whom have contributed essays to this volume.

We have tried to allow the contributors as much stylistic and rhetorical freedom as possible, within the constraints of available space. These essays vary in length, style, content, and teaching approach. Whatever the variations, however, the essays share an enthusiasm for, and commitment to, both the works of the writers discussed and the teaching process by which we are all engaged in preparing students to be better and more informed readers, not just of the works discussed here but also of literature in general. This dedication, which we have felt in everyone who has responded to this project, strikes us as a powerful sign that neither literature nor reading is dead: both are alive and well in the dynamic and innovative classrooms of colleagues everywhere. That being so, we hope all the more that the contributions here will fuel the fires of intellectual inquiry still further among our colleagues and their students, even as the essays invite a continuing dialogue about the work of the British women poets of the Romantic period and the ways in which we teach it.

Something Evermore About to Be:
Teaching and Textbases

Stuart Curran

Someone has to say it, so it might as well be me. The mere addition of Charlotte Smith to the course on British Romanticism, however much it may en-
large its historical and stylistic compass, will not effect a revolution in the
curriculum or in the canon. Not to be mistaken, on long reflection I believe
even more strongly than during the preparation of the edition of her poetry
that Smith was a pivotal figure in the development of Romanticism, setting
many of its agendas and achieving a marked influence on those male poets
who, until very recently, carried what one of them called its "banners militant"
(Wordsworth, *Prelude* 6.609). But if that tendentiously heroicized past seems
truly past, the thinking that created it is not, and Smith by herself cannot make
the difference.

Indeed, every time we consider who among the available women should be
added to our courses, we reflect that thinking—as if (I'll assume the male role
here) literature were a dance and, without even pretending to ask "May I?," I
am aware that I have the honor, first, to choose and, second, to lead. Canonizing got us into this masculinist fix, and substitute canonizing only entrenches it
further. I realize that our courses adhere to discrete time limits, that we all
have literary values we want to see upheld and even inculcated, that there is
only so much we can cover, that GREs lie ahead for some of our students and
quasi-intellectual game shows that make an occasional gesture toward a Keats
ode for many others, that anthologies are limited and our students' patience
with our experiments even more so, that life is short and art is long and the

need for coherence in all this welter is paramount. Still, I also realize that in 1810 Walter Scott was considered the major poet of the era, followed in popularity and claims on the national attention by Thomas Campbell, Samuel Rogers, and Robert Southey. Fifteen years later Scott had receded into The Great Unknown, and the indisputable major poet was Felicia Hemans. Canons are mutable, shaped by historical patterns, ideological programs, the sociology of reading, and academic convention. Move them about as we want, picking and choosing (or, in our privileged case, merrily expunging the historical record), the one assurance we have is that nothing we are doing is true to the facts. That should comfort us, then, as we contemplate introducing a non-Newtonian relativity into the curriculum.

Fortunately for us, technology is catching up with theoretical physics, and we are in the midst of an unstanchable flood of "textbases"—databases of text that can be accessed electronically—bypassing our absolute dependence on publications that reflect someone else's priorities. Whether anthologizers, editors, or publishing houses with one eye on the bottom line and another on market manipulation, the traditional producers of poetry collections share a common interest in fostering a stable, even rigidified, canon. They have promoted the addiction from which we are now becoming able to detoxify ourselves. We have a duty, all of us self-appointed guardians of the literary heritage, at least to try to liberate ourselves and our students from that template we have imposed on ourselves. Indeed, since our students experience little of this molding before they enter our classrooms, it is we who need liberation most. They may be induced to tag along for the fun of it.

And in one sense they might lead us. Because of their minimal investment in the canon and their considerable one in their own expressiveness, their sometimes maddening innocence may recapture the actual state of affairs of the period we purport to teach, for before there were canons or schools or even coteries there were solitary, generally young, inexperienced writers wishing to express something about their world, their thoughts and emotions, their associations and commitments. The writing scene into which poets of the late eighteenth century entered, marked by subscriptions and various other kinds of patronage, might seem very different from the conditions of today, but the fledgling poet's uncertainty about audience, voice, or remuneration has scarcely changed. Whether or not we can get our students to bridge two hundred years and establish a sense of identity with their compeers of another age, there would be a distinct value in the attempt. We might think of it as mainly salutary for students, but it should be for us as their teachers as well, restoring our sense of discovery, expanding our sense of the possible. In other words, to prick this balloon called the canon can paradoxically reaffirm our essential goals as educators, enlivening our teaching, enriching our sense of the literary, opening up rather than closing down our heritage.

Electronic textbases are proliferating at a breathtaking velocity. Many of them seem intended as modern equivalents of the Everyman Library, or perhaps the

Oxford World Classics—in other words, the standard canon. That may be thought a doggedly useful, if essentially reactionary, deployment of a radical technology. What most interests me, however, are those textbases that are truly realizing the liberating implications of technology. The textbases being produced by Chadwyck-Healey, for instance, while staggeringly expensive, are so inclusive that they resemble specialist libraries. Although they are dominated by male writers, that reflects as much the facts of literary history as commercial choice. Even so, there are enough women poets of the Romantic period in the *English Poetry Database* (AD 600–1900) to keep most of us wandering through an uncharted landscape for weeks. The expense of this library, however, whether subscribed to online or purchased as a CD-ROM, eliminates it as an option for most teachers of the Romantic period.

Nor, though they will likely remain crucial stopgaps as teaching aids even as more systematic collections become available, can we rely solely on the collections of women's poetry made freely accessible on the World Wide Web, notable examples of which include those promulgated at the University of Pennsylvania, containing line numbering for class use, and those disseminated by the University of Virginia in more experimental hypertext formats. Such efforts, however much they embody the value of the collegiality promised by the new technologies, are too minimal in their offerings to satisfy the large-scale demand for range and completeness that is altering the very conception of poetry of the Romantic era.

The textbase that was created specifically to satisfy that demand, a collection that has the capacity to serve at once as a reservoir for women's writing in English and as a platform for a continuous assault on a restrictive canonicity, is the Brown University Women Writers Project. Founded in 1986, the project is reaching maturity, expanding from the distribution of paper printouts to electronic availability, which should be sufficiently economical to allow many college and university libraries to purchase licenses to use the textbase. The project employs state-of-the-art electronic text encoding, which will aid researchers by enabling sophisticated search engines to work through the textbase in multiple ways. In the classroom this electronic dissemination should allow the process of historical discovery to become a norm in the study and teaching of literature.

Although I might seem to undermine my encouragement of individual creativity by making specific suggestions for use of the textbase, I present them only as a sample of the options the textbase provides; as the section editor primarily responsible for assembling the project's texts from 1750 to 1830 I know its holdings well. Indeed, a major principle of that selection from early on was to deposit distinctive work of many kinds and thus to offer readers an immediate sense of the variety and richness of women's writing in earlier cultures. Through the project's efforts such major, and perhaps now even canonical, voices of the Romantic period as Anna Barbauld, Mary Robinson, Charlotte Smith, and Jane Taylor were transposed from mere historical memories to classroom presences.

The suggested texts I offer here, however, are explicitly *not* intended to enter canonically into a curriculum, but instead are here to call attention to themselves because of intrinsic interest, idiosyncrasies, and artistry, as all writing is intended to do when you come upon it in a bookstore rather than the classroom. Although the texts are only available on paper printouts as of this writing, they should be close to electronic release by the publication of this volume.[1]

I begin with a group of writers who respond directly to some of the male poets who are never likely to be excluded from the canon. The writers of this group never intended their voices to compete with the male poets', though they may certainly have sought to be heard by them. They would enter a course as contributors not so much to the canon as to a dialogue. They are not poets of enormous pretension, but they have individual integrity and art.

Ann Batten Cristall, a few selections from whom first appeared in Roger Lonsdale's anthology *Eighteenth-Century Women Poets* and whose complete *Poetical Sketches*, aside from its inclusion in the Women Writers Project database, was also made available in 1995 from the Electronic Text Center of the University of Virginia, is that rarest of Romantic poets, a follower of William Blake. Her single volume of verse, published by Joseph Johnson in 1795, actually borrows the title of Blake's first publication. She even seems to make a direct allusion to the last plate of *The Marriage of Heaven and Hell*, ending her "To a Lady, on the Rise of Morn" "Singing the heavenly song of liberty" (the poems appear in the database literatim, without line numbers). Although Cristall adopts a male persona, the woman's authorial presence and the overt desire of the poem may implicitly evoke Oothoon in Blake's *Visions of the Daughters of Albion*. In her identification with nature in this and other poems, Cristall reflects Blake's early view of natural processes as beneficent, countering restrictive human systems of law and morality. Unlike him, however, she does not abstract natural rhythm into an antihuman system of its own. Rather, as is exemplified by her "Ode" ("Almighty Power! who rul'st this world of storms!"), Cristall embraces its sublime, dangerous yet inspiriting dynamicism, in which "Created matter in contention whirl'd / Spreads desolation as it bursts to life." Cristall gothicizes nature as well in her expression of the dynamics of eroticism—sexual politics, fear, desire, jealousy—areas seldom explored to this length by contemporary women poets and in the treatment of which her voice is noticeably younger and more attuned to actual life than Blake's is.

Two other women who are in dialogue with a canonical male writer are Isabella Lickbarrow (*Poetical Effusions*, 1814) and Mary Bryan (*Sonnets and Metrical Tales*, 1815). Both published in the years when Wordsworth consolidated his reputation by producing *The Excursion* and the recategorized collection of his *Poems*. Lickbarrow is perhaps the slighter poet, but she shares the mountain spirit of Wordsworth and often writes tellingly of the same scenery. She has an instinct for graceful simplicity, as is manifest in the unadorned quatrains of "The Mountain Flower," which takes its title from a plant known locally as "the grass of Parnassus," thus representing the unpretentious and natural poetic spontaneity flourishing in the mountain wilds. The subject of the poem is, indeed, its very expression, a common trope in women's poetry of the period. Balancing this ingenuous artistry are the ten strong poems in a distinguished blank verse with which she begins the volume, poems, such as "The Throne of Winter," in which she seems to attempt to mythologize and sublime this northern world. Wordsworth does not tend to feel comfortable in this métier, and thus the poems afford a valuable contrast to his usual practice.

Wordsworth was a subscriber to Lickbarrow's *Poetical Effusions*, but he is the dedicatee of Bryan's *Sonnets and Metrical Tales*. Whereas Lickbarrow endeavors to render the integrity of rural subjects, Bryan's take on Wordsworth is filtered through the Lucy and Matthew poems, and she captures with great skill their radically spare but suggestive language. Her poems often concentrate on the ultimately unfathomable recesses of the female psyche, as in "Julia" and "Anna," in which one uncannily hears the timbres of such later poets as Emily Brontë and Emily Dickinson. Several poems deal with real, strikingly unliterary insanity. Late in the volume stands a sonnet sequence supposedly extracted from a tale of village love but powerfully authentic in its representation of the narrator's passionate despair over the loss of love and self-hatred for being so demeaned. Wherever one looks in Bryan's volume, one encounters Romantic conventions as essentially female experiences.

But not all female poets of the era seem prompted into verse by the intellectual and stylistic strength of male poets of the canon. In Scotland before Scott's *The Lay of the Last Minstrel* (1805) Anne Bannerman had a virtually open field, and her incorporation of Gothic and folk elements into her *Poems* of 1800 is both idiosyncratic and free of competitive anxiety. Although the poetic scene is very different sixteen years later, still one senses in Dorothea Primrose Campbell's *Poems* (1816) a deliberate continuation of the line set in motion by Bannerman. We see an independent female energy arise even more strongly in Ireland in this period. The main instigator is Sydney Owenson, who later, as Lady Morgan, would have a distinctive effect on Anglo-Irish fiction and become a political gadfly against reactionary forces. Her *Poems* of 1801 and *Lays of an Irish Harp* of 1807 are instinct with the spirit and wit that would later drive her politics, but they are mainly expressive of youth, genius, and a passion for versification, and they are irresistible in their charm. If any teacher still introduces Thomas Moore to an American classroom, Owenson's influence on the *Irish Melodies* would be worth exploration. If not, there are other female Irish voices that could be incorporated. Catherine Quigley's two volumes *Poems* (1813) and *The Microscope, or Village Flies* (1819) share Owenson's wit and energy, but the voice is middle-class, natural, and strikingly modern. The poem in ballad meter with which she ends the second collection, "The Chase," tells how the spinster Miss Flacket takes an ostentatious outing on an ancient nag, and it is richly comic.

And then there is that true original Frances O'Neill, whose crudely printed *Poetical Essays, Being a Collection of Satirical Poems, Songs, and Acrostics* (c. 1800) appears to exist in a single copy in the British Library that lacks a central folding and thus dramatically testifies to the fragility of print. It is sad to think that in all probability we will never know how O'Neill's "On Being Refused the Patronage of Sir Joseph Banks" begins. No one, however, can mistake the power of its ending:

> For this great sir, nor can you blame,
>   When next we meet you in the square,
> I'll soon disrobe your ugly frame,
>   And leave your limbs expos'd and bare.
> With t—d I'll well bedaub you o'er,
>   In t—d I'll sink your bandy shanks,
> And every Muse that hears you roar,
>   Shal jointly plague Sir Joseph Banks.

This poem might fit in well after a discussion of Coleridge's secondary and primary imagination; perhaps it could be combined with a discussion of the opening satirical series that brings together Kelly the Irish butler and Sangster the Scottish cook in a bruising fight downstairs at the home of "a respectable family, No. 39, Great Charles Street, Berkley Square," in which most of the crockery is broken. Behind the raucous facade of this volume is a passionate, loud, willful, proletarian voice set within a complex literary sociology, as her self-description in her "Song" (of many pages in length) indicates: "Born with a mind / To write inclin'd, / This all the fates conspire to hinder; / In fame obscure, / In coin kept poor, / Gods! how I envy Peter Pindar."

There are many other proletarian voices of this period, both urban and rural. Frances O'Neill is a much better poet than Mrs. Cooper, but the latter's almost illiterate "Address to the People of Wapping" allows a fascinating inside view of lower-class London life in the late eighteenth century. Ann Yearsley, the "Milkwoman of Clifton," has herself become something of a canonical figure, if only through her problematic relationship with her patrons, Hannah More and Elizabeth Montagu. Her poems, however, have a real value, continually testifying to the psychological realities of the disadvantaged and thus putting a construction on Romantic self-consciousness very different from that conventionally offered in our courses. Ann Candler provides a complementary voice; her *Poetical Attempts* of 1803 opens with a rare and fascinating document, a proletarian autobiography. Her liberation from a drunken, abusive husband resonates tellingly today. Her poems are more conventional than those discussed above, but they reveal sharply the tyranny of subscribers over the objects of their charity.

I end these suggestions at the opposite end of the spectrum, with women poets who come from privilege and reveal independence and a feminist consciousness. Margaret Holford dedicates her epic poem *Margaret of Anjou* (1816) to her mother, also named Margaret Holford and the author of "*Gresford Vale," and Other Poems*, published in 1798. Although the daughter's epic is a poem of great strength, it will scarcely accommodate the schedule of a typical course; but her earlier collection *Poems* (1811) reveals many of the same poetic virtues. Such a mother-daughter link is not unique: a generation earlier there had been Mary Whateley and her daughter Elizabeth Darwall. Still, this kind of comparison offers rare opportunities for the classroom.

Another such chance is afforded by Jane Elizabeth Roscoe, the daughter of William Roscoe, the historian and dissenting intellectual. She, her father, and her older sister produced *Poems for Youth: By a Family Circle* in 1820; the next year she published a volume, *Poems*, that displays a refined, proto-Victorian sensibility caught between personal and religious desires. Finally, I would suggest a poetic drama of power and sweep that points the way to Matthew Arnold's *Empedocles on Etna*, Catherine Grace Garnett's "Sappho," published in a large volume called *"The Night before the Bridal," "Sappho, a Dramatic Sketch," and Other Poems* in 1824. In this version Sappho is forced to confront the nothingness of life and in the end commits suicide not from distraught love but as a means of rendering her spirit back into the pure elements from which it sprung. If you have found yourself tired of domestic affections, distrustful of the angel of the house, and bored by consumptive declines, you will find this heroine's taking charge and disposing of her genius something of a tonic. And if you began a course watching Wordsworth appropriate female sensibility in the late eighteenth century, you might appreciate the symmetry of seeing Arnold usurp the *poète maudit* from its female archetype at the end. There is more than one benefit to be gained from this dialogue between the famous and the unknown.

These suggestions are not prescriptive, nor do they mark the limit of what is available. The Women Writers Project will go on accumulating in its textbase collection what has been forgotten or almost lost, expecting that this exfoliation of the past will provide the basis for a cumulative exploration. These remarks present my perception of the project's capacity for opening up and keeping vital our sense of the potentiality of literature in the classroom. This process of discovery should be our reciprocal contribution to the literary period that, more than any other, is distinguished by its revolutionary energy.

NOTE

[1] Information about the textbase of the Brown University Women Writers Project can be secured by mail (Box 1841, Brown Univ., Providence, RI 02912), telephone (401 863-3619), or e-mail (wwp@brownvm.brown.edu) and is available at the project's Web site (www.wwp.brown.edu). The list of texts is also available at the site (www.wwp .brown.edu/textlist.html). Texts may be ordered by e-mail (wwp__orders@brown.edu).

How Their Audiences Knew Them: Forgotten Media and the Circulation of Poetry by Women

Paula R. Feldman

Because most of our encounters with poems of the Romantic era have occurred within the pages of printed books, it is natural to assume that audiences would have read the poems in the same format during the authors' lifetimes. But especially for women poets, that assumption is often incorrect. Exposing students to the now-forgotten ways in which verse once commonly circulated adds an important dimension to their understanding of the poems they read by women.

Early in our discussion, I tell my students how the values of the aristocracy caused women in that social class to be wary of allowing their names to appear in print and how working-class women usually had neither the means nor the social connections to publish their work. I talk about how the patriarchal structure of publication tended to exclude even middle-class women in subtle ways. "Modesty," too, was a highly valued female trait that prevented many women of all classes from "putting themselves forward" in print. But these barriers didn't stop women from writing poems, and if the authors were gifted, their poems circulated anyway through various media—songs, manuscripts, letters, albums, dramatic performances, literary annuals, broadsides, and newspapers. Sometimes these works became among the most well known and highly valued of the age. I offer here some examples of these forgotten modes of distribution from my teaching repertoire.

Song

Many romantic poems began life as songs, composed with original scores or as adaptations of traditional tunes. The playing of a musical instrument, often with vocal accompaniment, was among the most valued of feminine "accomplishments." I remind my students that before television and radio, women, especially those of marriageable age, were called upon to entertain guests or the family circle with musical performance. Students are often familiar with this aspect of eighteenth- and nineteenth-century life through novels and films.

Sometimes, a song by a particularly talented woman might be striking, moving, or delightful enough to catch on as a popular song and spread far abroad by word of mouth. That happened to Lady Anne Lindsay's "Auld Robin Gray" (1772), the most popular ballad of the English Romantic period, which William Wordsworth called one of "the two best Ballads, perhaps of modern times" (Wordsworth and Wordsworth 678). William Hazlitt remarked, "The effect of reading this old ballad is as if all our hopes and fears hung upon the last fibre of the heart, and we felt that giving way. What silence, what loneliness, what leisure for grief and despair!" (*Collected Works* 5: 141). Walter Scott called it "a real pastoral, which is worth all the dialogues which Corydon and Phyllis have had together from the days of Theocritus downwards" (8: 37).

"Auld Robin Gray" was not only sung throughout Lady Anne's native Scotland but also carried into England by balladmongers and strolling players and translated into French. It became such a craze that one season it even lent its name to the newest fashions, including the Robin Gray hat. Lady Anne observed some years later that it "had a romance composed from it by a man of eminence, was the subject of a play, of an opera, and of a pantomime, was sung by the united armies in America, acted by Punch, and afterwards danced by dogs in the street" (*Lives* 2: 333). It also found its way into other authors' literary works, including Mary Wollstonecraft's *Maria; or, The Wrongs of Woman*, where it is sung by a beautiful maniac (36). Its wide dissemination suggests it was printed on cheap broadsides, so ephemeral they have long ago disappeared.

Several people, including a clergyman, claimed authorship, for Lady Anne would not acknowledge her work. As she later observed, "I was pleased in secret with the approbation it met with; but such was *my dread* of being suspected of writing *anything*, perceiving the shyness it created in those who could write *nothing*, that I carefully kept my own secret" (3). Not until half a century after the song's composition did its author confess the truth to someone outside her family circle—Walter Scott, who had learned it from his aunt, a friend of Lady Anne Lindsay's family. He convinced Lady Anne to allow him to publish "Auld Robin Gray" with her name on the title page, in 1825, along with his introduction, for the members of the Bannatyne Club, a society for the preservation of Scottish literature and history. Thereafter it was reprinted in nearly every anthology of Scottish verse and was frequently the subject of commentary. In 1856 *Blackwood's Edinburgh Magazine* called it "one of those perfect and unimprovable works of genius which . . . the whole world receives into its heart" and noted, "there are lines in Lady Anne's ballad unparalleled, so far as we are aware, in depth of insight and perfect simplicity of expression" ("Family History"). In 1876 James Grant Wilson called it "perhaps the most perfect, tender, and affecting of modern Scottish ballads" (2: 334).

Carolina, Baroness Nairne, provides a similar example. She rewrote the earthy words to traditional Scottish national songs to make them suitable for the drawing room. Her new version of an old Scottish song, "The Ploughman" (1792), first sung, then circulated anonymously as a privately printed broadside, became an immediate hit, and unauthorized copies proliferated. Another of her well-loved compositions, "The Land o' the Leal" (1797), originated as part of a private letter of condolence. Lady Nairne wrote comic songs such as "John Tod" and "The Laird o' Cockpen" in the early 1820s, and her ardent Jacobite songs are said to be some of the best ever written.

Eventually, under the name of Mrs. Bogan, of Bogan, Lady Nairne contributed songs anonymously to a collection of national airs with words sanitized for polite company, entitled *The Scottish Minstrel* (R. A. Smith). She jealously guarded the secret of her authorship, even altering her handwriting and masquerading as an old country woman to meet the publisher. Only a few family members and close friends knew of her authorship during her lifetime. But shortly after her death, with the cooperation of her surviving sister, seventy of her songs, some written more than half a century earlier, were published in a book entitled *Lays from Strathearn, by Carolina, Baroness Nairne*. The *Dictionary of National Biography* maintains

> In her "Land o' the Leal," "Laird o' Cockpen," and "Caller Herrin," she is hardly, if at all, second to Burns himself. . . . Lady Nairne ranks with Hogg in her Jacobite songs, but in several she stands first and alone.

Some of Lady Nairne's songs remain among the most popular in English, and Scots schoolchildren still enjoy her enduringly humorous satire of the pompous, self-important Laird of Cockpen.

To give my students the flavor of these works, I have played in class Jean Redpath's excellent recordings. I have also supplied musical scores to our student organization, the Nineteenth-Century English Club, so that the group could perform them in a musical event. (We included selections by Felicia Hemans too.)

Isabel Pagan, a working-class poet, literally sang for her supper. My students are intrigued to learn about how she entertained her alehouse guests with improvised dramatic monologues and amusing songs, some old but many of her own making. According to James Paterson's 1840 account,

> [N]ight after night the vaulted roof of [Pagan's] humble dwelling rung with the voice of licentious mirth, and the revelries of bacchanalian worshippers, among whom she was the administering priestess. Famed for her sarcastic wit, as well as for her vocal powers, her cottage may be truly said to have been the favorite *howff* of all the drunken wags and 'drouthy neebors' in the district. She had no license for the retail of spirits, but usually kept a bottle for the supply of her customers; and by this means she contrived to eke out a subsistence which must otherwise have been sustained from charity. (116)

Her most famous song is "Ca' the Ewes to the Knowes." Robert Burns "discovered" it, according to his account when, in 1787, he heard it sung by the Rev. John Clunie. He had it transcribed, added a final stanza, "mended" others, and eventually published the poem in volume 3 of James Johnson's *The Scots Musical Museum* (1790), acknowledging Pagan's authorship only in later editions. "This beautiful song," he said, "is in the true old Scotch taste, yet I do not know that either air or words were in print before. It has a border sound . . ." (32).

It was not until 1803, when Pagan was over sixty, that her works were first published in book form under her name. *A Collection of Songs and Poems on Several Occasions* appeared in Glasgow and contained forty-six favorite songs from her repertoire, including many original works. Unable to write herself, she dictated the volume to her amanuensis. Not included in her book are her well-known songs "The Crook and Plaid" and "Ca' the Ewes to the Knowes." By 1845, Pagan's book had become so rare that Alex Whitelaw, doing research for a volume on Scottish song, was unable to locate a copy or even to confirm its contents. However, around the same time, Paterson recorded that "The Crook and Plaid" was still being sung (119). The persistence of Pagan's work was not altogether dependent on print media.

Manuscript Commonplace Books and Albums

Students are generally unfamiliar with the traditions of commonplace books and albums, so I have to start from scratch in describing what they looked like, why people kept them, and what they contained. I remind students that scribes copied books before the invention of the printing press and that the tradition did not entirely die out. I am fortunate in being able to show my students a manuscript album book dating from the 1820s that I bought at a flea market, but instructors who do not own one can still expose their students to this nearly forgotten literary medium. A special-collections librarian may be able to help: many libraries contain such items among eighteenth- and nineteenth-century family papers, whether British, American, or European. Instructors can also simply describe the books, as I did before I found mine. I compare them to childhood autograph albums or the blank books sold today in stores; they have pretty bindings (usually leather, which was sometimes gilt-embossed) and no printing on the leaves. I explain how before photography, people would go on trips and sketch scenes in commonplace books to remember them. At home, people might press leaves and flowers in their books or copy things they had read, usually epigrams, sayings, poems, or short quotes from favorite authors. They might ask visitors to write in their albums as a memento. Visitors would often set down favorite passages of poetry, but sometimes they would write original compositions; the latter would, naturally, be expected of a poet. Thus many poets who never wrote for publication had their writing preserved, and to some extent circulated, for everyone who subsequently wrote in a book might read it, and family and friends might have access to it. This practice explains the titles of published poems by canonical and noncanonical writers alike that begin "Lines Written in an Album. . . ." To demonstrate how pervasive this tradition was, I bring to class a collected edition of the poems of Samuel Taylor Coleridge, where students can scan the contents for such titles (e.g., "Lines Written in the Album at Elbingerode in the Hartz Forest" and "Lines Written in Commonplace Book of Miss Barbour"). One suspects that many poets had a memorized repertoire of album poems to "compose" on the spot. The album books that survive today provide us with a valuable record of popular poetic taste (rather than just what the critics approved). Some poems had a very wide circulation, almost exclusively in album books. For example, one popular selection was "Riddle on the Letter H," by Catherine Maria Fanshawe, retitled in many sources "Enigma" ("Riddle"). At a house party in Surrey, Fanshawe composed the poem late one night and read it to the assembled guests at breakfast the next morning. The poem was widely attributed to Lord Byron and even appeared in pirated printed editions of his work. Commonplace books often belonged to a whole family instead of one person. For example, Maria Edgeworth's family kept manuscript albums in which Edgeworth copied poems that she never published, alongside poems written by other members of her family. (Several Edgeworth family commonplace books are in the National Library of Ireland.)

It is because of a manuscript album book that the poetical works of Susanna Blamire were preserved and finally published. Like many women poets, Blamire wrote most of her compositions on the backs of letters, on receipts, or on handy scraps of paper; the only exceptions are her long and powerful poem "Stoklewath" and a few other songs found in fair copy after her death. Most Blamire poems were not published during her lifetime, but they were nonetheless extremely popular, sung as songs, copied into commonplace books, and circulated in manuscript form. A few were published anonymously as single sheets in the 1780s and then found their way into collections such as *Calliope; or, The Musical Miscellany* (1788). But most remained unpublished at her death in 1794. Many of her songs, especially "The Nabob," "What Ails This Heart o' Mine," and "The Chelsea Pensioners," continued to be sung in the Carlisle region of England for decades after she died.

Julia Thompson, a teacher, preserved fourteen of Blamire's poems in her commonplace book and taught them to her pupils. In the late 1820s, Patrick Maxwell decided to collect Blamire's poetry, which he knew from his childhood. He located Thompson in 1833, and she allowed him to borrow her commonplace book, which contained eleven poems he had never seen. Henry Lonsdale, one of Thompson's pupils, in 1839 met the poet's niece, who turned up a cache of Blamire manuscripts. These she entrusted to Lonsdale, who passed them on, with his notes on Blamire's life, to Maxwell. In 1842, nearly fifty years after the poet's death, Maxwell published a collected edition of her works, comprising eighty-five poems—some in standard English, others in Scottish and in Cumbrian dialect, including ballads, epistles, elegies, and other lyrics—as well as notes and a biographical memoir. An early review of the volume observes that her songs thrill "a sympathetic string deep in the reader's bosom. It may, indeed, be confidently predicted of several of these lyrics, that they will live with the best productions of their age, and longer than many that were at first allowed to rank more highly" (Chambers and Chambers). However, Susanna Blamire's writing is an exception. Most poems that circulated in manuscript never found their way into print.

Literary Annuals

Literary annuals were a major publication outlet for women poets, one whose requirements often affected the subject matter and form of their poems. The annuals, I tell my students, were the coffee-table books of the 1820s, 1830s, and 1840s. Their format was modeled after that of the manuscript album, and they were as sumptuously and beautifully made as possible, with tooled leather or silk bindings, gilt-edged leaves, and fine steel-plate engravings of works by the most popular and most well respected artists of their day. Some annuals contained only poetry; others included short fiction. Many canonized authors such as William Wordsworth, Samuel Taylor Coleridge, Alfred Tennyson, Mary Shelley, and Walter Scott contributed. I tell my students that for poets, publishing in the literary annuals was like publishing fiction today in *Esquire* or the *New Yorker* and even more lucrative. Especially in the early years of the craze, annuals paid their authors and engravers exceptionally well—better than any other print medium. Some editors, such as Letitia Elizabeth Landon, made extremely good livings from their work with the annuals. At the height of their popularity, Lady Blessington is said to have earned between two thousand and three thousand pounds a year from editing and contributing to them.

The books sold to a largely middle-class female clientele. They cost as little as eight shillings or as much as three pounds, depending on the binding and the quality and size of the paper. Because they were more elegant and more expensive than ordinary books, they were generally given only on special occasions to sweethearts, family, and close friends. Christmas and New Year's Day were the most popular occasions for giving annuals; as a result, they tended to be published around November expressly for the holiday season. They were often named after valuable and beautiful things, such as *The Gem, The Amethyst, The Pearl*, and *The Bijou*. The names reflected their function, too, for example, *The Forget Me Not, The Keepsake*, and *Friendship's Offering*. Most had a presentation plate on which the giver could write an inscription.

These books not only circulated poetry to a large, mostly female audience but also on a wide scale allowed middle-class households to own reproductions of great art. I remind my students that few art museums existed in those days. Most great art was housed in the private homes of the aristocratic and the wealthy, to which ordinary people had no access. Turner, Martin, Lawrence, Gainsborough, Reynolds, Opie, Landseer—most of the major artists of the period appeared in annuals. Many of the books were best-sellers—Alaric A. Watts's *Literary Souvenir* was selling ten thousand copies a year by 1830. Thus they are remarkable indexes to the popular culture and taste of the period. They document too the increasing economic importance of the female reader and her influence on the subject matter and style of poetry. Inexpensive examples of literary annuals still turn up in secondhand stores, for the craze leaped the Atlantic, and the books became as popular in the United States as in England. It is useful to bring a copy to class, so that students can appreciate the format. Knowing about literary annuals helps students understand otherwise puzzling aspects of the women poets we study. For example, why did Letitia Elizabeth Landon write so many poems about China and the Far East? I explain that in those days publishers of literary annuals often commissioned or bought engraved plates and then paid poets to compose works to go along with the engravings. So, as editor of *The Drawing-Room Scrapbook*, Landon often had the difficult task of writing poems about subjects she did not choose and might not even have had much interest in.

Felicia Hemans exploited the medium of the annual probably more than any other female poet of the period. Her poetry is ubiquitous in them, and they must have provided her a major portion of her literary earnings as well as helping to fan her fame. Understanding the peculiar sensibility of the annuals gives us insight into Hemans's poetry. Frequently she published works first in the annuals and then in books. But other writers are known to us as poets only by their occasional contributions to the annuals. Interestingly, perhaps because of the annuals' largely female audience and mass popularity, many now-canonized writers disparaged the books while, unable to resist the lucrative fees, condescending to publish in them. But most twentieth-century scholars have heeded what these writers said rather than what they did and thus have ignored the medium as the significant literary phenomenon it was and as the vehicle for much women's poetry.

These books are a treasure trove of potential research topics for students, especially for those interested in art or in the intersection of popular taste and women's poetry. The two best guides to these books are still Frederick W. Faxon's *Literary Annuals and Gift Books: A Bibliography, 1823–1903* (1973), which includes pictures, a descriptive essay, and a listing of individual titles that contains bibliographical information, and Andrew Boyle's *An Index to the Annuals* (1967), which lists contributions to annuals by poets' names.

My last suggestion for helping students get a feel for how the work of women poets circulated is an outing to a library rare-book room, where students can see how poetry physically looked to its contemporary audience. There, students can experience firsthand the difference between an expensive quarto volume—the format, for example, of Felicia Hemans's *Poems* (1808), with its lovely copper-plate engravings and large pages with expansive white space (Browne)—and the more constricted and plain duodecimo format of, for example, children's poetry books such as the many early editions of Ann and Jane Taylor's *Original Poems, for Infant Minds* (1804). They can also examine a subscriber's list at the front of a volume of poetry and admire the hand work that went into a contemporary fine leather binding. The experience will help them appreciate the high cost of many books, which meant that some women had to enlist many subscribers to have their poems published and which often made it difficult for a woman to amass a personal library or educate herself through access to private collections. Instructors can use any books from the period to demonstrate these concepts: the examples need not be especially rare or even by the particular poets the class is studying. It can be surprising to find how many examples are available even in the stacks.

Once students see how women's poetry often circulated in media we have long ignored as legitimate sources of literature—nonprint forms such as songs, albums, and manuscripts—and ephemeral print forms such as broadsides, literary annuals, and small private editions, they may be able to appreciate how so much poetry by women has been lost to us. Moreover, they may be better able to understand the challenge and excitement of current recovery efforts.

"The Choicest Gifts of Genius":
Working with and Teaching the Kohler Collection

Jane King and Kari Lokke

> Full oft beneath the steril soil conceal'd,
>   The richest veins of golden treasures lie;
> So genius may, her glory unreveal'd,
>   Be by the world neglected and pass'd by,
> While sunk in poverty's sequester'd shade,
>   Though the rough form no outward polish bear,
> And tho' in nature's rustic garb array'd,
>   The choicest gifts of genius may be there.
>   —Elizabeth Bath, "Sonnet II," *Poems*

When in 1983 the University of California, Davis, library purchased approximately nine thousand volumes of British poetry written between 1789 and 1918 and collected in the 1970s by the poetry lovers C. C. Kohler and Michèle Kohler, the library catalogued the poetry in four chronologically ordered bound volumes entitled *Minor British Poets*. Now the library staff has placed the collection on microfilm under the title *The Kohler Collection of British Poetry*. The omission of the word *minor* from the new title attests to the effects of a dozen years of changing critical perspectives on the poetry of British women writers of the Romantic era.

The library has made additional acquisitions only in the collection's earliest time segment, the Romantic era, which the library dates from 1789 to 1839. The library has added over 1,400 volumes to the holdings, doubling the original number, because the Romantic period is the era that has evoked the greatest scholarly interest among the faculty. It is the women writers of the era who have generated that interest, even though perhaps fewer than a fifth of the Kohler poets, whose gender is not always easy to determine by pen name alone, are female.

As of 1985, according to the preface to the 1840–1869 catalog, approximately forty percent of the collection's holdings were found in no other library in the United States (Kreissman), and, by the *National Union Catalogue*'s count, another twenty percent of its titles were available in only one other American library. Thus, in addition to works by such recently rediscovered and influential poets as Charlotte Smith, Helen Maria Williams, Mary Robinson, Charlotte Dacre, Mary Tighe, Mary R. Mitford, Letitia Elizabeth Landon, and Felicia Hemans, the Kohler collection holds fascinating volumes from more obscure authors like Jane Dunnett, Caroline Maxwell, and Mrs. W. Spencer, author of an 1812 volume entitled *Commemorative Feelings*. This mixture of poetry, some of it on the verge of—indeed in danger of—canonization and some of it still virtually unknown, presents serious challenges to the scholar wishing to write about and to teach it. We hope that our experiences with these poems can illuminate some of those challenges and suggest strategies for meeting them.

The first section that follows, Jane King's, concerns her research in the Kohler archives, supported by a grant from the UC Davis Humanities Institute, in 1988–89 (the year that Kari Lokke began teaching at Davis, excited by the terra incognita of the collection). The second section, written by King and Lokke, treats the teaching, at the graduate and undergraduate levels, of the diverse poetry that this research has unearthed.

King's Experience with the Collection

The problems one encounters in researching Romantic women poets, especially questions about selecting and organizing the material, anticipate some of the difficulties of teaching them. Alice was not more amazed and befuddled in Wonderland than I was when first confronted with the number and diversity of early Romantic women poets in the Kohler collection. I couldn't have known what to expect, because even feminist criticism before 1988 had emphasized the lack of poetry by women of this period. It never occurred to me, for instance, that women might have written epics, such as Lucy Aiken's *Epistles on Women* or Margaret Holford's *Margaret of Anjou*. (Emily Dickinson had, after all, written relatively short poems.) And there was so much poetry where I had expected to find so little; there was such variety where I had thought to find a certain sameness, both of genre and topic—comic poems, odes, ballads, satires, sestets, and more, poems about war, politics, nature, religion, education, love, the sublime. How could all this poetry have been utterly lost? How could one make sense of this body of work that refused to conform to notions of repressed or polite women authors? What I had thought would be a wasteland turned out indeed to be a wonderland; how delightful that the problem was not too few poets but too many.

Having identified from the catalog some two hundred volumes of poetry by women published between 1789 and 1839, almost all entirely unknown to me, the problem of reading order immediately presented itself. The only organizing information I could glean from the catalog was date of publication, so I decided to read chronologically. This approach proved generally helpful, though not entirely, because the poems were often published decades after their composition, and I found myself reading many poems written in the last half of the eighteenth century, which therefore reflected the tastes of an age earlier than the one I sought to study. Stuart Curran points to a related problem in "Romantic Poetry: The 'I' Altered": female Romantic poets, unlike most of their canonical male counterparts, often had very long lives and poetic careers, so that their poems span eras we have traditionally divided into separate literary periods. Therefore many traditional assumptions about literary history are unhelpful in studies of their work. During my research it became apparent that the history of women poets was distinct from that of canonized male poets and had to be created from the poems themselves.

Some contextualizing with the canon was, of course, possible and useful. For example, odes to personifications of ideals such as Modesty and Sensibility become less fashionable as the nineteenth century progresses (though they do not fade out entirely), and the influence of Pope, for instance, gradually wanes (fewer and fewer poems refer to him directly). But "Keatsian" diction and melancholy permeate this poetry long before Keats appears on the scene, which helps illuminate Keats's anxiety over feminine influence and readership. And Janetta Philipps's poems to transcendence and sublime visions found a clear devotee in Percy Bysshe Shelley, who ordered numerous copies of her book while at Oxford. Still, reading this bewildering assortment of unknown works created the overall impression of entering a literary landscape in which old rules no longer applied.

The specific problem presented by the dating of these poems illustrates the larger and more significant one concerning a body of noncanonical work, that is, how to contextualize it. Since most of one's prior assumptions prove wrong or incomplete in regard to the material, it becomes necessary to allow the poetry to teach one how to read it. Thanks to good advice from John Skarstad, the head librarian for special collections, I indexed topics and genres as I read. Recording information on theme, genre, allusions, references to other poets, influential subscribers, and publishers helped me sort out poems that were particularly worth writing about and teaching. For example, when I became intrigued by the symbolism attached to flower imagery, I was able quickly to assemble from my database an assortment of relevant poems to compare. The approach also helps with decisions regarding quality, because when poems are grouped like this, one or two will always stand out as exemplary or especially interesting. My index became a lifeline for making connections between poets when it came time to write about them and teach them.

Lokke and King's Experience Teaching the Collection

As often happens, teaching these poems proved enormously helpful in formulating and articulating our understanding of their intertextual significance. In a graduate seminar entitled Women Writers of Romanticism, the first challenge we faced was selecting poems to teach. We recognized the great variety—in theme, style, genre, length, poetics—of Romantic women's poetry, yet we still tried to create a fairly representative sample of fifteen to twenty poems. King assembled a group of poems (later expanded) that were individually interesting and that, taken together, provided a sense of the remarkable range of the poetry.

Several of our selection criteria may be useful to other teachers formulating syllabi. A number of poems that commented on other Romantic poems and poets—Mary Robinson's "The Poet Coleridge" and Mrs. Spencer's tribute to Charlotte Smith, for example—were essential to discussions of poetic influence and self-definition. We wanted the students to be able to contextualize the poetry, and therefore we included poems whose themes were familiarly Romantic, recognizably from the tradition of women's poetry, or both. To provide a gendered commentary on the role of the woman poet, we also sought poems written from a strong protofeminist perspective, such as Susan Evance's sonnet that opens, "Oh, Take me from the hated haunts of man," and the Elizabeth Bath sonnet that ends with the ringing assertion "Give me the mind where genius sits alone, / Creating worlds and kingdoms of her own." Anne Hunter's "A Ballad of the Eighteenth Century," an eerie and powerful prefiguration of *Jane Eyre*, and Smith's "Saint Monica" represented the Gothic. Then, for thematic balance, we added an antiwar poem, a love lament, a poem addressed to an infant, and a humorous poem. We also sought a mixture of poems by better-known authors and more obscure ones.

Once selected, the poems begin to work together and, in fact, to teach themselves. In an almost revelatory fashion, the bewildering profusion of information and insight sorts itself out, underscoring the importance of teaching these works in relation to one another. Poems that at first seem most notable for their perceived eccentricities open up to new and exciting readings in the light of works by other women poets. Similarities in diction, symbolism, and theme reveal themselves; political and aesthetic preoccupations become apparent; one sees new connections to canonical works of Romanticism and can begin to help students understand how gender inflects poetic voice.

Exploring with our students how these women wrote to and for one another and how thematically and stylistically this poetry belongs to the continuing tradition of women's writing makes clear that women's poetry of this period is not a gap but rather a firm link in the tradition. Poems about birds and cages, such as Maxwell's "Captivity: The Lamentation of a Canary Bird in His Cage," for example, correspond to what Cheryl Walker in her study of nineteenth-century American women poets calls the "free bird" poem. The great importance for this female tradition of the figure of Sappho and her incarnation in Robinson's work and Mme de Staël's *Corinne* becomes strikingly evident. Working with combinations of poems, students also discover the many intricate ways in which desire and the search for autonomy and artistic recognition are masked and encoded by techniques similar to those outlined in Alicia Ostriker's *Stealing the Language*.

We have devoted one three-hour class session to British women poets both times that the graduate seminar Women Writers of Romanticism was offered. Each time, the session has been a highlight of the seminar, affording students the exhilaration of discovering virtually unknown poetry. Undergraduates in upper-division courses on Romanticism are similarly receptive to reading and writing assignments involving these poets. The requirements of covering a large number of texts and authors in these courses make it impractical to focus solely on female poets. But it does work extremely well to set up provocative pairings of poems by canonical male poets with works by female poets. Susan Evance's "To a Violet" presents a picture of feminine obscurity and modesty different from that in Wordsworth's "She Dwelt among the Untrodden Ways," for instance, and Smith's portrayal of the relation of cultural memory to nature in "Saint Monica" reflects and challenges the assumptions underlying "Tintern Abbey." Similarly, Dunnett's angry, apocalyptic "On the First Eruption of Mount Vesuvius" provides a fascinating contrast to Byron's coldly cynical picture of the extinction of life in "Darkness," just as Maxwell's protest against women's imprisonment by cultural stereotype in "Captivity" illuminates Byron's metaphysical and existential vision of freedom in "The Prisoner of Chillon."

As the exciting work of Romantic women poets becomes more accessible, we hope that other scholars will turn their attention to it and begin to integrate noncanonical poets into their teaching and research. The richness and diversity of the Kohler collection illustrates the need for scholars to create innovative pedagogical and critical approaches to British women poets of the Romantic period, even as they expand their own horizons by exploring this and other archives that beckon them.

"In Tangled Mazes Wrought":
Hypertext and Teaching Romantic Women Poets

Joel Haefner

Midway the hill of science, after steep
And rugged paths that tire the unpractised feet,
A grove extends; in tangled mazes wrought,
And filled with strange enchantment:—dubious shapes
Flit through dim glades, and lure the eager foot
Of youthful ardour to eternal chase.
                    —Anna Letitia Barbauld

Anna Letitia Barbauld's 1797 warning to Samuel Taylor Coleridge could, with just a bit of retrofitting, seem a warning about the current juggernaut of instructional technology—that we need to beware of getting lost in digital space. And indeed a traditionalist might read in Barbauld's lines that romanticism is, or should be, grounded in the sensible world and that the study of romanticism should be anchored in the real world of the text.[1] The mainstream romantic writer, so the story goes, is adamantly antiscientific and antimechanistic.

But Barbauld's positioning—and indeed the whole issue of the machine in the romantic garden—is much more complicated. We note, even in the passage above, that the bower of temptation of which Barbauld warns Coleridge is "Midway the hill of science," a small part of that hill. Barbauld condemns this metaphysical false Eden, not science as a whole. Her poems addressed to and concerning Joseph Priestley's scientific experiments suggest not an outright rejection of the empirical and scientific but an insistence that we keep a balanced perspective. We should keep this warning in mind as we confront our digital future. The question is not whether computer-supported instruction has any place in the teaching of romanticism but how computers complement and transform our pedagogical and scholarly goals.

Computers and the Internet offer a range of applications to the literature classroom, a range I can only suggest here before focusing on a section of it. Some literature teachers use local area network (LAN) servers, CD-ROMs, and Internet hosts to give their students access to a wealth of online texts, especially texts by women that are difficult to find; the Women Writers Project at Brown University comes immediately to mind, as well as Jerome McGann's efforts to make more texts available on the Internet. Archives on the World Wide Web include graphic and textual resources that can complement the study of literature. Real-time conferencing can augment conventional class discussion. Finally, hypertext—the focus of this paper—offers one of the most exciting ways of restructuring and reconceiving a text.

Theodor Nelson coined the term *hypertext* in the early 1970s and gave a succinct definition: "an ongoing system of interconnecting documents" (*Literary*

Machines 2, 9). Hypertext became a technological reality in the 1980s, although Vannevar Bush had hypothesized a protohypertext, a "memex," by 1945. Many of us have become familiar with hypertext through the help features of programs like *Microsoft Word* or through CD-ROM encyclopedias: several key words in a passage are highlighted (or are "hot"); by clicking on one of these "nodes" with the mouse cursor, the user opens a new window, with additional text, graphics, or sounds. Several theorists of hypertext, such as Jay David Bolter, note that the concept of hypertext is not exactly new: footnotes, tables of contents, and indexes are all kinds of hypertext, systematically connecting documents within a single text (15). The two hypertext programs most commonly used in the classroom are Apple's *HyperCard* (for the Macintosh) and Asymetrix's *ToolBook* (for *Windows*).

Writers have identified a number of theoretical and pedagogical implications of hypertext. Most argue that hypertext undermines the traditional authority of the writer: "The author is no longer an intimidating figure, not a prophet or a Mosaic legislator in Shelley's sense," Bolter comments (153). And the reader assumes more agency. George P. Landow writes that "the figure of the hypertext author approaches, even if it does not entirely merge with, that of the reader; the functions of reader and writer become more deeply entwined with each other than ever before" (*Hypertext* 71). And the text becomes increasingly fluid and unstable. Some writers explicitly link hypertext to postmodernism and poststructuralism: Stuart Moulthrop and Nancy Kaplan call hypertext "an evolutionary outgrowth of late-modern textuality" (221).

At first glance, no two things could seem more incompatible than hypertext and the study of romantic poetry. Hypertext seems to subvert every precept romanticists bring into the classroom: the authority of the individual genius; the alienation of the writer from the reading public; the sanctity of the text. Yet these features make hypertext an attractive tool for teaching women writers from the romantic period because those writers and their texts challenge our preconceptions about romanticism and offer alternative aesthetics and epistemologies. The seeming contradictions and ambiguities of applying hypertext to the study of romanticism reflect not hardware or software limitations but our received wisdoms. Even the hypertext theorists are at odds: some label hypertext antiromantic because it undermines the romantic authorization of the author; others call hypertext romantic because it mirrors the associative theory of the mind that the early romantics espoused and gives voice to a new persona, the reader/creator (Charney 240).

To explore how hypertext might affect the study of romantic literature, consider two passages summarizing traditional romantic attitudes toward science and technology. In the first, John Turner argues that William Wordsworth condemns science's "habit of endless division and subdivision, its fragmentation of a single world into a multiplicity of fact, its process of systematic disintegration" (23). And here is the second, more global statement, from Hans Eichner:

> If the mechanical philosophy had sought to explain all phenomena, in-
> cluding those of life, by causal determination, by the motion of particles,
> and by the heuristic model of the machine, Romantic philosophy sought
> to explain all phenomena, including so-called dead matter, by freedom,
> by conscious or unconscious mental processes, and by the analogy of or-
> ganisms.   (15)

Wordsworth might well have hated hypertext, which fragments text into hot buttons, nodes, and links. But this fragmentation is not factual but interpretive, and a programmer can organize a hypertext document so that it is quite well structured. Eichner's comment highlights the "contrarities" of hypertext in the literature classroom: hypertext is indeed grounded in the "model of the ma-chine," and yet the use and ordering of text and data in hypertext are dynamic and are based on human epistemology. Catherine F. Smith, sounding much like a romantic organicist, refers to the "living form" and "cognitive architec-ture" of hypertext (269). In other words, we cannot claim that it is incongruous to support romantic literature instruction with hypertext. It's just not that sim-ple. In fact, as the last quote from Smith suggests, we can explicitly connect hy-pertext to romantic aesthetics and epistemology and to our own pedagogy.

First, and most important for the study of women poets during the roman-tic period, hypertext tends to undermine the hegemony of the canon. As John-dan Johnson-Eilola claims, "Hypertext threatens the privileged status of canonized works by unfixing them from their physical, unalterable status and placing them in the fluid medium of computer-based text" (210). The usual methods of canonization—the physical binding and table of contents of an an-thology—disappear in hypertext, and since hypertext documents are limited only by digital storage space and transmission speeds, the exclusion of women poets becomes more difficult to justify. Linking canonized and noncanonized texts stresses the common environment men and women wrote in as well as the similarities (instead of the differences) between widely anthologized texts by men and neglected texts by women. Landow, who has used hypertext to teach Victorian literature, points out that hypertext makes it easier to create a cus-tomized anthology that includes texts by women and writers of non-English ethnic backgrounds ("Hypertext" 87–91).

Second, hypertext replaces the paradigm of the writer-who-writes-alone with a collaborative interaction among a writer, other writers, and readers. The cross-fertilization that was truly characteristic of the romantic era may be bet-ter illustrated with hypertextual links among authors, across texts, genres, and geography. Stuart Curran has recently "recontextualized" the *Lyrical Ballads* by detailing its relation to Mary Robinson's *Lyrical Tales* ("Mary Robinson's *Lyrical Tales*"), and this kind of recontextualization can, with hypertext, be car-ried explicity into the classroom.

Third, as a corollary, a hypertext program that is accessible to students engages them in the conversation as well. An opportunity like this holds nearly as many perils as rewards. Through a *HyperCard* program I developed with Bill Prigge, an instructional technologist at Illinois State University, students can import texts, link texts to their essays, and attach comments. While some students revel in these powers, others feel that the space of the author—and of the text—has been invaded.

Fourth, hypertext can help instructors contextualize works culturally. Despite its name, hypertext can allow not only texts but also images and sounds to "enter" a text. Landow and others at Brown University, using *Intermedia*, a hypertext program developed there, have already illustrated how hypertext can enrich literary contexts and cross disciplinary boundaries ("Hypertext" 78–82). The integration of arts and media that has informed romantic pedagogy and criticism can be highlighted in ways that weren't possible before: slides of paintings, buildings, and portraits become immediately and repeatedly available to students, along with sounds and a plethora of other texts. And if students are allowed to participate in constructing a hypertext document, that integration can become increasingly complex and dense semester after semester. This feature of hypertext is particularly important for studying women poets like Barbauld, Charlotte Smith, and Felicia Hemans because many of their poems are already, in a sense, hypertextual: that is, they are heavily footnoted.

Fifth, hypertext may reinforce two closely connected aspects of romanticism: associationism and the aesthetic of fragmentation, what Thomas McFarland refers to as "diasparactive" thinking (4). The "multisequential" (Landow, "Hypertext" 70) linking of texts, images, and sounds is profoundly associative and preconscious; the product is broken text, jumps from idea to idea, image to image, voice to voice. And the size of a text is further constrained by the screen and memory size of the computer. Many teachers would see this as a major liability. But we could use that dimension of hypertext to explore the diasparactive nature of romantic texts like Smith's "Beachy Head," Percy Shelley's "The Triumph of Life," Wordsworth's enormous *The Recluse*, or the last volumes and texts by Felicia Hemans and Letitia Landon.

Finally, the use of hypertext in a literature class will create a different kind of learning community and alter the dynamics of the classroom, as my experiences and those of other hypertext users and as a number of writers, foremost among them Richard Lanham, predict. Hypertext is not, in the end, a new technology that we drag into the classroom to supplement our teaching while remaining unscathed. It is a new way of presenting, organizing, and accessing information within the context of higher education, and as such it is in essence a social institution. But although this view of hypertext is sure to irritate and frighten some readers, there are still sound pedagogical connections between hypertext and the teaching of romantic women poets. The innovation and fascination with change and revolution that characterized many of the writers of our period parallels the potential impact of hypertext. The generic experimentation of the period—Ann Batten Cristall's *Poetical Sketches*, for example, or Mary Robinson's *Lyrical Tales*—mirrors the textual changes hypertext creates. And instructors can discuss the social changes that affected many romantic texts within today's technological revolution. The limitations of gender, for example, that Robinson so eloquently attacked in "Thoughts on the Condition of Women" can be read in the context of gender disparities in computer technology, the Internet, and even hypertext specifically.

Imagine, for a moment, how this might work in the classroom. Let us suppose that, during a one- or two-week period, students focus on "Beachy Head," published in 1807, shortly after Smith's death on 28 October 1806. First, of course, one has to digitally scan the text, using Stuart Curran's *The Poems of Charlotte Smith* as the definitive text. Then the fun begins. Breaking into salons or writing circles of, say, six or eight in a class of twenty-four, students begin to forge links, to make digital connections to the poem. Perhaps the autobiographical core of the poem, lines 282 through 367, attracts the most attention and produces the greatest number of links. One circle, focusing on the visual arts, discovers that Smith was instructed in art by George Smith at the age of six, and links to the poem a passage from Florence Hilbish's biography of Smith; another student writes a short commentary on the use of light and shadow in the visual descriptions of "Beachy Head" and links that to the Hilbish quote; two others link John Constable's *Stour Valley and Dedham Church* (1814–15); another student finds two paragraphs from Vivien Jones's "'The Coquetry of Nature': Politics and the Picturesque in Women's Fiction" to link to some of the descriptive passages of Smith's masterpiece.

Another student circle takes a different tack, contextualizing the intellectual milieu in which Smith wrote. Curran's classic article "Romantic Poetry: The 'I' Altered" is a logical link, as is Judith Pascoe's article on botany and Smith's poetry ("Female Botanists"). Wordsworth's 1833 tribute to Smith, along with the "Fair seedtime had my soul" passage from book 1 or the end of book 7 of *The Prelude*, is also linked. One student, fascinated by the question of whether "Beachy Head" was a fragment, links the poem to other fragments, like Shelley's *The Triumph of Life*, and includes comments from Thomas McFarland's theory of romantic fragmentation. Yet another student, drawing on Marlon Ross's *Contours of Masculine Desire* and Eleanor Ty's *Unsex'd Revolutionaries: Five Women Novelists of the 1790s*, links Smith's experiences with the tradition of women writers from which Smith wrote. A third group explores the sociocultural context of Smith's representation of the rural poor, urban life, the Regency family, and the position of women, among other topics, and so provides links to Henry Mayhew's descriptions of London life (though those appeared considerably later), William Cobbett's *Rural Rides*, Leonore Davidoff's article "The Family in Britain," and Mary Russell Mitford's bucolic essays in *Our Village*.

The fabric of links that such a project would weave replicates, to some extent, the kind of analytic thinking and connection making that we want our students to do. Unlike a traditional research paper, however, a hypertext document does not present a thesis buttressed with sequential or causal reasoning. Hypertext accomplishes other things than a "solid" research paper: it reflects, in a modern vernacular, the intellectual exchange among women and men writers of the romantic period; it involves the students in the re-creation of the text; it re-contextualizes Smith's poem in the literary and social world in which it appeared; it establishes a parity and an interchange between Smith's oeuvre and canonical texts; it breaks down disciplinary lines by providing visual and audio links. And the hypertext document does not end with finals week: it can be perpetually supplemented by subsequent students and, if written in HTML, published on the Web for all to see.

An essay in *Newsweek* asks, "Is it possible to tell a good story interactively?" and goes on to worry about the effect of hypermedia and interactive digital texts on narrative (Robbins 16). The question is complex, but what is important is that it is being asked on such a public stage. Some form of that question will crop up soon, very soon, in romantic literature classrooms across the country, and when it does it will profoundly influence the texts, contexts, and pretexts of romantic studies. For us as teachers of romantic women poets, under the shadow of the canonized six, it may be liberating and invigorating to find ourselves confronted with the digital text, in tangled mazes caught.

NOTE

¹I here use *romantic* and *romanticism* with a lowercase *r* to call into question the premises that there was a single coherent ideological movement, a sharply drawn "Romantic" period, and that writers can be tagged "Romantic" or not with anything approaching confidence. To capitalize *romantic* reifies a very slippery concept and denies the multiplicity of romanticisms. A quick perusal of the *Oxford English Dictionary* suggests that during the nineteenth century *romantic* was more commonly lowercase than not and that twentieth-century writers in particular marked *romantic*, *romanticism*, and *romanticist* as capitalized words.

Teaching Alien Aesthetics:
The Difficulty of Difference in the Classroom

Scott Simpkins

When I teach Romantic literature, I explore why we refer to certain artists as Romantic and seldom (or never) apply that label to others from the same period. I question the notion that older canons simply reflected what was available or written at the time, as opposed to consisting of what readers, critics, reviewers, editors, and teachers agreed on as good representations. The latter explanation is often forgotten, I suggest, because over time the evaluative sense of the "good" reverted into the background and was replaced with the seemingly neutral tag of "representative." My approach reorients the "representative" by setting aside for the moment evaluative criteria and focusing on what existed or was read during the period. Unfortunately, this approach can elicit resistance, primarily because so many students have already internalized a set of criteria based on a hermeneutical morality that is often extremely attractive.

To overcome this resistance, I ask students to focus on what is truly and historically representative and to relinquish their customary and conditioned emphasis on high-level technical achievement. After examining, often for the first time, the origin of this evaluative criterion, they are much better able to challenge its sacrosanct status. Students may have grown comfortable with their aesthetic judgments, but instructors can reveal that these judgments are acquired, not the result of an essentialistic revelation. This unveiling can often dramatically demonstrate how students accumulate the critical paradigms they value and, more important, how they can modify these received beliefs to their benefit. By the end of the semester, students usually recognize the immense advantages of alternative views of the period.

To introduce students to the issues that have generated discussion about—and resistance to—modern efforts to introduce women writers into Romantic literature, I survey the current widespread concern about aesthetics, valuation, and canonicity epitomized by Arthur J. Weitzman's reactionary lament in 1994 that the "changing intellectual climate . . . seems increasingly eager to jettison aesthetics altogether as irrelevant" (3). We discuss the considerable canon-shaping power wielded by "ethical idealists" who possess a seemingly unshakable sense of hermeneutical propriety and find security within the confines of the old canons. To examine the origins of these canons, we investigate at length some particular aesthetic criteria. I ask students to consider how cherished God terms have been deployed to establish canons based on value. Students consult critics like Barbara Herrnstein Smith, who identifies two criteria—"structural complexity" and "information-richness"—typically used to establish a hierarchy of aesthetic accomplishment (51), and Jan Gorak, who surveys historically representative bases for criteria of merit such as difficulty and universality, concepts that my students then weigh in relation to different poets of the Romantic period.

The extensive canonical tradition derived from humanism, I demonstrate through illustrations, uses rather fuzzy terms to determine who and what merit inclusion, as Albert Cook reveals when he asserts that "in the ideal situation which we must be envisaging when we undertake to judge poems at all, they are finally conceived of as partaking in and communicating a wisdom encoded through the 'beauty' of the work" (15). Gorak does likewise when he proposes an "ineradicable cultural need" for the organizing support a canon provides (7), and so does Joseph Margolis, who defines *canon* as "a principled way of interpreting the normative import of an array of specimen cases" (161). As an exercise to illuminate the influence of personal preferences on the making of most canons (including my own noncanonical canon, of course), I ask students to compare these positions with their own aesthetic investments as indicated by their responses to poems introduced in class.

These preferences, I contend, are reconfigured through essentialist justifications that thereby mask their origins. To dramatize how individual taste is cloaked through the presumption of a seemingly impersonal aesthetics, we engage in exercises such as comparing the adult-child relations in poems that students usually praise as accomplished (Coleridge's "Frost at Midnight" or Wordsworth's "We Are Seven") with those in other poems (Felicia Hemans's "The Dreaming Child"). Initially, students argue that the familiar poems are obviously superior to the lesser-known ones. The evaluation changes quickly when I ask them to account for their response, which helps them realize that they have been taught to favor certain aesthetic orientations over others without relying on ostensibly intrinsic criteria.

More important, instructors can resituate a noncanonical poem so that students can see its contiguities with other Romantic texts instead of its differences. Because the Hemans poem, for example, portrays an adult speculating on the cause of a sleeping child's dream-related distress, it is arguably similar to the Wordsworth and Coleridge poems in theme and approach. However, since the adult narrator is the child's mother, who endeavors to spare her child premature exposure to the "human woe" adults suffer, students frequently consider her less significant than Wordsworth's and Coleridge's narrators, who usually assume greater status as patriarchs within the family dynamic. Yet others in class will trouble these observations and conclude that Coleridge's poem investigates a similar domestic affection. Wordsworth's poem likewise celebrates the preservation of childhood innocence, a theme that figures prominently in Hemans's conclusion, in which the mother gives thanks that she can still "win [her son] back from visionary strife!" ("The Dreaming Child" 34).

The class can examine irony in this way as well. Blake's social commentary in the *Songs of Innocence and of Experience* is typically viewed as an exemplary work of irony. Could the same be said, we consider in class, of something like Hannah More's "The Sorrows of Yamba, or the Negro Woman's Lamentation" and Anna Barbauld's "To the Poor"? Students' initial response to both works can be unfavorable: More seems to promote slavery and religious oppression through Yamba's seeming quietism regarding the promised reprieve in the afterlife, while Barbauld similarly appears to encourage the poor, "[B]ear thy wrongs" ("To the Poor" 11). Class discussion generates an amazing shift in perspective, though, as students move from dislike of these seemingly heavy-handed, even mean-spirited, poems to formulate intriguing alternative readings. What cues, I ask, suggest that Blake is actually critical of his narrators' opinions? And what prevents us from considering these other poets capable of an ironic stance too?

I continually emphasize the historical range and diversity of Romantic literature, asking questions like Anne Mellor's: "What happens to our interpretations of Romanticism if we focus our attention on the numerous women writers who produced at least half of the literature published in England between 1780 and 1830?" (*Romanticism and Gender* 1). Not surprisingly, students are often shocked to discover that there is much literature from that time besides the poetry of canonized writers like Wordsworth. So, I ask further, is it responsible or ethical to ignore such works that were excluded from the canon simply because of their aesthetic difference? Hélène Cixous, who has wrestled with the issue of gender-specific criteria at length, concludes that the "infinite richness" of women's "individual constitutions" leads down a blind alley: perhaps "you can't talk about a female sexuality, uniform, homogeneous, classifiable into codes—any more than you can talk about one unconscious resembling another" (1233). Yet one can produce revelations by exploring this gender distinction, and that may be the greatest benefit to a revisionary Romantic poetry project.

For instance, I contend in class that women writers of the Romantic period offer a literature that merits consideration simply by virtue of its existence; if this writing seems inferior to my students, we then trace how they acquired the aesthetic criteria they use to make that assessment. Why do we view William Wordsworth's descriptions of a mind interacting with nature, for example, as superior to similar descriptions by Dorothy Wordsworth? To illustrate this comparison I point out William Wordsworth's famous description of a group of daffodils (in "I Wandered Lonely As a Cloud"):

> All at once I saw a crowd,
> A host, of golden daffodils;
> Beside the lake, beneath the trees,
> Fluttering and dancing in the breeze.
>
> Continuous as the stars that shine
> And twinkle on the milky way,
> They stretched in never-ending line
> Along the margin of a bay:
> Ten thousand saw I at a glance,
> Tossing their heads in sprightly dance.
>
> The waves beside them danced; but they
> Out-did the sparkling waves in glee.
>> (*Poems* 619, 3–14)

Then Dorothy Wordsworth's description, from the *Grasmere Journals*:

> They grew among the mossy stones, about and about them; some rested their heads upon these stones as on a pillow for weariness, and the rest tossed and reeled and danced, and seemed as if they verily laughed with the wind that blew upon them over the lake. They looked so gay—ever-glancing, ever-changing.   (Wu 496–97)

The first response from students on this comparison usually centers on genre and the common elevation of poetry over prose. I note that William Wordsworth himself supported a nonevaluative distinction between the two forms in the preface to *Lyrical Ballads*. Students usually then find Dorothy Wordsworth's text potentially far more engaging and fruitful than they had before. After all, I ask, do the texts differ that much in depicting an arresting image derived from the everyday? If so, does that difference necessarily involve aesthetic merit? Some students inevitably maintain the conventional position and give William Wordsworth the nod, but others recognize the benefit of at least entertaining these alternative views.

One can also foreground Dorothy Wordsworth's verse by comparing her commentary on the moments when mutability seems especially overwhelming with William Wordsworth's similar explorations (in the Intimations Ode) or with other parallel examples (Keats's "Ode to a Nightingale," for example, or Letitia Elizabeth Landon's "Lines of Life"). In "Thoughts on My Sickbed" she writes:

> has the remnant of my life
> Been pilfered of this sunny spring?
> And have its own prelusive sounds
> Touched in my heart no echoing string?
>   (Wu 502)

I stress that such comparisons were common (especially among reviewers) during the Romantic period, and I cite the dueling quotations William Wordsworth used in the prefaces to the *Lyrical Ballads* and *Poems* (1815) as representative attempts to situate comparative aesthetic fields by evaluating one against another.

Studies like Marlon Ross's *The Contours of Masculine Desire* help illuminate the bias against women's poetry because of its difference. Ross observes that "Romanticist critics have made women writers of the period an extension of male Romanticism" (5), praising certain women writers only for being like their male counterparts. I have used Anna Seward's sonnets to illustrate the opportunity that this apparent problem provides. Those sonnets can come across as overly sentimental, pedestrian, or technically lacking, in comparison with the more familiar (male) poetry associated with Romanticism, especially when placed beside the "soul-animating strains" of some of William Wordsworth's sonnets such as "The World Is Too Much with Us; Late and Soon." But one can introduce students to canonized authors' poetry, conveniently left out of anthologies, to demonstrate that these poets wrote similar work. Compare Wordsworth's "It Is a Beauteous Evening, Calm and Free" with Seward's "Sonnet 91" and their similarities become clearer. In the opening locodescriptive lines Wordsworth's placid landscape contrasts with a strong emotional response by the narrator:

> It is a beauteous evening, calm and free,
> The holy time is quiet as a Nun
> Breathless with adoration; the broad sun
> Is sinking down in its tranquillity;
> The gentleness of heaven broods o'er the Sea:
> Listen! the mighty Being is awake,
> And doth with his eternal motion make
> A sound like thunder—everlastingly.   (1–8)

The first eleven lines of Seward's poem describe an emotional field remarkably like that in Wordsworth's:

> On the fleet streams, the Sun, that late arose,
>   In amber radiance plays; the tall young grass
>   No foot had bruised; clear morning, as I pass,
>   Breathes the pure gale, that on the blossom blows;
> And, as with gold yon green hill's summit glows,
>   The lake inlays the vale with molten glass:
>   Now is the year's soft youth, yet one, alas!
>   Cheers not as it was wont; impending woes
> Weigh on my heart; the joys, that once were mine,
>   Spring leads not back; and those that yet remain
>   Fade while she blooms.   (Breen 37)

Is this really so different from Wordsworth? Yes, but perhaps only in that it articulates an aesthetic distinction attributable to gender; we need not label it inferior according to aesthetic standards derived from the work of male poets like Wordsworth. Different, not less valuable, in other words.

Another classroom strategy can also reveal how the new space opened by women Romantic poets is merely a different facet of Romanticism, one that has been silenced through a long history of canonical omission to the point that it seems inferior to, rather than merely different from, that inscribed by poems in the canon. Because this difference offers much territory to explore as we try to broaden our perspective upon the nature of literature actually written and published during the period, students can be encouraged to approach that poetry from a descriptive, instead of a prescriptive, standpoint seeking to identify the salient characteristics of that poetry based on aesthetic qualities rather than on an ostensibly evaluative standard. To investigate the *difference* of women Romantic writers, my students read criticism that focuses on apparently distinct features of women's works, such as emphasis on the everyday, on the political economy of the domestic sphere, and on the psychosexual implications of operating within a socially marginalized space. Joanna Baillie's "A Winter's Day" and "A Summer's Day," which present unremarkable descriptions of daily routines among rural workers, may seem stiflingly dull to a reader schooled on arguably more exciting depictions of apocalypse, robber clans, insanity, and intense self-scrutiny. Yet the difference in subject matter illustrates an aspect of the difference of an arguably feminine Romanticism. In class I also cite observations like Lawrence Lipking's assertion that women challenge the value of authorial objectivity often privileged in male-based aesthetics concerned with context. "A literary theory true to women's experience . . . is likely to view 'aesthetic distance' as a sham, a denial of women's rights to literature," Lipking asserts. "A reader absorbed by a text finds her own identity there, and a man who tells her to stand back probably does so because he is after her place" (94). I also direct my students to many recent studies as useful models for new, representative readings of the period and encourage them to itemize the often differing responses to poems they are studying. However, at the same time I prod students to remain tentative about all presumed distinctions, reminding them of the temptation to reductively totalize a field or entity by assuming that it has essential, objectively identifiable features.

In effect, we try in my classes to set newer views of Romanticism in dialogue with older ones. I point out the views of critics like Stuart Curran, who observes that "to look with attention and historical discrimination is to realize that some of the genres we associate most closely with British Romanticism . . . were themselves strongly impelled by women poets; that some of the distinctive preoccupations of women poets eventually color the landscape we think of as Romantic; and that others are so decidedly different as to suggest a terra incognita beneath our very feet" ("Romantic Poetry: The 'I' Altered" 189). I contrast those views with revealing remarks like John Hodgson's approving assertion that "in the typical Major English Romantic Poets course [c. 1986] Wordsworth's poetry comes early, looms large, and, if we teach it at all well, persists stubbornly and vividly" (130). Students begin to see how ultimately unhelpful judgments like Hodgson's are when I ask them to discuss how they would formulate a semester's reading list from an ever-increasing body of available writing.

My students realize that previous courses seriously misrepresented a period that produced a startlingly diverse body of writing, and, more important, they understand that adding selections by writers like Hemans and Barbauld will require deleting selections by writers like Wordsworth and Coleridge. Some of them remain unwilling to make this trade-off (arguing, e.g., that poetry from the older tradition is simply too good to omit even small amounts), while others see that a blend of marginalized and traditional poets can offer a much more nuanced sampling of the period. Some even argue for entirely new renditions of Romanticism that entail reading little or no poetry by those who once "loomed large." But most students recognize the difficult choices involved in accommodating classroom limitations. In fact, they quickly come to agree with Herbert Lindenberger's observations that "a new challenge [to the older canon] is far more likely to extend the canon than to allow its present membership to be shrunk" and that "the power struggles that must be waged to achieve canonical status for a particular figure require a redistribution of what often turns out to be limited resources: just as the manufacturers of consumer products struggle for supermarket shelf space, so those who seek to expand the canon must compete for limited space" (41, 145).

As the class explores the etiology of our attitudes about Romantic aesthetics and the current debates about them, I urge my students to consider how they would situate the canon in their research and teaching. I suggest the possibility of adopting "something like a transient literary *canon*" (Margolis 139) or constructing multiple canons in accordance with Arthur O. Lovejoy's pluralistic notion of "Romanticisms," a strategy that, in Lipking's words, offers us a way to "put women back into time" (102).

It is undoubtedly worth the effort, and it may even be an ethical responsibility, to show our students different registers of Romanticism that include aesthetic considerations seemingly distinct to women's writing. While using a priori evaluative criteria to construct a canon certainly has its merits, there is much to be said for directly involving students in deciding for themselves what typifies Romanticism. As Lindenberger suggests, this undertaking can effect significant paradigm shifts for those who believe specific works are more representative than others. "With sufficient rhetorical skill we can persuade others to love, revere and enshrine the works we ourselves have decided to treasure," he argues, "and we can even—as those who revise the canon have normally done at all times—persuade them to question their earlier commitments, indeed to change the objects of their literary affections" (147).

Strategies for Replacing the Six-Poet Course
Judith Pascoe

It has never been possible to teach a semester-long course in Romantic-era literature without being acutely aware of all that one is leaving out: one rarely plumbs the depths of a Romantic anthology. The study of Byron has a tendency to get compressed or even omitted in the end-of-semester crunch, and Blake's later, self-referential works are conjured through broad gestures rather than perplexing details. A new attention to the works of women writers merely exacerbates the situation, and women are not the only ones who have traditionally got short shrift in the undergraduate classroom. The names John Clare, Robert Bloomfield, and George Crabbe remind us of Romantic-era experience not easily subsumed under the rubric of the greater Romantic lyric.

I propose some alternatives to the six-poet class here, offering up my experiences in teaching classes focused on (to use convenient labels) genre, history, and theory. In the first category I include two lower-level undergraduate classes, one devoted to Romantic-era autobiography and another organized around particular poetic forms (sonnet, epic, romance, etc.). The classes both carried the title Selected Works of the Romantic Period. Because students at the University of Iowa, where I teach, are not required to take survey courses (instead they must take courses in several categories such as pre-1800 literature, literature and culture of a historical period, and cultural studies), the course can be fairly flexible. In the second category falls an undergraduate honors seminar entitled Romantic Revolutions, which focused on prose responses to the French Revolution and efforts to bring about a revolution in poetry, and a graduate seminar on the 1790s. In the final category, I discuss another graduate seminar, entitled Romanticism and Gender, which used gender and performance theory to grapple with the place of both women and Woman in Romanticism.

A class on autobiography can capitalize on students' prurient interest in the often scandalous lives of Romantic-era writers while tempering their enthusiasm for biographical readings of literary works: by the end of the semester they will have ample evidence of the fictiveness of all literary representation. I began my class on autobiography with Jean-Jacques Rousseau's *Confessions* and Mary Robinson's *Memoirs*, focusing particularly on the style of narration and the concern for audience; we lingered on the passages in these putatively private texts where the authors' attention to their readers is most clear. For the first writing assignment I asked students to examine how a particular moment in one of the texts is described and how the author's concern for his or her audience affects self-construction. The pairing of Dorothy Wordsworth's *Grasmere Journals* and William Wordsworth's *Prelude* also forced students to focus on style more than story (thus avoiding plot summary in their critical writing). What students originally saw as Dorothy Wordsworth's plain style, her quotidian register of events, supplements William Wordsworth's more self-consciously artful mode of writing; her completeness calls attention to his omissions. But we also came to question the seeming artlessness of Dorothy Wordsworth's writing, noting her dramatic, although abbreviated, enactments of desire.

The course encompassed texts that are autobiographical though they are not autobiographies (for example, Byron's *Don Juan*) and fictional works that incorporate elements of autobiography, such as James Hogg's *Confessions of a Justified Sinner* and Mary Hays's *The Memoirs of Emma Courtney*. A Tilottama Rajan essay on *Memoirs* provides a useful framework for works of what Rajan calls a "(post)romantic intergenre" characterized by "transgressive miscegenation of private and public spaces" (149, 158–59). Hays's text and its reception (which Rajan helpfully reviews) underscore the ways in which women's autobiographies and literary works are inextricably bound. Moira Ferguson's edition of *The History of Mary Prince*, which includes documents relating to the work's publication, conveys to students the kinds of mediation that influence the publication of works by writers out of the cultural mainstream. That Prince's abolitionist mentors transcribed and rectified her narrative makes it impossible to establish an authoritative text. Prince's work thus resembles many other Romantic texts, most notably John Keats's "Ode on a Grecian Urn," whose final lines are variously punctuated.

The writing assignments included both critical writing (for example, students wrote about the effects of large-scale omission and small-scale revision in book 9 of *The Prelude*) and autobiographical writing (students wrote a journal entry on a day in their lives and then revised it into an autobiographical essay, which had the unintended but bracing result of confirming what a small star my class was in the constellation of my students' social lives). The contrast between the ease with which they wrote about their lives and the awkwardness with which they wrote critical essays underscored that, for many students, academic writing is like composing in a foreign language. Toward the end of the class, we read Jane Tompkins's essay "Me and My Shadow" and discussed the possibility of merging academic and personal writing. One of the options for the final paper was to attempt such a merger in an essay on Byron's *Don Juan*. Just as Byron's narrator provides a running commentary on his performance, students provided commentaries on their own critiques, interweaving critical analysis and personal meditation. The class ended with an autobiographers' party, where students dressed as their favorite autobiographers or literary characters so as to conjure up a particular moment in one of the autobiographies we read—a dashing Lord Byron and a blind beggar were among the guests.

An undergraduate class I organized around poetic genres started out promisingly but foundered mid-semester (I drew on Stuart Curran's *Poetic Form and British Romanticism* to organize the syllabus around the sonnet, ode, pastoral, romance, epic, composite poem, and elegy). I chose the generic organization because I wanted to use an anthology (Duncan Wu's *Romanticism*) while drawing attention away from the anthology's comparatively scanty samplings of works by women. By beginning the class with a discussion of sonnets, rather than a particular writer's work, I was able to demonstrate the importance of Charlotte Smith's *Elegiac Sonnets* in the development of a Romantic ethos, to trace the influence of Smith and William Bowles on the sonnets of Samuel Taylor Coleridge, and to explain the usefulness of the sonnet as a vehicle of both sensibility and political sentiment (in Wordsworth's 1802–03 sonnets). The focus on different writers' work in a particular genre of poetry often helped underscore the interrelations of these writers and the malleability of the form. Wu's anthology proved particularly replete with elegies. We read Wordsworth's "Elegiac Stanzas, Suggested by a Picture of Peele Castle in a Storm, Painted by Sir George Beaumont" against Mary Shelley's "On Reading Wordsworth's Lines on Peele Castle." Most interestingly, we situated Felicia Hemans's elegiac poems (e.g., "The Grave of a Poetess") against Letitia Landon's "Stanzas on the Death of Mrs Hemans" and Elizabeth Barrett's "Stanzas Addressed to Miss Landon, and Suggested by Her 'Stanzas on the Death of Mrs Hemans.'" The comparisons made clear the primary preoccupations of late-Romantic-era women and the lines of influence among these writers. I assigned portions of Paul Fussell's *Poetic Meter and Poetic Form* periodically, using it during the sonnet section to help students learn how to scan poetry. I think there were many virtues to this class's design, but I have to admit that I lost my students in the middle of the ode section and had to keep scrambling to win them back. Reading lots of odes in a row, or for that matter reading epics back to back, is probably not a good idea with undergraduates. The design also underscored my students' lack of familiarity with poetic genres; I had to describe traditional pastoral, epic, and romance poems to demonstrate how Romantic-era practitioners deviated from poetic conventions.

Romantic Revolutions, an undergraduate honors seminar, began with group projects aimed at providing a historical context for the debate over the French Revolution carried out in England by Edmund Burke, Thomas Paine, Mary Wollstonecraft, and (less directly) William Godwin. Groups of three students each made time capsules containing four or five artifacts illustrative of the key social and political events of 1789–90, 1791–92, and 1793–94. The artifacts could be photographs, portraits, excerpts from key texts, or anything else that would give the class a vivid sense of French and British history. Students were asked to distribute a chronology of the two years they were responsible for and a bibliography of sources. The assignment brought the class up to speed on the major historical events that shaped the debate, but, perhaps more important, it established collaboration as the primary pedagogical mode for the class. After this project, interest groups formed and re-formed over the semester to deliver reports on such persons and topics as Marie Antoinette, Napoleon Bonaparte, and the aftermath of the Revolution.

I followed the project with readings from Helen Maria Williams's *Letters from France.* The collection is, of course, too lengthy to assign in its entirety; we concentrated on her opening letters' descriptions of the preparations for the federation festival (1: 1–17), her depictions of the assassination of Jean-Paul Marat and the execution of Charlotte Corday (2: 1–17), and her account of the trials and deaths of Marie Antoinette and Mme Roland (2: 147–207). Mary Favret's essay "Spectratrice as Spectacle: Helen Maria Williams at Home in the Revolution" helped introduce Williams's theatrical staging of revolutionary martyrdom, which was a primary focus of our discussion.

We then read most of Burke's *Reflections on the Revolution in France* and Paine's *The Rights of Man*. Students wrote short papers contrasting Burke's and Paine's positions on issues. We discussed the writers' efforts to construct their arguments as "natural," a term that surfaced again when we moved on to an excerpt from Godwin's *Enquiry Concerning Political Justice* (we paid particular attention to Godwin's definition of his title phrase and his controversial examples of its practice—e.g., the decision of whom to save from a fire: the archbishop of Cambray or the archbishop's valet). After Godwin, we read Wollstonecraft's *A Vindication of the Rights of Woman*; students were most interested in her delineation of the ideal marriage relationship (one of friendship) and the problematically antisororal aspects of her feminist polemic (her disdain for women as they are intrudes on her speculations about how they might be).

The second half of the class was devoted to poetry, beginning with Blake's *Songs of Innocence*, *Visions of the Daughters of Albion*, and *America* and moving through Wordsworth's *Lyrical Ballads* and books 1 and 9 of *The Prelude*. We used Shelley's "Ode to the West Wind" and "A Defence of Poetry" (and intended to use parts of "The Revolt of Islam," which was eliminated in the end-of-semester crunch) as well as Byron's "Ode to Napoleon Buonaparte," *Manfred*, and *Don Juan* to talk about the construction of heroism in the aftermath of the Revolution. While the class read less poetry than is usual in a Romantic literature class (and nothing by Keats and Coleridge), students got a solid sense of the period and its aesthetic and political preoccupations.

My advanced graduate seminar on the 1790s took up many of the same texts I used in the undergraduate seminar, but we supplemented the readings with a greater number of critical and theoretical texts. In addition to reading Burke and Paine, my graduate students read excerpts from Lynn Hunt's *Politics, Culture, and Class in the French Revolution*, Dorinda Outram's *The Body and the French Revolution*, and Jay Fliegelman's *Declaring Independence*. Mary Wollstonecraft's *Vindication* was combined with Cora Kaplan's important essay on Wollstonecraft, "Wild Nights: Pleasure/Sexuality/Feminism," and Tom Furniss's "Nasty Tricks and Tropes: Sexuality and Language in Mary Wollstonecraft's *Rights of Woman*." There is no single text that can represent the complicated rhetorical debate around the 1794 treason trials involving the leaders of the radical corresponding societies, Thomas Hardy, John Horne Tooke, and John Thelwall (who, to the government's considerable embarrassment, were acquitted); instead of assigning reading, therefore, I asked students to become authorities on particular facets of the trials. Suggested sources included the trial transcripts (compiled in T. B. Howell's *State Trials*), caricatures of the trial participants from contemporary periodicals, memoirs of participants or witnesses (such as Hardy, Thelwall, Thomas Holcraft, Lord Eldon, Amelia Opie, and Henry Crabb Robinson), Godwin's writings on the trial, newspaper accounts, and transcripts of Parliamentary proceedings. The students' research provided the grounding for an in-class roundtable discussion of the trials.

The graduate seminar Romanticism and Gender emphasized the contributions women writers made to Romantic-era literature but also focused on the status of women in Romantic poems. I attempted to juxtapose men and women writers in ways that would provide new insight into the writings of both and to supplement literary texts with critical and theoretical works that grappled with gender issues both in Romanticism and in general. We read Blake's *Visions of the Daughters of Albion* and *The Book of Thel* with Mary Wollstonecraft's *Vindication* and Thomas Laqueur's chapter "Representing Sex" in *Making Sex*. We accompanied Mary Robinson's *Lyrical Tales* and Wordsworth's *Lyrical Ballads* with Stuart Curran's essay "Romantic Poetry: The 'I' Altered" and Julie Ellison's discussion of the parallels between Romanticism and feminism in the introduction to *Delicate Subjects*. A class meeting devoted to political poems took into consideration Percy Shelley's "England in 1819" and *Queen Mab*, Felicia Hemans's "Casabianca," "Woman on the Field of Battle," "Stanzas on the Death of Princess Charlotte," and "Stanzas to the Memory of the Late King," as well as Anna Barbauld's "On the Death of the Princess Charlotte," "On the King's Illness," and *Eighteen Hundred and Eleven*. Excerpts from Judith Butler's *Gender Trouble* and Mary Ann Doane's *Femmes Fatales* exploring the performative aspects of a gendered subject position helped structure discussions of Germaine de Staël's *Corinne; or, Italy* and Byron's *Don Juan*. By the end of the semester, students were well equipped to debate the merits of Anne Mellor's discrimination of a "masculine" and a "feminine" Romanticism in *Romanticism and Gender*, the final text on the syllabus.

The most tightly focused and historically grounded classes I have taught have been the most successful ones. Students like a grid in which to place the knowledge they are accumulating, and by concentrating on the French Revolution or on a particular decade, for example, one can provide such a structure without resorting to simplistic generalizations about writers who can be only forcibly yoked together under a single definition of Romanticism. Students tend to desire a unified explanation of Romanticism; the confusion they express at mid-semester or, unhappily, sometimes even at the end of a course organized around a few authors or poetic genres, is perhaps a salutary confusion that accurately reflects the variousness of the era. However, I have been able to suggest some common preoccupations and aesthetic dilemmas of Romantic-era writers, to give Wordsworth his due in class time without allowing him to become too normative a model of the Romantic poet, by paying greater attention to the specific historical moments out of which Romantic literature emerged.

Distinguishing the Poetess from the Female Poet

Anne K. Mellor

What major stylistic and thematic differences exist among the women poets of the Romantic era? By raising this question with my students at the very beginning of the course, I alert them to the need not only to distinguish women's poetry from the canonical male Romantic poetry with which some students are already familiar but also to be wary of grouping all female poets as an undifferentiated whole. With the advent of Stuart Curran's edition of the poetry of Charlotte Smith, William McCarthy and Elizabeth Kraft's edition of the poetry of Anna Barbauld, and, most recently, Richard Matlak and my anthology *British Literature, 1780–1830*, it is now possible to show students that there were at least two very different kinds of poetry by women in the Romantic period.

Most recent classroom discussions of this poetry—especially those that have relied on Duncan Wu's *Romanticism: An Anthology*, Jerome J. McGann's *New Oxford Book of Romantic Period Verse*, and Andrew Ashfield's *Women Romantic Poets, 1770–1838*—have represented it as the production of what I shall here call "the poetess." The discussions have been guided by the excellent recent critical studies of Felicia Hemans and Letitia Elizabeth Landon by, among others, Isobel Armstrong, Angela Leighton, Anne Mellor (*Romanticism and Gender*), McGann ("Literary History"), Glennis Stephenson (*Letitia Landon*), and Cheryl Walker. Rightly recognizing that the Victorian literary establishment defined Hemans, Landon, and their female peers as poetesses, distinct from the male "poet," these teachers and critics have explored and acutely defined the literary conventions that governed the productions of these poetesses and helped construct a feminine music of their own. These conventions encompassed the adoption of the mask of the improvisatrice, the insistence that love and the domestic affections are primary to a woman's happiness, the rejection or condemnation of poetic fame, the embracing of Edmund Burke's aesthetic of the beautiful as the goal of female literary desire, and the acceptance of the hegemonic doctrine of the separate spheres. At the same time, in extremely subtle ways these poetesses rhetorically subverted and resisted the representation of feminine subjectivity as entirely private and domestic. They did so by identifying with such female personae as Philomela's Nightingale, the Greek Pythia, or the inspired Sappho, figures that empowered their criticisms both of masculinity and of the havoc wrought by men within the public sphere.

Poetess seems appropriate for women like Hemans and Landon, who self-consciously embraced an aesthetic of the beautiful; who celebrated, as Lydia Sigourney writes of Felicia Hemans, "the whole sweet circle of the domestic affections—the hallowed ministries of woman, at the cradle, the hearthstone, and the death-bed" (qtd. in Walker 32); and who saw themselves as writing a specifically feminine poetry, however much they questioned the category. Responding to my opening question, however, my students very soon recognize that a great deal of poetry by women from this period does not conform to this poetic practice. Here I focus on this alternative tradition of Romantic women's poetry, which—for want of a better term—I call the tradition of the female poet.

The Origins of the Tradition of the Female Poet

The literary tradition of the female poet is explicitly political; it self-consciously and insistently occupies the public sphere. It originates in the writings of the female preachers or prophets who embraced seventeenth-century Quaker theology and a belief in a divine inner light that authorized them to speak in public at Quaker meetings. In *Writing Women's Literary History* Margaret Ezell draws attention to the numerous seventeenth-century Quaker women who preached in public and who published over one hundred religious tracts and epistles containing accounts of their conversions, persecutions, and transcendent visions, as well as sacred verse, written in a plain and supple style. Christine Krueger documents in her study of women preachers, women writers, and nineteenth-century social discourse, *The Reader's Repentance*, that by the end of the eighteenth century women preachers invoked scriptural authority for the right of women to speak in public, citing the prophet Joel, who describes a time of special blessing as one in which "the sons and daughters shall prophesy" (Joel 2.28). They further reminded their listeners that even Paul acknowledges that in Christ "there is neither Jew nor Greek, there is neither bond nor free, there is neither male nor female" (Gal. 3.28).

Identifying themselves as the voice of Christian virtue, answerable to no mortal man, scores of female evangelical preachers such as Mary Bosanquet

Fletcher, Sarah Crosby, Susanna Wesley, Sarah Cox, Frances Pawson, Hester Ann Rogers, and Mary Tooth, many of whom published autobiographies, memoirs, and polemical tracts, had by 1780 established the social practice and the literary precedent of women's speaking publicly on both religious and political issues. They had claimed and achieved the right to comment on the rectitude or unrighteousness of the government, the military, the legal and medical professions, and especially commerce and to condemn the sins of men in the name of the highest authorities, God and Scripture. Encouraged by John Wesley, the Methodists, and the Dissenters, women preachers grew in number and influence throughout the early nineteenth century.

These female preachers taught that a careful reading of the Bible provided telling precedents for female judges (Deborah), for female rulers (Queen Esther), and for female military leaders and saviors of their people (Judith). The Bible also provided women the authority to resist fathers, brothers, and husbands who might lead them astray, to leave the family home in pursuit of a life of greater sanctity, to gather in communities independent of male control, and even to laugh at God (as did Sarah).

Just as the canonical male Romantic poets claimed divine authority or poetic genius as the inspiration and origin of their writing, so did the tradition of the female poet claim divine authority, grounded in a revisionist reading of Holy Scripture, for its prophetic verse. These female poets frequently defined themselves as the mouthpieces or vessels of the Divine Word, invoking not only the Bible but also examples from written and oral history (such as Queen Elinor, Gertrude von der Wart, and the female Christian martyrs) to argue that, as women, they had demonstrated a fidelity (to Christ, a child, or a husband) superior to men's. Moreover, they pointed out, Christian women were traditionally responsible for the inculcation of virtue in the domestic sphere and for the moral and religious instruction of young children. Citing this practice, they laid claim to a more refined virtue than the average man could attain, a capacity for "right feeling" that combined a highly developed sensibility with practical morality. Again and again, the female poet insisted that she spoke on behalf of Virtue, which she consistently gendered as female; because Virtue must, in a Christian nation, govern both the private and the public sphere, it takes precedence over all political and commercial expediencies.

Since female preachers typically spoke to the uneducated, to children, and to the working classes, they consciously used a vernacular or vulgar language. Against the prescriptions of Samuel Johnson's *Dictionary* (1755), Bishop Lowth's first comprehensive grammar of English (1762), and James Harris's grammatical treatise *Hermes* (1751), all of which attempted to regulate proper or polite speech on the basis of rules derived from Latin that only classically educated men could comprehend, they insisted on the capacity of Virtue to speak in plain, everyday language that even a child could understand. Implicitly they engaged in the class politics that Olivia Smith describes in *The Politics of Language*, in a democratizing movement that undermined the religious and social authority of learned men over the unlettered working classes and less well educated women.

Before we present our students with examples from the tradition of the female poet, we need to make clear the ideological limitations inherent in a female literary tradition that derives its authority from the practice of the evangelical or dissenting female preacher. First, because she spoke on behalf of *Christian* virtue, because she invoked the Bible as her final textual authority, the words of this preacher could easily be heard as an affirmation of patriarchal Christianity; indeed much of the energy of this dissenting tradition was by 1840 absorbed within a specifically Anglican evangelicalism that operated comfortably within the established church. Second, the writings of the Christian female poet were often co-opted in the name of a British imperial expansion that also defined itself as Christian. The female poet's jeremiads were frequently used to justify a missionary movement that imposed on African, American, and Asian nations and cultures the assumptions of what Winthrop Jordan has called "Anglo-Africanism"—that "to be Christian was to be civilised rather than barbarous, English rather than African, white rather than black" (94).

Nonetheless, the female poet could and did claim a moral and literary authority equal to—or even greater than—that of the male poets who worked within a neoclassical literary tradition that looked to the battlefields of the *Iliad*, the *Odyssey*, and the *Aeneid* for inspiration, that produced an inherently competitive and self-aggrandizing ideology, and that consistently sacrificed Christian virtue to national conquest or personal glory. By equating virtue with moral rectitude, the refusal to compromise, the willingness to suffer for one's beliefs, personal self-sacrifice, compassion for others, and, above all, spiritual liberty and peacefulness, the female poet aligned herself with Christ and his martyrs, with those who had an obligation to speak out for the greater good, even the salvation, of the nation.

However relentlessly didactic much of this poetry seems today, I always remind my students that it inaugurated a tradition of explicitly feminist poetry, poetry that insisted on the equality of women and men and on the right of women to speak publicly about good government and how best to educate children to achieve a moral society—subjects on which they had a unique, valid perspective and that affected their daily lives.

Defining the Tradition of the Female Poet

The female poet's writing is political and didactic. It typically responds to specific political events; argues for wide-ranging social and political reform; or attempts to initiate a social revolution, what Mary Wollstonecraft in *A Vindication of the Rights of Woman* (1792) called "a REVOLUTION in female manners," a redefinition of gender that will ensure equal rights for women (192). The female poet grounds her social analysis in a specific political or religious ideology that entitles her to stand in moral judgment of events.

Several poems written by women between 1780 and 1830 specifically addressed the two most important political events of the period, the French Revolution and the campaign to abolish the slave trade. One might teach a poem such as Charlotte Smith's "The Emigrants" (1793) as a critique of the pro-Jacobin sympathies of Blake, Wordsworth, and Coleridge. (All the poems discussed in this essay are in Mellor and Matlak.) For powerful condemnations of the slave trade and the institution of slavery in the British West Indies, one might look to Hannah More's "Slavery" (1787; later expanded and retitled "The Slave Trade"), to Ann Yearsley's "A Poem on the Inhumanity of the Slave Trade" (1786), Helen Maria Williams's "A Farewell, for Two Years, to England" (1789), or Amelia Opie's "The Black Man's Lament; or, How to Make Sugar" (1826). These poems can fruitfully be contrasted to such poems by men on the slave trade as William Cowper's "The Negro's Complaint" (1788) and "Pity for Poor Africans" (1788) or Robert Southey's "The Sailor, Who Had Served in the Slave Trade" (1798). Gender played a significant role in the poetic arguments for the abolition of slavery (Mellor, "Am I Not a Woman"). The most prominent male abolitionist poets, such as Cowper and Thomas Day, tended to attack slavery as an offense against natural law, the principle that all men are born equal and have certain inalienable rights. Female poets tended to condemn slavery because it violated the domestic affections by separating mothers from their children and husbands from their wives and subjected black women to sexual abuse from their white masters. I also remind my students that all the abolitionist poems written during this period, by women and by men, embraced the discourse of Anglo-Africanism, as More's address to British slave traders in "Slavery" makes clear:

> Barbarians, hold! th' opprobrious commerce spare,
> Respect *His* sacred image which they bear,
> *Though dark and savage, ignorant and blind,*
> They claim the common privilege of kind;
> Let malice strip them of each other plea,
> They still are men, and men should still be free.
> (Mellor and Matlak 208; my emphasis)

For a more broad-ranging condemnation of colonial imperialism and bourgeois capitalism that urges social reform at home and political restraint abroad, one might turn to a poem like Helen Maria Williams's *Peru*. In this, her first major poem, published in 1784, Williams fiercely attacks the devastations wrought by Pizarro's invading troops on the fertile lands and contented people of Peru (Richardson gives a fine analysis of this poem in "Epic Ambivalence"). Or one might teach Anna Letitia Barbauld's *Eighteen Hundred and Eleven*, a brilliant denunciation of England's decline and fall as a consequence of commercial greed.

Lucy Aikin's *Epistles on Women* (1810) is a brilliant example of a poem by a woman that offers a political rationale for a social revolution, specifically a redefinition of the construction of gender in England in the nineteenth century. In this 1,200-line poem, written in heroic couplets, Aikin rewrites the history of humanity from the Garden of Eden to 1750, attributing all the major advances in civilization to "Maternal Love" and the social practices of women (2.124; on this poem, see Mellor, "Female Poet"). She also presents an alternative poetics based on a concept of poetry as conversation or linguistic mothering, which vividly contests the Wordsworthian concept of poetry as the overflow of powerful feeling in a solitary, contemplative mind.

Whichever poems one chooses to represent the tradition of the Romantic female poet—and Mary Robinson, Helen Maria Williams, Charlotte Smith, Anna Barbauld, Ann Yearsley, and Amelia Opie, among many others, provide numerous additional examples—one should enable one's students to recognize the differences among Romantic women poets as well as their similarities, differences in the use of literary conventions and in the conceptualization of the audience, of the social goals of poetry, of the appropriate themes for women's poetry, and of the subjectivity of the female poet. Students who recognize such differences will attain a far more nuanced and complex view of the rich and varied outpouring of poetry by women in the Romantic period.

Romantic Women's Poetry as Social Movement

Mary A. Favret

> For on earth there's something new appears.
> Since earth's foundation plac'd I tell you here,
> Such wondrous woman never was below.
> —Joanna Southcott

Joanna Southcott's verse puts a special twist on the familiar strain of Romantic prophecy tied to self-congratulation. Here "something new appears"—a woman stakes her claim not simply to the hearts of her readers but also, through them, to the future of humankind:

> The Wars, her tumults they shall never cease
> Until the hearts of men shall turn to me
> And leave the rage of persecuting thee.
> (Thompson 384–85)

In Southcott's invocation of divine inspiration, in her topical reference to a world at war and her suggestion of a feminine alternative, and in her explicit, almost enforced, reliance on a gendered position, we see many of the ingredients of Romantic women's poetry as it has begun to be canonized and anthologized. The prophetic verse also exemplifies a feature of women's poetry that newly canonized writers such as Anna Letitia Barbauld, Charlotte Smith, and Felicia Hemans share with anonymous or less celebrated "poetesses": the poet understands her writing as joined to social movement and therefore constructs for it a role in history. In the fierce satire *Eighteen Hundred and Eleven*, for instance, Barbauld introduces a historiography of the future. Her poem simultaneously presents Britain with a vision of its demise—"Ruin, as with an earthquake shock, is here, / . . . Thy baseless wealth dissolves in air away" (152–53)—and, from an imagined position in the future, applauds the enduring wealth of British culture, including the writings of her friend Joanna Baillie: "While wide o'er transatlantic realms thy name / Shall live in light and gather all its fame" (154–55). Whether allegorizing social concerns, as Southcott does, or, like Barbauld, intervening directly in topical debates, women poets of the Romantic period allow themselves a prospect on and a range of motion within history.

It is worth impressing on students that in the Romantic era poetry was thought to have cultural and political clout; poetry presented itself as an effective means for women to address, instruct, woo, and chastise their audience. Introduced as a movement with historical vision and ambitions to transform society, these women's poetry raises at least two important general questions about poetry: what effects does poetry imagine for itself, and how do we measure these (and other, unanticipated) effects? Such questions redirect us from a narrow focus on aesthetic or literary value; they also encourage students to consider the vagaries of canonization, that is, the shifting ideologies that assign value to literature—a crucial issue in the study of women's literature. More significant pedagogically, these questions raise the political stakes of writing and reading poetry. What consequences arise because of who writes, who reads, and who chooses what is read? It may be instructive to point out that nineteenth-century anthologies of women poets, for example, Alexander Dyce's *Specimens of British Poetesses* (1827) and Frederic Rowton's *The Female Poets of Great Britain* (1850), routinely neglect the political engagement of such writers as Hannah More and Helen Maria Williams, emphasizing love songs and hymns over satire and prophecy. As Rowton states, "Man's Poetry teaches us Politics; Woman's Morality. In all the poems contained in this volume, it would be difficult to find a passage written to accelerate man's political advancement; whilst every page will display some effect to stimulate his moral progress" (xxxix). Of course, his division avoids the historical implication of the language of moral progress with the political advancement of women as well as men.

I propose to teach the poetry of Romantic women poets as the work of a particular movement—the rising identification of women with poetry—that is intertwined with the work of other social and political movements. Following my interests, I focus on the antislavery movement and the debate over England's involvement in the wars with France. In both issues poetry and women claim privileged roles, though in the first the women's influence makes antislavery a feminized movement whereas in the second the gendering of the war vexes women's response. But the tones and themes specific to the campaigns color even the poetry that pretends to distance itself from public debate. One could just as well concentrate on the politically weighted trends toward children's education, which prompted many women to publish songs and hymns for children; toward Christian evangelism, many varieties of which authorized women's voices; toward parliamentary reform, a movement that inspired both Chartist poetry and the vogue for poetry about the rights of man, woman, and indeed animals; or toward the definition of the nation itself, which prompted interest in "the genius of our country-women in the department of poetry" (Dyce ii). All these movements are, to a certain degree, inextricable. They share, moreover, a faith in the power of poetry, especially poetry written by women.

In the classroom I begin with an introductory section on the rise of women's poetry in the late eighteenth century, paying special attention to how various women represented themselves as poets and how they represented the work of poetry. Entitled Poems on Women Writing: From Patronage to Print, this section spans a range from Phillis Wheatley's "To Maecenas" to Felicia Hemans's "On the Grave of a Poetess," about Mary Tighe. A recurring characteristic of the Romantic women's poetry movement is the women's praise for and response to one another in verse, which reinforces their poetic accomplishment and exploits the medium to create a women's dialogue. The following list of suggested poems can be extended or cut to suit particular courses (e.g., courses on Romantic women poets or a general survey course on Romantic literature). Its advantages are the range of occasions presented for embarking on poetry, the various poses the authors of the poems adopt or are assigned (from the patronized phenomenon of Wheatley and later Ann Yearsley to Ann Radcliffe's fictional girl-poet to the outraged voice of "A Lady" to Mary Darby Robinson's erotic appropriation of Sappho), and the persistent suggestion of an audience that needs convincing or of no audience at all (as in Radcliffe's "Song" and Hemans's "Treasures of the Deep"). I selected these poems partly as precursors to the next two sections; certain writers reappear in each section, and certain themes—freedom of movement and constraint, expansiveness and inwardness, the visionary and the material—recur, accumulating greater resonance. The list is as follows: Wheatley, "To Maecenas" (1773); Yearsley, "On Mrs. Montagu" (1785) and "From Clifton Hall" (1785); "A Lady" and "Sedition Act" (both anonymous; 1796); Barbauld, "Washing Day" (1797) and "A Summer's Evening: Meditation" (1792); Radcliffe, extract from *The Romance of the Forest*, including "Song of a Spirit" (1791); Southcott, selections from *A Word in Season* (1803) or *A Word to the Wise* (1803); Baillie, "The Kitten" (1840); Robinson, selections from "Sappho and Phaon"; Hemans, "Treasures of the Deep" (1823) and "On the Grave of a Poetess" (1828) (or "Last Song of Sappho" [1831]).

I provide the students background on the publication of each poem and basic biographical information on the authors. I ask the students to read the poems carefully and to answer the following questions about each: What is the position of the speaker? What goals does the poem set? What methods does the poet use or suggest to achieve those goals? What role do women (or feminine figures) play in the poem or its goals? How does poetry itself serve the poem's goals? As we answer these questions, we can begin to map the woman poet onto a variety of material and imaginary positions. To consolidate these answers into a description of the poetic landscape as women viewed it, we end with a single question: What, literally or figuratively, is the place of poetry? I may ask students to select a poem and write a short (one- or two-page) analysis of the significance of its setting or positioning (e.g., outer space in Barbauld's "A Summer's Evening," the fireside in Baillie's "Kitten," or the graveside in Hemans's "On the Grave").

The figuration of place and position is crucial for the second part of my approach, in which we examine poems on war and imperialism. The imaginary travels of Barbauld's "A Summer's Evening" and Hemans's "Treasures of the Deep," for instance, now seem to resonate with a certain geopolitical ambition. The potential list for this section is enormous, so I vary it often. Sometimes I add Anna Seward's "Verses Inviting Stella to Tea on the Public Fast-Day," a wickedly biting poem in protest of the "American War," written in 1781 but not published until 1791; if we have a lot of time and photocopying resources, I might assign Hemans's troubling "Siege of Valencia" (1823). But one can also give the class a fairly short list and ask them to supplement it with their own discoveries from Betty Bennett's anthology of war poetry of the Romantic period or other available anthologies or collections, particularly those of women's poems. Here are some of my standards: Hannah More, "Sensibility: Epistle to Mrs. Buscamp" (1782); Charlotte Smith, "Fragment Descriptive of the Miseries of War" (1793, rev. 1797) and "Beachy Head" (1807); Yearsley, "To Mira, on the Care of Her Infant" (1796); Barbauld, "Written on a Marble" (before 1802) and *Eighteen Hundred and Eleven* (1812); Radcliffe, "To the Winds" (1796); Hemans, "The Call of Liberty" (1809) and "To My Younger Brother" (1809). I like to pair the More and Yearsley poems, because Yearsley uses the violence of the intervening years to critique More's popular verse epistle, redefining the relation of the maternal to the nation and the military. Barbauld's and Hemans's two poems demonstrate the poet's fluctuating responses to the war. Both Smith and Radcliffe meditate on the distant, invisible violence and, in doing so, find violence to be everywhere and nearly inescapable.

In class discussion, we apply the questions from the first section to each poem and probe the significance of place and position to issues of war and empire. (Here brief rundowns of political-religious and class differences and of historical shifts in the war effort are often necessary.) But we also consider a new question: How does the author depict war or violence? The question magnifies the pragmatics of describing foreign wars, which most women could not witness, and the politics of imagining war on the domestic front. I strongly recommend having the students assemble their own collections of war poems or poems that rely on war motifs (Michael Scrivener's collection is another good source). The alternations within poets' careers, not to mention the spectrum of responses over time and across classes, prevent any easy equation of women with pacifism or of peace with domesticity.

Having created a repertoire of tools for analyzing the purposes, rhetorical positions, and imaginary-political maps that women poets articulate, we turn to the social movement most strongly identified with women's writing, the antislavery movement, in its several manifestations between the 1780s and the 1830s. These poems arguably reveal women poets at their most ambitious. Moira Ferguson's *Subject to Others* offers an overwhelming number of antislavery poems (and prose works) and reads them with acuity, emphasizing the connections between the antislavery movement and the ideological war with France, as well as the campaign for women's rights (Donna Landry's *Muses of Resistance* also offers valuable material from the point of view of laboring women). From Ferguson's compendium I select a few long poems for class discussion, believing that the length of the poems is itself a sign of the seriousness with which the authors entered this civic, commercial, and moral debate: Wheatley, "To . . . the Earl of Dartmouth" (1773); More, "Slavery," (1788), "The Sorrows of Yamba" (1795); Yearsley, "A Poem on the Inhumanity of the Slave Trade" (1788); Williams, "A Poem on the Bill . . ." (1788); Barbauld, "To William Wilberforce" (1791).

A potential stumbling block for this section, which may arise in the other two as well, is the overwhelming repetition of figures and set pieces. Ferguson quotes a contemporary review that sniffs, "The subject itself [slavery] precludes any novelty of ideas" (156). To forestall such criticism and to remind students that originality is not always the goal of poetry, I begin the section by asking the class to specify an urgent topical issue or two hotly debated in the media. I assign the students to spend a weekend studying one debate and then to write a poem that engages it. Rather than sort through the poems myself, I divide the class into groups to read one another's poems. They look for repeated language, figures, or arguments: How much of the poem makes use of the common discourse? How much can the author claim as original after reading a dozen others on the subject? The assignment is enlightening. By demonstrating how public discourse circulates, it requires students to examine how poetry can address contemporary politics, and it produces a certain amount of respect for the poets we study.

One can adapt the strategic questions of the earlier sections to the antislavery poems, asking students to investigate the visibility of slavery and of slaves. How much do the poems tell us about either? How and where does the speaker position herself in relation to slavery? By this point, the class should be familiar enough with the language of war and empire and the classed and gendered issues of literacy and of asserting a public voice to trace their inconsistencies or affinities with various aspects of the antislavery cause, especially as it is advanced by women. I end this section with a deceptively simple poem, written after the wars with France and during a lull in the antislavery conflict. Hemans's "Statue of a Dying Gladiator" (1826) is infused with the rhetoric of abolition and of military heroism; the poet's fixed contemplation of the male body problematically holds the two together.

There are several advantages to teaching Romantic women's poetry in this manner. If we are careful, it will help us avoid three common problems: exceptionalism, ghettoizing, and an essentializing treatment of the poets that looks more like beatification than canonization. A historical recognition of women's poetry as a literary and social movement guards us from a Romantic tumble into exceptionalism, wherein we single out individual women artists for transcending the limitations of their social position. Yet while acknowledging the rise of women writers and their complex relation to literacy and publication somewhat justifies our considering women poets as a distinct group, by doing so we risk simplistically differentiating the two groups and thus, most likely, minimizing the accomplishments of the historically marginalized. I find it valuable, therefore, to examine the poets' engagement not just in the social movement that is women's writing but also in the other movements that defined their work and their era. Placing More and Yearsley in conversation with each other as well as with a wide public discourse makes sense as we watch them respond to particular events, such as the defeat of the Slave Trade Bill or the resumption of war after the Peace of Amiens.

The troubled relationship between the prosperous More and her once-destitute protégée Yearsley, moreover, reminds us that the work of these writers does not constitute a homogeneous representation of the Romantic woman poet. Not only are the poems shot through with disturbances, but such social movements necessarily prompt a variety of jostling, uneasily accommodated, if not contentious gestures. Women poets are too often portrayed as angels in the house of literature, mitigating or correcting the errors of overly ambitious or selfish men (as in Rowton's account). I would not deny the gendered force of domesticity or "moral progress" but rather insist that it fails to explain Barbauld's ambition and satire, the compelling if gloomy wanderers popularized by Smith's verse, or the fact that two morally earnest women (say, Barbauld and Hemans) could find themselves on opposite sides of a political question. And while the women poets and their contemporary champions often resound the angelic strain (and here we might find the salvific Southcott in league with More), we should realize that critics often direct this corrective music against other women writers. Richard Polwhele's hysterical poem *The Unsex'd Females* is an extreme example of such beatification joined to demonization; but we hear milder echoes of it whenever a critic suggests that a feminine Romanticism will counteract the evils of canonical masculine Romanticism.

Women Poets and Colonial Discourse: Teaching More and Yearsley on the Slave Trade

Alan Richardson

One of the challenges in teaching Romantic-era women's poetry is to avoid replicating the split between "public men and private women" characteristic of that era's dominant ideology by concentrating too exclusively—in however revisionary a spirit—on poems written in a lyric voice and featuring domestic subjects. Unfortunately, for reasons both pragmatic (lyric poems are shorter) and ideological (women are held to have faltered in the more "ambitious" genres because of their "relatively constricted" social experience [Lonsdale xliv]), anthologists have to date included little in the way of poetry explicitly concerned with national public issues, despite the acknowledged importance of poems like Anna Barbauld's *Eighteen Hundred and Eleven* and Charlotte Smith's *The Emigrants*. Two unabashedly ambitious poems, however, publicly addressing one of the most critical and widely social issues of the era, Britain's notorious role as the dominant slave-trading nation, have been available for some time: Ann Yearsley's *A Poem on the Inhumanity of the Slave-Trade* and Hannah More's *Slavery: A Poem*. Teaching these poems together can provide a rich opportunity for discussing issues of the overtly political aspects of women's poetry and of the relation of women's writing to colonialist discourse and the construction of racial difference. In addition, the juxtaposition of antislavery poems by the laboring-class poet Yearsley and her one-time patron More broaches the issue of class differences among women writers and the question of how to account for such differences in our interpretation of their works.

As a pretext for discussing the question of class differences I assign, in addition to the two poems, the "Narrative" on her break with More, addressed by Yearsley to the subscribers to her first collection and intended to counter More's charge of "ingratitude" in their eyes. The details of their rift, which has been helpfully discussed by both Elizabeth Kowaleski-Wallace (3–5) and Donna Landry (16–22), are contextualized in terms of the working-class poet's continued dependence on an increasingly archaic patronage system and the bourgeois woman poet's strategic extension of the domestic role into various kinds of "social work": educating and writing for children, setting up schools and pioneering a literature for "the poor," fostering the "native" genius of lower-class poets like Yearsley. To what extent does the seemingly inevitable hostility between More and Yearsley over the latter's growing desire for economic and intellectual independence suggest a need for wariness in regard to any generalizing about women's poetry or (for that matter) women in this era? Is there a relation between the sort of cultural project represented by More's patronage and tutelage of Yearsley and the woman writer's engagement in the antislavery cause? Is there a subtler relation between More's angry characterization of Yearsley as "monstrous" and as a "savage" ("Narrative" 382, 385) and

the tension between the Christian universalist ethos and the Eurocentric prim-
itivist tropes found in More's antislavery writing?

Whether or not my students have been primed by reading Moira Ferguson
(*Subject to Others*) or Linda Colley on British women's extensive involvement
in the antislavery cause and the opening it made for cautiously overt political
engagement, they are quick to perceive how More makes use of a domestic
voice to validate her entry into political and economic debate: she cites the
mother-infant bond as an example of the "social life" disrupted by the slave
trade (115), roots local identity in "home" and national identity in the "parent
soil" (134, 144), appeals to feeling over reason as ground of both the slave's humanity and the reader's sense of justice (181–84), constructs an alternative
male heroism exemplified by the "gentle" Cook and "peaceful" Penn (277,
288), and composes a paean to the "soft contagion" of Mercy (314). The students can adduce all these strategies as examples of a "feminine" reformist discourse that would relate More's antislavery poem to other instances of domestic
rhetoric and of a "relational" ethos in women's writing of the era. The discussion can be redirected at this point to the invocation of Liberty that opens the
poem, where More seems forced to split Liberty into Liberty proper ("pure
daughter of the skies") and her evil twin, "mad Liberty," a potentially "wild" and
uncontainable force associated with magic, madness, disease, and "prostituted"
verse (1-50), suggesting that More's reformist rhetoric, though "feminine," may
require an inaugural gesture of a distinctly antifeminist tenor.

A comparable sense of ambivalence emerges from further discussion of the
poem's relation to contemporary colonial and racial discourse. Students readily perceive a contradiction between More's condemnation of African slavery
and her support for European missionary activity and for a "fair Commerce"
dominated by Britain (173) and may even see this as aligning More with a "liberal" version of colonialism destined to prevail in the nineteenth century (and
since). At the same time, they are impressed with More's Christian sense of
an equal claim to humanity under differences of climate and skin color and
with her reversal of the "savagery" trope to characterize the slave trader rather
than his human commodity (164, 249). Pressing on this very issue, however,
can make for a productive discussion of how readily even explicitly antiracist
rhetoric can take on racialist associations in the discourse of this era. More's arguments for equality under the skin ("Though few can reason, all mankind can
feel" [184]) manifest an unquestioned sense of cultural superiority and a near
monopoly on civilization (despite the barbarity of the slave traders) on the part
of Europeans generally and the British in particular. Terms that in isolation
may not strike students as especially problematic—"native genius" (76), "rude
energy" (87), "the wild vigor of a savage root" (90)—reveal more disturbing
tonalities when read in tandem with the poem's insistence on African illiteracy
and passivity, its problematic opposition (in this context) of light (enlightened,
British) and dark (benighted, African) images, and its more obviously ethnocentric passages: "Though dark and savage, ignorant and blind, / They claim

the common privilege of *kind*" (165–66). The point isn't to convict More of simple hypocrisy but to consider her poem as embodying the ambivalence and self-contradiction of Romantic-era antislavery discourse generally; not to induce the easy complacency of historical hindsight but to ask instead whether any post-Enlightenment discourse assuming stable racial categories, however self-critically, can altogether avoid racialist associations.

Students may turn at this point to Yearsley in search of a way out of this discursive bind. If More's status as woman under patriarchy facilitates sympathy but not identification with her enslaved African subject—if to the contrary her uneasy cultural position seems finally to demand an assertion of difference from the "dark and savage" other—what of Ann Yearsley, whose double "alterity" as an impoverished working-class woman might enable her, as Ferguson argues in *Subject to Others*, to see the slave as "class ally" (170)? Is Yearsley better positioned, having herself felt the weight of an increasingly commercialized system of social relations, to criticize colonialism and trade imperialism along with colonial slavery and the traffic in human flesh? Yearsley's attack on the British slave trade in the context of a larger network of "Custom" and "Law" that also render the English subject mentally "enslav'd" (20) and her indictment of "English law" not only for upholding colonial slavery but for being framed by the "few" nobles, clergy, and franchise holders "deem'd / The fathers" of their country (384–85) indeed suggest a more radical critique than More's, one that refuses to separate gender and class oppression from the signal injustice of the slave trade. Students also tend to remark on the contrast between More's essayistic, propositional approach and Yearsley's greater reliance on pathetic narratives and vignettes, again suggesting less distance and a greater sense of identification. They may also note (if pressed a bit) a much greater preponderance of performative language generally and apostrophes (often addressed to the reader as fellow "Briton") in particular, features that lend Yearsley's poem a greater sense of urgency and immediacy.

Students will notice continuities between the two poems as well. Yearsley also draws on a rhetoric of "social love" (389) to engender sympathy in her English reader for the slave, portraying how the latter is torn from a matrix of familial and erotic ties no less sacrosanct and deeply held than the reader's own. She too appeals to the reader's presumed Christianity throughout the poem, although she does not share More's nationalistic sense of British superiority and ultimate moral ascendancy, remarking on how the "Spaniard" shows more concern for the spiritual (if not bodily) good of his slaves; both the English and Spanish slaveholders are shamed, moreover, by the "Mussulman" who "frees his slave / Who turns to Mahomet" (322–24). Yearsley's poem also underscores the provisional character of the racial categories relied upon by More, reminding us that "race" was an unfixed concept very much under construction and subject to debate throughout the late eighteenth and early nineteenth centuries. Yearsley in fact fails to discriminate between black Africans and "Indians" (natives of the Caribbean islands) in this poem, equating "Indian" with

"Coromantin" (340–45, note to those lines) and attributing African beliefs and terms (such as "buckera") to her "Indian" characters (174–76, note to 209). Lest students attribute this confusion to Yearsley's alleged ignorance as what Robert Southey would soon term an "uneducated poet," it may be helpful to point out that aboriginal West "Indians" (enslaved and eventually eradicated in large numbers by the Spanish) and the West African slaves who were brought in to replace them are frequently confounded throughout eighteenth-century antislavery writing (Sypher).

Students should not, however, be left with the impression that racialized categories are any less invidious for being indefinite and unstable. Whether African, Indian, or both, Yearsley's "native" subjects are given epithets from the same colonialist lexicon drawn upon by More: "savage" (351), "artless" (125), "barb'rous" (316), denizens of "the wild" (148) with "dingy" skin color (52). Few readers will have failed to notice the lines describing the grief of an enslaved "Indian"'s father:

> horrid and dark
> Are his wild, unenlighten'd pow'rs: no ray
> Of forc'd philosophy to calm his soul,
> But all the anarchy of wounded nature.
>   (170–73)

The class must confront the question as to whether Yearsley adopts an ethnocentric vocabulary despite her own experience of oppression or indeed because of a compensatory need to buttress her own hard-won and provisional cultural position—"Miss More appeared to be greatly moved, and told me imperiously, that I was 'a savage'" ("Narrative" 385)—by contrast with a "wild, unenlighten'd" colonial other. Do More and Yearsley both manifest, in their antislavery verses, cultural anxieties that they displace onto their colonial, racialized subjects, even as their own experiences of cultural oppression facilitate sympathy and suggest appeal to what Yearsley terms "social laws" (113) that stand above the partial laws of England's so-called "fathers"?

A final question to discuss in a class on this topic is whether the racist and colonialist moments in these texts cancel out their reformist impulses; whether, to put it somewhat differently, the acts of conscience that they embody are altogether vitiated by the cultural anxieties they display and displace. Again, the arrogance of hindsight needs to be confronted, as must the continuing implication of our thinking in racialized categories even as we seek to analyze the racism and colonialism of new as well as received literary canons (Michaels; Young). No one (least of all the instructor) should walk out of this class feeling too comfortable.

Of course, what I have outlined above is only one possible way of putting these texts to pedagogical use. One might also teach the antislavery poems of More, Yearsley, or both in tandem with William Blake's "The Little Black Boy" or *Visions of the Daughters of Albion*, Mary Prince's *The History of Mary Prince, a West Indian Slave*, Maria Edgeworth's "The Grateful Negro," or the antislavery poetry of Anna Barbauld or Helen Maria Williams. This suggestion brings me to a last point concerning women's antislavery writing generally, one that concerns the perceived "marginality" of Romantic-era women writers. On issues of empire, slavery, and colonialism, women writers of this period frequently seem more directly engaged with the pivotal issues of their time than do the canonical male Romantic poets. As we rethink the relation of metropolitan "center" to colonial "periphery," of England (or is it Britain?) to the revived empire, in the cultural history of the late eighteenth and early nineteenth centuries, our notions of what constitutes culturally "central" writing need rethinking as well.

Understanding Cultural Contexts:
The Politics of Needlework in Taylor, Barbauld, Lamb, and Wordsworth

Carol Shiner Wilson

For several years in my scholarship and classes I have found needlework, the female quotidian, a fascinating lens into women's lived experience and imaginative literature in the Romantic period. Needlework—dismissed by some in Georgian England as "trifling" and railed against by others as "dangerous"—also provides a powerful trope with which writers like Jane Taylor, Anna Letitia Barbauld, and Mary Lamb illuminate intense debates about women's roles and women's potential for artistic and political expression in the period. Needlework figured prominently in what Leonore Davidoff and Catherine Hall call the development of "professional motherhood" (175). Writers serious about women's economic, political, and artistic opportunities had to negotiate the powerful icon of the Good Mother, often depicted as sewing or knitting for her family. Tracing her lineage to the revered, virtuous, and industrious spinning and weaving wives depicted in the Bible, the Good Mother was diligent, frugal, moral, selfless, and devout. The needle of this Protestant Madonna was like the needle of a compass, guiding family and nation on the path of virtue. Patient and silent, hunched over samplers as soon as they could hold a needle, all girls prepared to become Good Mothers by sewing detailed designs, including mottoes honoring God, parents, and nation. Reinforcing the identification of women, sewing, and domesticity, the very sewing case that a woman carried was known as a "housewife." Needlework, absent or constructed as reassuring domesticity in writers like William Cowper and William Wordsworth, is an important device with which women writers complicate, subvert, or challenge the ideal of domesticity. Moreover, as Stuart Curran argues in "Romantic Poetry: The 'I' Altered," analyzing the female quotidian in Romantic poetry—minutely observed flowers, the plaiting on a Sunday cap, needlework—helps us rethink the concept of vision (really visionary flight) that we have inherited from conventional Romantic thought (189–90).

I examine needlework in Taylor's "Accomplishment," Barbauld's "Characters," a two-page selection from Jean-Jacques Rousseau's *Emile*, a short story for children by Mary Lamb ("The Little Mahometan"), and Wordsworth's "We Are Seven." I use these works—and refer to other works, including conduct manuals, Mary Wollstonecraft's rebuttal to Rousseau, and British paintings of women sewing—in two single-semester courses, day and evening, in a liberal arts setting: the 300-level course English Romantic Writers (usually about one-half English majors) and the 200-level course Women Writers (usually one-third or one-quarter English majors). Both classes study the Wordsworth poem in conjunction with Mary Robinson's "All Alone" and "The Savage of Aveyron" (in *Complete Poems*). From the beginning of English Romantic Writers, students examine dimensions of the slippery category "Romanticism" and become more aware of a variety of poetic forms and their importance in British Romanticism. Early in Women Writers, through reading poetry and watching the video *Hearts and Hands*, students explore women's lives and writing by examining sewn work. The video focuses on quilts as narrative texts by women in nineteenth-century America: the needlework records marriages and birth, slavery and the hope of freedom, the perilous trek west, and the temperance and suffrage movements. Students always look dazed at the end of the showing and say, "I never realized all that about quilts." They are particularly impressed by the account of quilts being hung outdoors to designate safe houses for runaway slaves. During discussions in both classes, we revisit material previously read and anticipate material yet to be covered.

The syllabus is elastic: works may be added or subtracted, depending on the time available and the course. For example, one can extend discussion of the limitations women felt as artists by including Felicia Hemans's "Prosperzia Rossi." One could add Taylor's "World in the House" to underscore the religious dimensions of needlework and domesticity or shift the discussion altogether toward spirituality and religion; Romantic studies have, after all, traditionally neglected the Dissenting heritage. In Women Writers, I always include Ingrid Wendt's poem "Dust" (a wonderful window on the female quotidian), and I sometimes include Susan Glaspell's *Trifles*. American needlework has also worked well as an early discussion subject in another course I teach, Introduction to Women's Studies.

To encourage close reading and good discussion, I ask students to write focused journal responses of approximately 250 words to Rousseau's view of needlework in "Sophy, or Woman" in *Emile*, to Taylor's "Accomplishment," or to Lamb's "The Young Mahometan." I also ask them to reconsider for discussion the passage in Wordsworth's "We Are Seven" that depicts the little girl sewing by her siblings' graves. I ask two or three students to start off discussion by reading or summarizing their responses to the Rousseau passage. Usually, students are outraged by—or, worse, incredulous and dismissive of—the essentialist view of women that underlies Rousseau's essay: it is girls' nature to "dislike learning to read and write" and to prefer learning sewing "for their adornment" (331). Moreover, he claims, needlework teaches little girls the docility and restraint they will need as women to be subordinate to men (332–33). At some point just before or during the discussion of Rousseau, students examine their own assumptions of sewing as primarily a woman's activity for loved ones within the home. Inevitably, students mention—with great fondness—quilts lovingly stitched by mothers and grandmothers. These personal associations help students understand that the assumptions underlying needlework and domesticity remain. I tell them that in the Middle Ages, men were exclusive and honored embroiderers of ecclesiastical garments; that in turn-of-the-century America immigrant men sewed clothing in garment factories; and

that today men work as tailors of fashionable suits in London. I also refer to
Roosevelt Grier, the former Los Angeles Rams and New York Giants tackle
who was famous in his time, though students rarely know his name today, and
who became even more famous when he announced in a book and on numerous talk shows that he did needlework—mostly, he insisted, masculine or neutral designs such as Japanese warriors, gangsters with bombs, monograms, and
semaphore flags. I then pass around Rosey Grier's *Needlepoint for Men* so they
can see the designs and Rosey himself, stitching away.

We then turn briefly to the Wordsworth piece, in which the wise little girl is
a junior version of the sweet domestic sewing icon, and to "Accomplishment,"
which we use to examine the intersection of gender and class through material
culture. The poem depicts the costly education of a middle-class girl, especially
her needlework, valued in her social-climbing milieu as proof of her mar-
ketability as the future bride of a man of substance and standing who needs a
"finished" wife to signify his success. By the 1790s *accomplishment* was a code
word for unproductive pastimes of upper-class women, self-absorbed and ne-
glectful of their families: dance, drawing, music, French, and embroidery
rather than wholesome plain sewing. The Good Mother was the upper-class
woman's antithesis and became her successor as England grew more conservative. Radicals like Wollstonecraft, moderates like Barbauld and Taylor, and
conservatives like Hannah More all attacked accomplishments (M. Myers,
"Reform" 201).

The poem has a powerful effect on students. Taylor draws them in through
a relentless accumulation of details, concrete and lush diction, and compressed
quatrains punctuated by couplets that stop the reader after, for example, a seductive absorption into "clusters of roses full-blown and red hot" or the brutal
personification of "Art tortur'd, and frighten'd half out of her wits." The students identify how the shape, tone, and progression of the poem come together
much like the pieces of a patchwork. And they see how the patchwork pieces
violate the beauty and order of Nature, God's handiwork: far too numerous
stars and exaggerated, eroticized tulips that are crammed into a "labour of
years" that is a "mass unharmonious, [an] unmeaning . . . show void of intelli-
gent grace; . . . not a landscape . . . not a face" (*Essays* 83). The students also
identify how the accumulation of details depicts the way this education shat-
ters the girl, leaving her without any possibility of mind or soul. By the end of
the poem, she is like the patchwork itself: torn pieces of expensive fabric,
painfully stitched together. Inevitably, students comment that they felt a disturbing shift in their position as readers: they start out as observers and end by
feeling the needle pierce them as it does the girl. "Accomplishment," they conclude, exposes the moral and spiritual costs of a world that values display and
money over simple, honest spirituality.

I next introduce Taylor's ambivalence toward domesticity, including sewing.
Taylor never married and continued to write. Her sister Ann, with whom she
coauthored beautiful hymns for children (including "Twinkle, Twinkle, Little

Star") early in her career, married and relinquished her writing career for a life of unrelenting domesticity. After Taylor's death, her brother wanted to assure the world that she valued domesticity over her fame as a writer, citing as evidence her skill in needlework (*Writings* 1: viii). Taylor's letters, however, reveal that she detested domestic tasks, in large part because they took away from her writing. She speaks of herself as two very different Jane Taylors. The morning Jane is "an active handy little body, who can make beds or do plain work [such as sewing shirts or hemming sheets] . . . but the last mentioned lady never troubles her head with these menial affairs;—nothing will suit her but the pen" (*Writings* 1: 168). The second Jane seeks refuge from domestic chores in her secluded attic room, which holds "one chair for [her]self, and one for [her] muse" (1: 85). Taylor's letters reveal the extent to which domestic labor is ignored in idealized domesticity.

We ask, then, what the ideology of domesticity suggests about women's creativity. Is there necessarily a conflict? We turn to Barbauld's "Characters," in which the poetic voice indicates that the writer is very much a poised lady with a composed soul. In "Characters," the artist's pencil, the housewife's needle, and the writer's quill rest equally, without tension (McCarthy and Kraft 41). Like Taylor, the voice of "Characters" identifies the moral realm as woman's natural domain and calls for a world more consistent with Christian principles. Morality, generosity, and grace are, Barbauld notes in her corrective to Wollstonecraft's *Vindication of the Rights of Woman*, woman's true realm of activity (90). I cite or put on the board brief quotations from Barbauld's letters that problematize her claims of the sweetly balanced pencil, needle, and pen: "I am full well convinced that to have a too great fondness for books is little favourable to the happiness of a woman" (*Works* xix); "the thefts of knowledge in our sex are only connived at while carefully concealed and if displayed, punished with disgrace" (xviii). The statements are part of a letter in which Barbauld refused to establish an academy that would provide girls with an education like hers, in serious subjects like Latin and Greek, which were almost exclusively reserved for boys. She argues that such an education, which she acquired through her father, a teacher at a distinguished Dissenting boys' academy, would bring misery to girls, who ought to be educated to be wives and mothers. We conclude from this letter and others by Barbauld that she believed women should use the pen only when it is clear that they are primarily defined by the needle or another symbol of domesticity. Moreover, a woman writer should never display equality with or superiority to men, lest she be "punished with disgrace."

The most sobering work relating to needlework, class, and a girl's potential for learning and creativity is Lamb's tale "The Little Mahometan," from *Mrs. Leicester's School* (1809). I mention that children's stories were a particularly acceptable genre for women in this period and that Mary Lamb contributed most of the pieces in this collection, which she wrote with her brother Charles. In their journals and discussion students identify the extreme social control manifest through needlework. In the tale little Margaret, who lives with her widowed mother as the dependent of Mrs. Beresford, is virtually abandoned because her mother is forced to spend all day stitching a carpet with her employer, who is literally and figuratively blinded by years of such useless work. Finding her way to the forbidden library of the house, Margaret is enchanted by reading tales of the world of Muhammad. Found out, she falls ill and is ostensibly cured by the doctor's wife, who guides Margaret from the dangerous world of imagination and heresy to the supposedly safe—and numbing—world of domesticity, submission, and Christianity by buying her a needle case, a pincushion, and a sewing basket. Because Margaret is female and working-class, the creative life is closed to her. Students are often disturbed by the bleakness of the tale, and they resist the idea that nineteenth-century readers, child or adult, could have found it pleasurable reading. Students find particularly chilling that we see Margaret's world closing down but that she does not seem to realize that it is happening.

At the conclusion of the discussion in both courses, I ask students to sum up the ideas in these works and place them in the context of those we have discussed earlier in the course. The students note that needlework—whether samplers, shirts, embroidery, or quilts—was lived reality for women of all social classes, including the women writers we have studied. Dismissed as trifling or overvalued as emblematic of domestic virtue, needlework was a site of powerful debate about women's fulfillment and limitations as wives and mothers, about their roles as producers of literary texts, and about the nature of vision and ways of seeing.

Transatlantic Cultures of Sensibility: Teaching Gender and Aesthetics through the Prospect
Julie Ellison

Happily, it is difficult to introduce poems by Anna Letitia Barbauld, Charlotte Smith, Joanna Baillie, Dorothy Wordsworth, Mary Tighe, Hannah More, and Felicia Hemans into courses on Romantic poetry without challenging the notion of Romanticism itself. One can elaborate such challenges further by including the poets of British North America and the early Republic, such as Phillis Wheatley, Sarah Wentworth Morton, Mercy Otis Warren, and Ann Eliza Bleecker. The more noncanonical writers I teach, the more Romanticism appears to me to be a local phenomenon, one of a number of related subcultures within the British literary scene between 1790 and 1825. And the more closely I link the 1790s to the preceding decades, the more I am convinced that Romanticism, however we define it, is one several cultures of sensibility—by which I mean cultural conventions that foreground the social, or relational, experience of feeling. These cultures begin much earlier, persist in multiple forms throughout the period, and thrive long after the ostensible end of Romanticism, as close study of the popularity of sentimental writing after Byron's death suggests. In sum, because of the current scholarly rage for sensibility, noncanonical writers have taken on new stature and canonical poets have assumed less grandiose proportions.

The culture of sensibility understands emotion as social energy that moves through persons, speech, objects, places, and texts as they are viewed, read, or remembered. The ethical core of sensibility is a narrative characterized by cross-class and often cross-racial spectatorship and sympathy. Sensibility includes philosophies of benevolence and moral sentiment; "Whig Sentimentalism" (Silverman 82–87); narratives of the man and woman of feeling; the Gothic novel and poem; the elegiac but critical locodescriptive poem featuring vignettes of suffering others; much abolitionist literature; poetic allegories, marked by fancy or the depiction of the sublime, in which poetic diction and deep subjectivity choreograph feeling; the sentimental novel; and the quasi-narrative essay, such as Richard Steele's *Spectator* rendition of the story of Inkle and Yarico. It is traditional to date the emergence of the "Age of Sensibility" somewhere after the death of Pope (1744) and before the French Revolution (1789). Alternatively, and with quite a different inflection, this period is referred to as the age of Johnson, as in many course titles and *The Concise Cambridge History of English Literature*. The age of sensibility has been treated as an interlude of minor writers (with the exception of Johnson) between the eighteenth century and Romanticism (though the minor is a category that Gilles Deleuze and Félix Guattari have defamiliarized). Sensibility and Romanticism, according to both of these temporal constructs, are mutually exclusive.

When, with the help of friends and colleagues including Marlon Ross, Adela Pinch, and Nanora Sweet, I started assigning in linked clusters poems by Barbauld, Samuel Taylor Coleridge, Wheatley, and Philip Freneau, for example, or William Wordsworth, Hemans, and Henry Wadsworth Longfellow this chronology ceased to work. My contemporaneous research, aimed at reading late-eighteenth-century North American and British poets in relation to one another, further helped break down the distinctions among the Age of Sensibility, the Age of Johnson, Romanticism, and, for good measure, the early Republic and the antebellum period. At least in the beginning, both the students and I found the women poets more continuous with Thomas Gray, James Thomson, William Collins, and Oliver Goldsmith than with the authors of the greater Romantic lyric. My students felt disoriented reinterpreting as historically simultaneous cultures they were used to understanding as separate in time. They thought that women's poetry "of the Romantic period"—as the present volume puts it—was stale and formulaic and was justly superseded by the psychological and political torments of Romantic subjectivity. These reactions provided occasions to work through the impression that all allegorical personifications, say, look alike (a variant of the "all couplets sound alike" charge concerning Swift and Pope) and to question the students' sense that Romanticism is modern or intuitively accessible to the twentieth-century reader in a way that poetry classed in an earlier or different school is not.

In the available space, I can only sketch out two sequences of assigned readings that illuminate an array of complex relations between the hypothetical cultures of sensibility and Romanticism. In my honors course Questioning Romanticism, I teach texts that showcase the poetic uses of the prospect. It is a choice of topic greatly helped along by John Barrell's *English Literature in History, 1730–80: An Equal, Wide Survey*. Barbauld's *Eighteen Hundred and Eleven* employs the prospect in the service of historical retrospect and prophecy, offering a bird's-eye view of imperial expansion in the New World and decay in the Old. Coleridge's political prospect poems use the same combination of prosopopoeia and elevation to dramatize the poet's ambivalent attraction to public sympathy, historical grandiosity, and critique. My selections included "Life" (1789, 1834), "Reflections on Having Left a Place of Retirement" (1796), "Religious Musings" (1796), "Destiny of Nations" (1796, 1817), "Ode to the Departing Year" (1796), "Fears in Solitude" (1798), and "France: An Ode" (1798). I might then draw on book 6 of *The Prelude*. The account of travel through France and Switzerland (342–556), which we typically rush through on our way to Wordsworth's sublime reaction to crossing the Alps, and the posttraumatic interlude that follows this crisis (649–726) shift among several modes, constituting a virtual anthology of later-eighteenth-century poetic language: the picturesque, the pastoral genre scene, the beautiful. These modes are accompanied by an appropriate range of tonalities from "a Poet's tender melancholy" (366) to the genial male bonding of "gilded sympathies" (552) and by an array of figures from personification ("the lady Sorrow" [555]) to gothic simile ("a dull red image of the moon / Lay bedded . . . / Like an uneasy snake" [705–07]) (citations from the 1850 text). And if ambitious I may also include Freneau's two versions of "The Rising Glory of America" (1772, 1786), a dialogue between two male friends who survey the fate of European colonies in North and South America in a hyperkinetic rendition of fanciful nationalism.

I was able to teach these materials in part because our honors program in English was then organized as an intensive, two-year march through literary history from the Middle Ages to Joyce; I could rely on my students' having taken a good course on the eighteenth century in the preceding term. This well-prepared group and I could quickly address the alienation prompted by poetry that seemed dated to the students in a way that the greater Romantic lyric did not. Our honors program now allows greater curricular flexibility and foregrounds the senior thesis, and so not all the honor students have such a deep background in poetry. For these students I would probably combine the poetry with fiction (Henry Mackenzie's *The Man of Feeling*, William Hill Brown's *The Power of Sympathy*, Radcliffe's *The Mysteries of Udolpho*, Wollstonecraft's *Wrongs of Woman*, Charles Brockden Brown's *Edgar Huntly*, Jane Austen's *Persuasion*), a more accessible genre in which to work through the idioms of the sublime and the beautiful, of locodescription and the prospect, of the actively interpretive protagonist, and of imperial content.

Using the prospect as the common element in these poetic texts accomplishes several things: the prospect links epistemology to history by making the view from on high the occasion for reflections on great public affairs and the poet's relation to them. Furthermore, it shows how a single poetic convention adapts to occasions that are bound up with aesthetic vocabularies and taste, with class, gender, national, racial, and psychological meanings. The comparison across traditional temporal boundaries helps students discriminate among unfamiliar works while clarifying how the representational or ontological questions raised by allegory, personification, and the prospect illuminate the cultural history of feeling.

A second cluster of poems I have taught probes the associations among Catholicism, the dislocated or ungrounded feminine cut loose from the patriarchal family, elegiac tones, narratives of quest and exile, and the aesthetics of the beautiful. Neither Hemans's "The Forest Sanctuary" (1825) nor Longfellow's *Evangeline* (1847) belong to the canons of British or North American Romanticism, yet both narrate dramas in which reactionary state-sponsored violence splits families along sexual lines, leading to uncanny wanderings in American interiors far away from the Catholic homeland. The focus on the traumatic aftermath of the Inquisition (in "The Forest Sanctuary") and on British imperial intervention in Arcadia (in *Evangeline*) aligns these poems with Byron's *Childe Harold*, insofar as either the content or the composition of all three works bears a historical relation to the Napoleonic wars. I might also teach them Wordsworth's *The Ruined Cottage / The Excursion*, book 1 (1814), in which the female gaze fulfills some of the function of Evangeline's quest and in which war occurs offstage; Percy Shelley's "The Triumph of Life" (1822), particularly to compare the remarkable processions featured in Shelley's, Hemans's, and Longfellow's poems; or Walter Scott's *Lay of the Last Minstrel* (1805), surely a model for all later costume dramas in verse, a poem that operatically combines war, memory, religious difference, and the uncanny. These materials present complex family melodramas and have a narrative momentum that makes them more accessible to undergraduate readers. They do not pose the same difficulties for a mid-level college English course, therefore, that the poetry of prospect does (although I wouldn't teach them in the course, Introduction to Poetry, a prerequisite for our major).

These assignments are designed to help the poetry of sentiment become more Romantic and Romantic poetry become less so. They have three goals, aimed at helping students become better critical readers. First, the assignments challenge all established chronologies and curricular habits rather than substitute some newly prestigious notion of sensibility for a dethroned Romanticism. Second, they integrate the issue of gender into all discussions of literary types and cultural periods. Most students of Romanticism still tend to consider feminist work—including the pathbreaking contributions of Stuart Curran, Margaret Homans, Mary Jacobus, Anne K. Mellor, Adela Pinch, Marlon Ross, Karen Swann, and Susan J. Wolfson—as an avoidable subspecialty. Third, they help students to understand that the rise in the academic popularity of eighteenth- and nineteenth-century sensibility is a function of our present cultural situation. The tone of United States culture in the 1980s and the 1990s can be construed as incorporating both a revival of and an attack on certain forms of sensibility. Confirming this trend are the turn to emotion studies in fields from psychology to history, anthropology to communications; the marketing—and debunking—of the sensitive male; the fraught legitimacy of public weeping; the heavy investment of mass media in therapeutic discourse; and the astonishing success of autobiographical writing, which increasingly focuses on social experience. By confronting the revised relation between Romanticism and sensibility during the present phase of postmodern emotionality, students can see for themselves how cultural history is revised in accordance with the changing needs and values of reading audiences.

Staging History: Teaching Romantic Intersections of Drama, History, and Gender

Greg Kucich

I always begin my course on Romanticism and gender by emphasizing the tremendous scholarly excitement about the new Romanticisms emerging from our gendered revisionings of the traditional canon. Students find this spirit of enthusiastic discovery contagious, whether or not they are familiar with Romanticism, and I channel the resulting excitement toward several specific gender-related projects: recovering the texts of the period's many women writers, investigating these writers' ideological challenges to masculine Romanticism, and rethinking the achievements of Romanticism's canonical male writers. One intriguing way to integrate these activities is to focus students' attention on the provocative intersections of dramatic, poetic, and historical writing among the era's women authors. We are just beginning to recognize, as Stuart Curran notes, that a pervasive "engagement with history" ("Women Readers" 191) makes up one of the strongest characteristics of Romantic women's writing. I stress that fact at the outset of the course, pointing out the voluminous amounts of historical writing British women produced during their first rise to prominence in various branches of historiography: Catharine Macaulay, Mary Wollstonecraft, Helen Maria Williams, Hester Piozzi, and Mary Shelley in political history; Lucy Aikin, Anna Jameson, and Mary Hays in women's history; Hannah More and Harriet Martineau in social and economic history; and Mary Howitt and Charlotte Smith in natural history. I also encourage students immediately to consider how such historical outlooks conditioned much of the poetry written by Romantic-era women, particularly their verse drama. To demonstrate that unique integration of history, drama, and gender, I assign Joanna Baillie's "Introductory Discourse" to her *Series of Plays*, in which Baillie grounds her theory of an alternative dramaturgy critical of masculine ideologies in the work of the "historian" (17). I follow up on the implications of Baillie's strategy with a series of questions and challenges to guide students in their work on women's texts: what motivates so many Romantic women writers to engage with history, and why do they so frequently connect history with poetry and verse drama? In what ways do their historical outlooks and dramatic procedures contest masculine practices in both genres? Can we delineate in these challenges types of feminine historiography, poetics, or dramaturgy? And, finally, can we relate these questions to recent developments in the practices of contemporary feminist historians, philosophers, poets, and dramatists?

I do not expect definitive answers; rather, the questions introduce readings and discussions that generally frame the broader issues of my course on Romanticism and gender. I begin by asking the related questions of why historical writing attracted women and how their poetic experiments with it responded to masculine historiography. First of all, I alert students to the rise of history as a discipline in the eighteenth and early nineteenth centuries that claimed to replace religion as the ground of modern truth. To demonstrate the specific political functions of such representations of truth, I assign excerpts from Hume, Gibbon, Burke, Paine, Godwin, Malthus, and Condorcet and ask students to explore the ideological implications of the purported truths revealed there. Students are often particularly intrigued by the class biases of Malthus's population theory and the gender subordinations of Paine's arguments for the rights of *man*. At this point, I also assign the opening chapters of Christina Crosby's *The Ends of History* and Margaret Ezell's *Writing Women's Literary History*, both of which demonstrate how the "truths" of eighteenth- and nineteenth-century historiography systematically excluded women from historical, cultural, and political life. These exclusions generally took the form of abstract models of historical motion—such as the liberal progressions of Whig history, the perfectibility scenarios of Godwin and Condorcet, and the oscillations of dearth and supply in Malthus's population narratives—whose universalizing emphases dismiss the presence of individual subjects, particularly marginalized ones like women and racial minorities, from the grand sweep of historical development. Students thus learn that if history had become the guardian of truth by the late eighteenth century, the revelation it proffered was, in Crosby's phrase, "man's truth" (1).

Yet histories of truth, as William Blake reminds us in *The Marriage of Heaven and Hell*, frequently become the sites of party contention. I draw on that reminder to suggest why, as movements for female empowerment intensified in the late eighteenth century, so many women writers entered into the lists of history to protest against rights and truths reserved for "man." To highlight the reluctance of many women writers to embrace the epistemological and political structures of mainstream historiography, I specifically emphasize Catherine Moreland's response to what she calls "solemn history" in Jane Austen's *Northanger Abbey*. "[H]istory, real solemn history," she declares, "I cannot be interested in. . . . The quarrels of popes and kings, with wars or pestilences, in every page; the men all so good for nothing, and hardly any women at all—it is very tiresome" (123). I direct students to various echoes of Catherine's irritation in the works of eighteenth- and nineteenth-century women commentators on the writing of history: Mary Astell argues as early as 1705 that history never "record[s] the great and good Actions of Women" (293); Mary Wollstonecraft generally denounces the systematic exclusion of women from the writing and "study of history" (*Vindication* [Polity] 108); Anna Jameson more specifically laments that "history never heard [of] . . . or disdains to speak" of women (xvii). And Jane Austen begins her wickedly parodic *History of England* (always a big hit among students) with an ironic point about the invisibility of women in conventional historiography: "It is to be supposed that Henry [IV] was married, since he had certainly four sons, but it is not in my power to inform the Reader who was his Wife" (xvi).

After we examine these protests, I urge students to consider how women writers more subtly critique the general priorities of masculine historiography that foster such exclusions. I direct students to excerpts from selected texts (assembled in a course packet) that reveal broad tendencies among women writers to criticize masculine history's emphasis on political or military abstractions and its persistent inattention to the interior lives of the individual subjects who are perilously swept up in the relentless march of history. More, for instance, rebukes Hume in her essays on English history for his distortive indifference to the "character" and "ruling principle[s]" of historical agents. His more abstract concern with the "general" forces of historical causation, she concludes, "is the too prevailing method of historians . . ." (*Complete Works* 73). Maria Edgeworth, in the preface to *Castle Rackrent*, similarly argues that "the professed historian" deals only with "public" events and "sublime" heroes, leaving readers completely uninformed of "the feelings" of common individuals (2). Baillie, in her "Introductory Discourse," also denounces "real" or public history for its tendency to obscure the inner lives of those who suffer through the ravages of time (*Series* 18). When students have learned from these selections that women's resistance to "real" or "solemn" history does not only respond to its suppression of female characters but also to its elimination of subjectivity, I raise the question of why emotional interiority became so important for women writers.

That question usually provokes a lively discussion, drawing from Anne Mellor's theories of "feminine Romanticism" (*Romanticism and Gender* 3), about the inclination of many Romantic women writers to prioritize emotional sympathy as the basis for a feminine ethic of care that promotes benevolent interpersonal relations and harmonious domestic community in opposition to the combative economic, political, and military dynamics of the masculine public sphere. Critically sophisticated students sometimes find such a binary model of separate spheres reductive, and vigorous debate often emerges over the usefulness of Mellor's categories. But I usually turn these discussions, in the end, toward a general recognition of the political importance of women's resistance to the impersonalities of masculine historiography. To insist on the "feelings"— hence the presence and the rights—of individual subjects in history is to challenge the basic principles of an entire social system based on hierarchies of class, race, and nationality as well as gender—to create, as Wollstonecraft would put it, "a REVOLUTION in female manners" (*Vindication* 113).

I focus discussion of such a revolutionary, interiorized historicism on the various shapes it could assume: Wollstonecraft's outbursts of pity and "Weeping" in *An Historical and Moral View of the Origin and Progress of the French Revolution* for the victims of revolutionary violence (163); Edgeworth's attention in *Castle Rackrent* to the "domestic lives" of historical characters, disclosed "behind the scenes . . . [of] the great theatre of the world" (2); Baillie's "sympathetic curiosity" toward the "dispositions and tempers" of history's "feeble" individuals, whose agitations of soul she wishes to delineate in a drama of the domestic closet (*Series* 4, 16, 21). Students find an important example of the political implications of this personalized form of historicism in Baillie's argument for its capacity to open the hearts and deepen the sensitivities of political leaders (12–14). They also notice how Baillie and Edgeworth connect such a politically transformative historicism with modes of theatricality.

One of the most striking examples of this intersection between historicism and theatricality can be found in Macaulay's *History of England*, which I present in selected excerpts that include its brief but critically significant theoretical preface on historical method (6: v–xiv). Students find Macaulay a fascinating transgressor of conventional gender boundaries in her controversial emergence within the masculine field of political history as the period's leading republican historian and one of its most passionate champions of representative government. Macaulay not only challenged Britain's aristocratic political institutions but also, identifying herself as a "female opposer" radically entering "a path of literature rarely trodden by my sex" ("Account" 331; *History* 1: x), critiqued the gender-coded systems of knowledge produced by masculine historiography. While self-consciously establishing herself as a rational thinker intellectually equal to male historians, Macaulay constructed a theoretical model for the kind of alternative history of the human heart promoted by other women writers. I point out to students that her theoretical preface locates the sources of historical knowledge in human "character" (6: v), which reveals a sorrowful record of individual suffering throughout time. Macaulay regards this poignant record with "sympathising tenderness" (students often note the similarity to Baillie's "sympathetic curiosity"), and she admits having "shed many tears" (students recall Wollstonecraft's "weeping") while immersing herself in the lives of historical subjects (6: 21, xii). This kind of historical "sympathising" leads Macaulay to focus on the domestic situations of ordinary subjects in their communal relations—what she calls elsewhere "the situation of sufferers" (*Letters* 177).

I encourage students to associate this interiorized focus on communal relations with the historicism of Baillie and Edgeworth, especially in the way that Macaulay equates such a domesticated historical method with theatricality. Conceptualizing her sympathetic record of human fragility as a "horrid theatre of human sufferings" (*History* 2: 9), Macaulay frequently highlights the experience of individual anguish by staging dramatic spectacles like her description of Henry Vane's execution:

> On the scaffold his countenance and manner were so serene and composed, that whilst he was talking to a knot of his friends, the spectators cried out, "Which is the man who is to suffer? which is Sir Henry Vane?" On this the prisoner, stepping forward, saluted the multitude on each side the scaffold with his hat off, and then returned to the company. [Sound of trumpets; then with his head on the block, Vane prays aloud:] Bless the Lord who hath accounted me worthy to suffer for his name. . . . Whilst the hand of the executioner was suspended over the head of this illustrious sufferer, it was remarked by the spectators, and, in particular, by a curious and ancient traveller, "That his countenance did not change,

and that his nerves were as little affected by the violent and fatal stroke, that contrary to every other instance where he had seen the same kind of death inflicted, his head lay perfectly still immediately after it was separated from the body." (6: 123–25)

The emotional impact of this sort of personalized historicism depends on its sensational theatricality, which freezes the abstract narrative flow of public history in a stunning tableau of particularized suffering and communal sympathy. Students are delighted to test the arresting stageworthiness of this scene by mounting it in class as a *tableau vivant*. Their exuberant demonstration drives home the point about women historians' characteristic recourse to theatrical practices in order to stage spectacles of emotional intensity that stop the abstract narrative trajectory and contest the truths as well as the politics of "solemn history."

As students learn about the political importance of these theatrical strategies in such a contestatory historicism, they begin to understand why so many of the period's women poets and dramatists resort to historical paradigms. I direct students to critics like Marjean Purinton (133–34) and Anne Mellor ("Joanna Baillie" 565) who draw specific links among women poets, women dramatists, and the feminist historians and polemicists of the 1790s. But it is not always necessary to seek direct lines of influence among these groups. It may be more productive in the end for students to use their knowledge of female historians as a guide for comprehending the aims and limitations of historical poems and dramas by women. Yet at the same time we should also urge students to ponder the viability of critical attempts to formulate categories such as "feminine historiography," "feminine dramaturgy," or even "feminine Romanticism." They should juxtapose the methods of male and female historians, male and female historical poets and dramatists, always considering gender as a social construct rather than a biological fact while tracing the gender crossings as well as distinctions among male and female poets, dramatists, and historians.

With those warnings in mind, I encourage students to explore the patterns in women's poetic and dramatic writing that replicate the theatrical strategies of female historians like Macaulay. Although teachers should be creative in choosing from among the many women poets and dramatists of the period, I focus attention on Joanna Baillie and Felicia Hemans because they were particularly immersed in historical readings and projects. Their plays and poems are also relatively accessible in facsimile reprints as well as early and modern editions (Cox; Burroughs, "English Romantic Women" 296). I encourage students to develop their own connections between these works and those of the women historians they have studied, but I find it useful to emphasize both writers' frequent deployment of the kind of arrested spectacle of suffering and sympathy that informs Macaulay's historicism. Baillie, in fact, theorizes this practice in the preface to volume 3 of her *Series of Plays*, conceptualizing the ideal stage as a kind of framed picture. She constructs such a frame in *Basil* by freezing the play's action before the impending death scene in order to sculpt the following arrangement, elaborately detailed in her stage directions, of characters bound together in shared sorrow for the fallen general, Basil:

> (*Enter* Soldiers, *who gather mournfully round* Basil, *and looking mournfully upon him; he holds out his hand to them with a faint smile.*)
> BASIL. Ah, my brave soldiers, this is kindly meant. . . .
> (3d. Soldier *endeavours next to speak, but cannot; and kneeling down by* Basil, *covers his face with his cloak.* Rosinberg *turns his face to the wall and weeps.*)   (1: 185)

This arrested moment of shared mourning and weeping among Basil's soldiers prioritizes sympathy over military action in a domestication of public history that recalls Macaulay's pausing to shed tears for "the situation of sufferers." I illustrate the comparison by having one set of students stage the scene as a *tableau vivant* alongside another group doing the same with Macaulay's vision of Vane's execution. I also have students mount an even more striking *tableau vivant* of communal sympathy from the scene at the end of Baillie's *De Monfort*, in which Jane De Monfort grieves over the body of her dead brother while surrounded by a group of sorrowing friends and attendants who "gather round her, with looks of sympathy" and literally prop her up in their supporting arms (1: 408). Staging these scenes sometimes provokes divided judgments of their lachrymose quality. But I emphasize the important political implications of stopping the flow and domesticating the values of public action. In *De Monfort*, for instance, the concluding exercise of communal affection humanizes the Officer of the Law, who relinquishes his stern public duty to sympathize with "the situation of sufferers."

I urge students to make discriminations between Baillie's practices and those of other women poets and dramatists, but they often find that Hemans's work clarifies their sense of how Baillie's kind of dramatic spectacle can revise masculine history and its political priorities. They learn that Hemans's writings are overwhelmingly preoccupied with history and its recurrent subordinations of women. Her critiques of what she calls the "fearful history" (*Complete Works* 1: 456) of political power and military conquest appear throughout her poetry, especially in the portraits of shattered women that fill her *Records of Woman*. But she also seeks "history's reconstruction," and she frequently draws on Baillie's type of historical dramaturgy to formulate an alternative "gendered aesthetics of history" (Sweet 182, 175). Students can learn from Marlon Ross that Hemans studied Baillie's plays to develop a similar dramatic practice of "stress[ing] plot as *suffering action* rather than plot as a burst of grand, varied activity" (*Contours* 287). That emphasis on "suffering action," or the freezing of narrative and historical action to foreground a revisionary chronicle of emotional exchange, gives rise to numerous spectacles of suffering in *The Siege of Valencia* and *The Vespers of Palermo*. Hemans tantalizingly suspends the imminent collapse of Valencia in one final battle, for instance, while Gonzalez views the execution of his eldest son from the city walls and cries out amid his anguish, "My son! my son!—Mine eldest born! . . . my brain whirls fearfully . . . my boy! my boy!" (1: 455). Similarly, the triumphant revolution of Palermo swings to an abrupt halt when Procida, as the stage direction indicates, "throws himself upon the body" of the son he had doomed to execution and cries out, "My son, my injured son!" (2: 69). Emphasizing the obvious parallels here with Baillie's dramatic spectacles, I focus on similar effects in Hemans's nondramatic poetry—particularly "Joan of Arc in Rheims" and "The Bride's Farewell"—to indicate how such theatrical displays of communal suffering pervade the various forms of historical poetry composed by Romantic women writers. Finally, I prod students to consider the political possibilities and limitations of this dramatic-historical style. Hemans's displays of anguish, especially female suffering, both challenge hegemonic patriarchal systems and lament, with crushing but politically ineffectual poignance, their persisting destruction of women's aspirations and lives. As Susan Wolfson concludes, Hemans's spectacles ultimately yield "a perspective that effaces . . . [female] heroism in the pace of men's history" ("Domestic Affections" 152); the same might be argued of Baillie's spectacles.

In the end I ask students to relate these political contradictions to the aesthetic differences between dramaturgical principles realized on stage and carried out in nondramatic poetry. The experience of mounting *tableaux vivant* usually leaves students questioning the dramaturgical efficacy—and the impact of related political imperatives—of halting stage action in such a manner. They are usually not surprised to learn that the plays of Baillie and Hemans failed on stage while generally succeeding as reading texts. Pitched disputes often emerge over the relative political effectiveness of dramatic and nondramatic poetry by writers like Hemans and Baillie. Yet much as students question the political results of these problematic stage practices, they learn, by now, to resist associating such liabilities with artistic ineptitude. Instead, they see clearly how women's stagecraft, whatever its limitations, performs calculated strategies to alter dominant structures of history, knowledge, and power—strategies, moreover, that could succeed in an appropriate theatrical space. Staging these scenes in a small classroom setting reveals that their disruptive impact on plot development, as Baillie suggests in the preface to volume 3 of her *Series of Plays*, can work with startling effectiveness in a small theater space to disturb conventional audience expectations and outlooks. Students are always intrigued to learn from Catherine Burroughs ("English Romantic Closet") that such strategies anticipate major innovations in contemporary lesbian and feminist theater theory. Discussion about Baillie's relevance today can lead to broader considerations of the links between the contestatory historicism of Romantic women writers and the epistemological theories of women's time, and women's ways of knowing and seeing, developed by contemporary feminist philosophers, social historians, and standpoint theorists (see, e.g., Kristeva,

"Women's Time"; Donovan; Showalter, "Women's Time"; J. Scott; and S. Harding). These contemporary applications may never settle the problem of delineating a coherent "feminine" historicism, poetics, or dramaturgy among Romantic women writers. But they do highlight the enduring significance of these writers' efforts to integrate various forms of writing in the service of contesting the masculinist ideologies of their time.

The Aesthetics of Loss: Charlotte Smith's *The Emigrants* and *Beachy Head*

Kay K. Cook

A major challenge for scholars and for teachers who are integrating the "new" British women poets into their work is to draw attention to gender differences without dividing the period into a male Romanticism and a female Romanticism. Such polarization misrepresents literary production in the early nineteenth century and marginalizes writing by women new to the institutionalized canon.

My approach has been to place newly recovered authors "in conversation" with more established ones. In my senior-level British Romanticism course, for example, I have created a series of assignments involving clusters of authors and works that I arrange around certain genres, subjects, time periods, and the like. Below I discuss one such cluster, in which I put the works of Charlotte Smith in conversation with those of Mary Wollstonecraft and William Wordsworth. I focus on Smith's *The Emigrants* (1793) and *Beachy Head* (1806) from *The Poems of Charlotte Smith* (Curran); Wollstonecraft's *Letters Written during a Short Residence in Sweden, Norway, and Denmark* (1795; pub. 1796) and her letters written to Gilbert Imlay (1793–95); and Wordsworth's two-part *Prelude* (1799).

These three contemporaries serve well to introduce the Romantic period and its troubled relation with the French Revolution as well as to initiate a discussion of Romantic identity. I group their works under the topic The Aesthetics of Loss. An aesthetics, of course, is not ahistorical, as Jerome J. McGann (*Romantic Ideology*) and Marilyn Butler (*Romantics*) pointed out in the early 1980s. That is precisely why it is interesting to look at the works of three people decisively influenced by the Revolution and its aftermath. Their contemplation of deep personal loss, either resulting from the Revolution or finding its objective correlative in that event, leads them to meditate on the mind's relation to the external natural world and the capacity (or failure) of that world to offer solace and healing. The excursive poems of Wordsworth and Smith and the Scandinavian letters of Wollstonecraft, each representing an attempt to position the self publicly, spatially, and historically, provide the student with a historicized, individualized aesthetics that helps identify some of the literary impulses of the late eighteenth and early nineteenth centuries in England that we later came to identify as Romantic. Moreover, by examining a gendered aesthetics of loss grounded in the poets' narrative and autobiographical strategies, we broaden our critical concepts of British Romantic identity, most of which are based historically on a document published after the Romantic era, Wordsworth's 1850 *Prelude*.

Smith, Wollstonecraft, and Wordsworth found themselves inextricably involved with matters political and personal pertaining to France before and during the Revolution. Wollstonecraft had replied to Edmund Burke's *Reflections on the Revolution in France* with *Vindication of the Rights of Men* (1790) and subsequently with *A Vindication of the Rights of Woman* (1792); Wordsworth had written his "Letter to the Bishop of Llandaff" (1793); and in *The Emigrants* Smith had taken on the plight of those people, especially women and children, exiled by the upheaval in France. Yet while writing in these public, historical modes, the authors were enduring personal distress that contributed to their development of an aesthetics of loss.

During his residence in France, about which he would later report in verses describing the bliss of being alive and his subsequent despair and breakdown over the failure of the Revolution (1850 *Prelude* 11.302–05; 105–09), Wordsworth met Annette Vallon, who gave birth to his child Caroline after he returned to England. Mary Wollstonecraft began her association with Gilbert Imlay and later, while in France, gave birth to his daughter, who accompanied Wollstonecraft on her tour of the Scandinavian countries. She also witnessed and wrote about the procession leading Louis XVI to the guillotine. Smith accompanied her husband to France in 1784 when he fled from debtors; there she witnessed his continuing philandering and squandering of money. Childbearing had become a way of life for her by this time; during the period in question she was the only one of the three authors who had children within the bounds of marriage. She too saw the effects of the war on the innocent.

For all three writers, France became a political emblem of danger and a personal emblem of anguish. The channel, Calais, Beachy Head, Havre, and Dover figure into the works of these emotional exiles, who position themselves in many of their writings as solitary figures on the shore of one country looking across the channel toward the other. Wollstonecraft, moreover, extended her solitary wanderings and writings to Scandinavia, all the while painfully looking toward England and France.

Some examples from the works illustrate how I use the clustering approach in class. Smith positioned the narrator of *The Emigrants* on the cliffs overlooking the channel to reflect on the French Revolution's effect on exiles, from women, immigrating to England alone or with small children, to the clergy. As a parade of exiles passes before the reader's eyes, Smith locates and allegorizes human actions within the expanse of history, speaking out against the ravages of war and the intolerance of her own country: "Flush'd with hot blood, the Fiend of Discord sits / In savage triumph; mocking every plea / Of policy and justice" (2.52–54). The political turns personal for Smith when she explains her empathy for the French Catholic clergy against whom the English bear animosity: "I mourn your sorrows; for I too have known / Involuntary exile; and while yet / England had charms for me, have felt how sad / It is to look across the dim cold sea" (1.155–57).

In *Beachy Head*, an unfinished and more complex poem, Smith likewise overlooks the channel, contemplating the sweep of time, diurnal and geological, and the great events witnessed by the promontory on which she stands. A compendium of history, geography, natural history, and geology, *Beachy Head* also echoes literary works from the classics, recounts tales of the sea and of hermits, and ruminates on the life of the shepherd who has no appreciation of the history of the ground on which he walks. The poem catalogs the learning of a classically educated woman without university training. Yet, Smith's central question, posed midway through the poem, defines the self's core—"Ah! Who is happy?" (255); she answers the question, "I once was happy" (282). Interestingly, Smith's placing her personal despair historically does not diminish the personal much as one might think. Instead, the poignant "I once was happy" underscores how impersonal is the cosmic scheme against which the personal is positioned.

In both poems Smith uses a remarkable rhetorical strategy that Wordsworth and Wollstonecraft do not; she includes copious notes to each poem. The reader must therefore work back and forth between two texts; the result is a reader-constructed version of the text that extends beyond the generic boundaries of poetry, prose, autobiography, and scientific writing.

Although he does not refer specifically to the poems' unusual annotation, Stuart Curran remarks on the "multitudinous, uncanny particularity [that] represents a counter reality to that of human society and history" and that "testifies to an alternate romanticism that seeks not to transcend or to absorb nature but to contemplate and honor its irreducible alterity" (*Poems* xxvii–xxviii). In *Beachy Head* proper, for instance, Smith remarks on "the strange and foreign forms / Of sea-shells" that mingle "with the pale calcerous soil" on the promontory (373–74). The notes to these lines report, "Among the crumbling chalk I have often found shells, some quite in fossil state and hardly distinguishable from chalk. Others appeared more recent" (232).

I try to help my students appreciate that Smith's alterity is manifested both visually and structurally in *The Emigrants* and *Beachy Head* through the verse and notes, as well as substantially through the diarylike quality of several of the notes, which contrasts with the formal tone of the poem proper. Smith's strategy presents the private (diary), or conversational, form and the public (poem) as one text, but she deliberately refuses to blend or merge the two. (In my work on Dorothy Wordsworth I argue that this strategy is a gendered resistance to dominant male Romantic forms of poetry, especially the forms that valorize the sublime ["Immersion"; "*I*"; "Self-Neglect"].)

How does Smith's poetry echo, answer, oppose, or relate to Wollstonecraft's and Wordsworth's? Writing letters that evoke the travelogue, Wollstonecraft suppresses the anguish of her long separation from Imlay and of the knowledge that he will not marry her. While she is commenting in the Scandinavian letters, for example, that "Norwegians are fond of music" (70), she is writing privately to Imlay, "I could not help feeling extremely mortified last post, at not receiving a letter from you. My being at _____ was but a chance, and you might have hazarded it; and would a year ago" (131). Less willing than Smith to document her loss publicly, Wollstonecraft nonetheless privately inscribes it as a footnote to her travelogue. The author of *A Vindication of the Rights of Woman* was at the time a self divided, and students find her eloquent recounting of her tour all the more powerful when they read the love letters as subtext.

In the 1799 *Prelude* Wordsworth elides present personal loss and sexual tension (as does Wollstonecraft in her letters to Imlay) because the work is a public poem. Placing himself within the tradition of the (male) epic poem, Wordsworth consigns any present loss to his mythologically produced, sublime "spots of time" (2.287). Characterizing himself as "Two consciousnesses—conscious of myself / And of some other being" (1.30–31), he disconnects not only from his former "self" but also from former passions that quite probably extend into the present. Wordsworth had fathered an illegitimate child, and he wrote the poem while living isolated in Germany with his sister. He had passionately supported the French Revolution (a passion also displaced in this version), passionately loved a woman, and passionately pursued the living arrangement with his sister. And yet in this autobiographical piece all such passion is displaced (and disguised) in "spots of time," far back into childhood, far back into "some other being."

Smith, in contrast, subverts the public form of the epic poem and checks the inclination toward the sublime while establishing her connection with—and alterity to—the natural world. In her textual self-formation, she announces her relation to love, loss, and exile by embedding her feelings into the ode and the epic. Like Wollstonecraft and other women, Smith cannot emotionally or socially distance herself from the offspring of her passion. The reminder of that love, although fraught with bitterness, is ever-present in her life and in her work.

Thus, whereas Wordsworth employs one text (which he then continually revises) and Wollstonecraft writes two separate texts, Smith seeks to define herself in relation to national, historical, and natural definitions by encompassing, in a single text, poetry and prose, the public and the private. Formed by the French Revolution and its bloody aftermath, understanding that political despair and private despair are one, these three authors helpfully introduce the British Romantic period to students.

Clustering "new" women poets with their more familiar contemporaries enables instructors and students alike to reformulate the canon themselves and to participate in the creation of literary history while resisting the temptation reductively to polarize Romanticism along strict gender lines, opting instead to recognize how different social and cultural positions reflect the complex dynamic of gender that characterized the period.

Hemans's "The Widow of Crescentius": Beauty, Sublimity, and the Woman Hero

Nanora Sweet

I teach British Romanticism to English majors at an urban campus of our state university. Our Romanticism offerings are divided into two courses—on early and on later Romantic writers—leaving room to teach several women writers and provide ample cultural context. Male and female students enjoy Romantic women writers, whose involvement in battles over gender and class links their period with our own. To reveal the culture that distinguishes the Romantic period from ours, I ask each student to report on a text used as a source by Romantic writers. A report on Petrarch's *Rime Sparse*, for example, accompanies Percy Shelley's *Alastor* and brings Petrarch's influential poetics of gender into the course. Both courses unfold as dialogues among writers or between writers and their culture. These dialogues are always finally gendered, be the participants men, women, or both. Thus women poets are not intruders in my courses, but full and necessary participants.

When I teach Felicia Hemans in Later Romantic Poetry and Prose, she appears as a typical later Romantic, the author of long poems written in dialogue with Lord Byron, Shelley, and John Keats and covering matters of material interest to women. Thus my teaching of Hemans contrasts with current scholarship in which she appears as a lyricist of the years 1825 to 1835 (McGann, "Literary History"; Tucker) or as a key member of a women's countercanon (Mellor, *Romanticism and Gender*; Ross, *Contours*). My course devotes one class day to Hemans, and we read three poems that range in length from 206 to 618 lines. We concentrate on "The Widow of Crescentius," a highly colored Byronic tale published in Hemans's *Tales, and Historic Scenes, in Verse* (1819), and discuss *Dartmoor* (1821), a Romantic triumph poem written on the occasion of Napoleon's death. *Dartmoor* attacks the Titanism of Napoleon and Byron and argues for a woman-centered culture of peace. We mention but do not discuss "The Bride of the Greek Isle" (1825), which as a Byronic tale that invites comparison with Keats's "Ode on a Grecian Urn" supplies a popular paper topic. I reproduce these pieces in a course pack, using the Oxford edition (*The Poetical Works of Felicia Dorothea Hemans*) for the poems because its lines are numbered and drawing Hemans's substantive notes from the Philadelphia edition (*The Poetical Works of Mrs. Felicia Hemans*). I also include a Hemans chronology and other poems that students can use in their papers.

Our class on Hemans is the last before midterm. By then, we have covered Jane Austen's *Mansfield Park*, Byron's *Childe Harold's Pilgrimage* and *The Giaour*, and Shelley's *Alastor*, "Hymn to Intellectual Beauty," and "Mont Blanc." In the process we have encountered increasingly difficult notions of politics and poetry, gender and aesthetics. Shelley's "Hymn" and "Mont Blanc" and Byron's *Childe Harold* 3, for instance, have introduced us to the aesthetics of beauty and sublimity and *Childe Harold* 4 to Italian republicanism. In a very welcome way, Hemans makes these notions more concrete and meaningful for students. "The Widow of Crescentius" dramatizes and genders Romantic beauty, sublimity, and republicanism. In turn, the literary background that students studied to prepare for *Childe Harold* 4 supports our reading of "The Widow": one student has reported on sources for that canto's allusions to Numa and Egeria (Plutarch's "Life of Numa" and Ovid's *Metamorphoses* 15), another on Germaine de Staël and her *Corinne; or, Italy.*

The protagonist of "The Widow," Stephania, is the young bride of Crescentius, a tenth-century Roman who seeks to revive classical republican government. When the poem opens, in 998, Rome has been taken by the Saxon emperor Otho III, and Crescentius's party is besieged in Hadrian's tomb. Promised amnesty, Crescentius and his lieutenants leave their sanctuary only to be betrayed and taken prisoner by Otho. As his wife and supporters look on, Crescentius is executed. Now a widow and political exile, Stephania disappears at the end of part 1, leaving us to doubt her survival.

Part 2 takes place in 1002. It begins with a study of two other exiles in Italy's lush countryside, Cicero in the Roman republican past, Otho in the German imperial present. Seeking solace for his remorse, Otho is soothed—but also seduced—by the equivocal melodies of the boy minstrel Guido, whose face bears "the stamp of woes" (2.152). For diversion, Otho holds a banquet where Guido —who is Stephania, of course—assassinates Otho by poisoning his wine. She claims the deed, then turns the spotlight on the treacheries of Otho and his Italian supporters. She embraces an execution that matches Crescentius's, and asks to be entombed with her husband.

At the outset of discussion several students usually comment on the poem's immediate appeal. Some volunteer that "The Widow" is like a Byronic tale, and a couple may notice that its tetrameter couplets are the form Byron uses in *The Giaour*. More students point to the sharp contrast between the independent heroine and the repressed or victimized heroines in Austen and Byron. Hemans's protagonist reminds some of the Byronic hero himself, for like Childe Harold she is a bitterly emotional exile who, in her minstrel persona, arguably becomes the author's alter ego. "The Widow of Crescentius" thus quickly highlights two of the course's more accessible themes—heroism and gender—and a more difficult one, the poet as hero.

The poem's provocative heroine and its subversive plot prompt further discussion. Students note Stephania's real limitations and dangers as a civic wife and widow, but they observe her powers as well, a discussion that I direct toward further commentary on matters of gender, poetry, and politics. When Stephania cross-dresses as a boy minstrel, she reminds students of Byron's experiments with gender reversal. She is like Leila in *The Giaour*, who escapes her harem by dressing as a page, and even more like the Maid of Saragoza of *Childe Harold* 1, who replaced weaker men on the barricades in the Spanish War of Independence (stanzas 54–58). Her use of minstrelsy to achieve political ends opens the question of Hemans's own career as a woman poet in the politicized milieu of later Romantic poetry. I talk about Hemans's ambitious career under the Regent and later the Tory press and mention that both Stephania and Hemans wrote for the ear of governance, neither of them in a simple or straightforward way.

As Susan Wolfson ("Domestic Affections") and others do, I cover Hemans's agonies over fame and explain the difficulties for women who court ill fame as public writers. I suggest that both Hemans and her heroine were driven to compose a disguised poetry of intimations and implications. I point to Hemans's headnote to "The Widow," which she represents as a direct translation from the German historian and economist J. C. L. Simonde de Sismondi's *Histoire des républiques Italiennes* (1809–18), and note that Hemans has revised Sismondi in one important way. She has edited out his suggestion that Stephania "could still dazzle with her charms" and acted as Otho's "mistress or as his doctor" (Sismondi 1: 111; my trans.). Hemans avoids this ill fame for her heroine by disguising her as a poet whose killing charms are those of Italian song, wine, and poison.

As we speculate about the insidious poetry and imagery that Hemans and Stephania both use, I turn our discussion from author and plot to aesthetics (see Sweet for a fuller argument). Stephania's association with lush Italian imagery is obvious to my students: they smile at the descriptions of the glowing eyes and flowing hair of this heroine, in whom "[l]ives all the soul of Italy" (1.39, 45, 142). I suggest that Stephania embodies not simply exotic Italy but a feminine and republican beauty that in part 2 will overpower the masculine and imperial sublimity in Otho. On closer reading we find fresh passages that depict Hemans's Italy as anti-imperial: Italy's vegetation "[u]surps the vanished column's place" (1.12), Stephania is successfully concealed in a land "[w]here flowers luxuriate o'er the brave" (2.6), and there she garners the song, wine, and poison that she uses against a foreign emperor. Students have been introduced in *Childe Harold* 4 to a wronged Italy whose poets are exiles, whose personifications are feminine ("Niobe," "Hope"). Reading Hemans, students begin to understand how a feminized Italy might fulfill the revolutionary purposes that Byron and Shelley share with Hemans.

I then move on to the further republican and feminist arguments that the poem makes through its allusions and through its sixteen substantial notes, which I include in the course packs. The text cites richly from the Bible, Milton, and other texts but most persuasively from Germaine de Staël, Sismondi, and Plutarch. Especially important for teaching this poem are the epigraph from Staël's *Corinne; or, Italy*, the headnote from Sismondi's *Histoire*, and footnotes from these works and Plutarch's *Lives*. Hemans carefully orchestrates these notes to demonstrate that her intentions are calculated and—in a distinctively Romantic-republican way—feminist.

The poem begins with a quotation from *Corinne*. The equivocal motto "L'orage peut briser en un moment les fleurs qui tiennent encore la tête levée" (Staël 54) is rendered divergently by Avriel Goldberger and other translators.

I offer my class my own literal reading of the line and point to its paradox of vulnerability and resurgence: "The storm may in a moment break the flowers who again hold their heads raised." At the end of part 1 we read that, as in Staël's motto, Stephania "sinks . . . a blighted flower," "A broken gem, whose inborn light / Is scatter'd—ne'er to re-unite" (1.281, 1.283–84). But as the motto foreshadows, in part 2 the broken flower will "again raise its head." Staël's motto reaches across the two parts to foreshadow Stephania's resurgence and to unite the poem.

Stephania's heroic resurgence raises legitimate questions about the destructiveness and self-destructiveness of her heroism—and also rouses the persistent worry in our culture over feminism and negativity. It is as though in Stephania the feminine beautiful becomes a scourging sublime. Hemans's citations from the historians Sismondi and Plutarch help my class frame Stephania's dark deeds in historical and feminist terms.

Hemans draws her political history and the sublime dimensions of her aesthetic from Staël's colleague Sismondi, who argues explicitly that Italian republicanism emerged in the Middle Ages and implicitly that it should return to Napoleonic Europe. He charts medieval history as a series of sublime moments in which upper-class republicans go to the scaffold and urban throngs assemble and reassemble. For Sismondi, the execution of Crescentius is a key early moment in the growth of Italian republicanism, a movement recurring in the nineteenth century as the Risorgimento (literally "rising again"). Throughout her *Tales, and Historic Scenes, in Verse* and its sequel, *The Vespers of Palermo* (1823), Hemans replaces Sismondi's male scaffold figures with heroines whose entry into history as women is especially arresting and sublime. When her Crescentius is condemned and executed, Hemans assembles a throng characteristic of Sismondi's moments and allows it to bear Crescentius's "anxious bride" (1.121) from convent confinement into the streets and into history. Hemans strengthens her allusion to the Sismondian throng by including in note 5 the scaffold crowd from an episode later in his *Histoire* (1: 266). Like Sismondi's heroes, Stephania will perish in the throes of political action—but if Staël's aesthetics and Sismondi's history are correct, the woman republican will "again raise her head."

Hemans cites Sismondi in the service of her historical argument that Stephania's immolation might reap positive results, and she uses Plutarch to point to a time when a female figure guided Rome in good governance. Crescentius has tried to revive classical Roman republicanism, but Hemans's poem accepts that attempt as a "[v]ain dream" (1.217). In part 2 she cites Plutarch on the great republican Cicero in his exile and near death (n11). It is vain to revive classical republicanism, Hemans's line explains, because "the sacred shields are gone" (1.217). Note 8 glosses these "bucklers" by citing from Plutarch's "Life of Numa." During a pestilence, the original buckler fell to the feet of Rome's second king, the Sabine Numa, in the Campagna. His consort, the nymph Egeria, "and the Muses" counseled him to conceal the shield among twelve more and then establish a shrine at a spring: thus the pestilence ended. Plutarch argues elsewhere in the "Life" that Numa had a long pacific reign largely because of such salubrious rites suggested by Egeria. When finally the shields are stolen from the temple of Mars, Hemans implies, Rome's republican dreams fail, and the healthful measures offered by Rome's female counselors give way to poisonous ones.

Teaching "The Widow of Crescentius" shows Hemans to be a poet well in control of her tone, structure, and text. The poem also serves canonical Romanticism by dramatizing beauty as indeed the unsettling, and feminine, power that Shelley tells us about figuratively and philosophically in his "Hymn to Intellectual Beauty." The poem is eminently teachable, and its powers to educate the student of Romanticism are certainly not exhausted here.

Teaching the Poetry of Mary Tighe:
Psyche, Beauty, and the Romantic Object

Harriet Kramer Linkin

By the time my students and I get to the poetry of Mary Tighe in the middle of my semester-long course on British Romanticism, the students are fully prepared to appreciate the sophisticated critique her *Psyche; or, The Legend of Love* offers of masculinist Romanticism's objectification of the female. Indeed they are eager to hear a strong female voice break through the silence imposed on all the Wordsworthian and Coleridgean maidens presented as objects of aesthetic gratification. Although I begin the semester with a chorus of female voices from the late 1700s articulating poetical and political positions, I organize portions of my syllabus to replicate the canonical Romanticism that so long elevated the writings of the major six male Romantic poets; I think it is important for students to gain a visceral sense of that canon even as our recuperation of women's literary history changes it. During the first three weeks we examine careful groupings of poems by Charlotte Smith, Anna Seward, Joanna Baillie, Hannah More, Ann Yearsley, Anna Barbauld, and Mary Robinson on such matters as war, education, intolerance, domesticity, maternity, nature, and writing; then we focus for the next three weeks on work from the first generation of male Romantic poets, William Blake, Samuel Coleridge, and William Wordsworth. I do not set the women and men exclusively in polarization—we read Coleridge's "Kubla Khan" with Robinson's "To the Poet Coleridge" and "The Haunted Beach" as well as Barbauld's "To Mr. C" and "Washing Day"— but I do try to re-create the canonical polarities of my training through the syllabus's weekly emphasis. So we turn from the opening immersion in the visions written *by* the daughters of Albion to the masculinist visions *of* the daughters of Albion, in which Blake, Coleridge, and Wordsworth erect the great platforms of their inspired truths to view rather than hear the voices of their sisters. As we move from William Wordsworth's "Lucy" poems and "Nutting" to Dorothy Wordsworth's journals and poetry, we revisit the territory Margaret Homans charted in exploring the romanticized female who seeks to write the self, and we ask, as Homans did, where and how the female poet locates her voice after *Lyrical Ballads* (*Bearing*; *Women Writers*). And then we read Mary Tighe, whose *Psyche* makes the act of challenging the masculinist objectification of the female her very means of communing with the muse, as she offers up a new version of the story of Cupid and Psyche that repositions not only Psyche as quester but also the Romantic woman poet as visionary.

To begin our weeklong discussion of *Psyche* I ask my class two simple questions: what reading the poem was like and what readers know or should know about *Psyche* before reading. I mean to invite commentary on Tighe's use of language and of source material and on how it affects the poem's intellectual accessibility. *Psyche* is, and is not, easy to read: while its narrative proves eminently accessible, the convoluted language Tighe uses to construct her version of the myth is certainly not. My students happily identify their discomfort with Tighe's language immediately and cite the opening stanza of the argument as an initial point of resistance; their resistance provides a point of entry as we look together at that first stanza:

> Let not the rugged brow the rhymes accuse,
> Which speak of gentle knights and ladies fair,
> Nor scorn the lighter labours of the muse,
> Who yet, for cruel battles would not dare
> The low-strung chords of her weak lyre prepare;
> But loves to court repose in slumbery lay,
> To tell of goodly bowers and gardens rare,
> Of gentle blandishments and amorous play,
> And all the lore of love, in courtly verse essay.
>
> (1.1.1–9)

When I ask my students to unpack the complicated syntax, the variant glosses they offer enable them to see how Tighe's syntactic play encodes a sharp critique of the stylistic assumptions that link gender with genre. Does the rugged brow accuse the rhymes that speak of gentle knights and ladies fair, or do the rhymes accuse the rugged brow? Given the grammatical ambiguity of the loaded verb "accuse," Tighe's language destablilizes interpretation even as her narrative unstages masculinist Romanticism. Once students recognize method in Tighe's verbal technique, they enjoy stumbling on syntactic roadblocks because they rightly suspect these seeming impasses may present opportunities to puzzle out secondary meanings.

One such opportunity only a few stanzas into the poem provides a kind of key philosophical statement that epitomizes Tighe's larger project, when the narrator describes Psyche's lack of haughty pride, even "[t]hough men her wondrous beauty deified" (1.7.3). Students are quick to double gloss this line, so that on the one hand readers learn that Psyche's male admirers deify and thereby objectify her for her beauty, but on the other hand these men are deified and objectified in turn through their very admiration of her beauty. It is through syntax that my students first encounter how Tighe rewrites the male Romantic aesthetic that objectifies the female as a reciprocal process that fixes both admired and admirer, a reciprocity Tighe brilliantly captures in her syntactic construction. The very difficulty of the language cues my students to read Venus's subsequent demand for revenge against Psyche's beauty as another instance of what I term "reciprocal objectification" ("Romanticism" 72); when Venus tells Cupid to sting Psyche's heart, her words ambiguously command, "Deep let her heart thy darkest arrow sting" (1.14.3). Students already know that Cupid will sting Psyche's heart, but Tighe's language enables them to anticipate that Psyche's heart will also sting Cupid's arrow. So Tighe demonstrates through magnificent wordplay in her rendering of the scene where Cupid is frozen in admiration as his gaze fixates Psyche, where the typically ravishing power of the male gaze redirects itself from the gazed on to the gazer: "And half relenting on her beauties gazed; / Just then awaking with a sudden start / Her opening eye in humid lustre blazed, / Unseen he still remained, enchanted and amazed. / . . . As o'er the couch he bent with ravished eye" (1.27.6–28.2). Tighe predicts, "Nor, though a God, can he presaging tell / How he himself shall mourn the ills of that sad spell!" (1.26.8–9), but she demonstrates and analyzes what male Romantic artists have not yet seen: the reciprocity inherent in aesthetic objectifications of the female. Tighe's linguistic and narrative strategies enable students to see how a woman poet can issue a feminist critique of the Romantic aesthetic as a way to position herself within it. Students note, however, that Tighe does not exempt herself as gazer from the dilemma that reciprocal objectification poses to the artist. Indeed Tighe's narrator confesses that "The dreams which hold my soul in willing thrall, / And half my visionary days deceive" (5.2.3–4) ravish her. She continues, "Even now entranced her journey I pursue, / And gaze enraptured on her matchless knight" (5.4.6–7). Such confession firmly situates Tighe as a visionary poet within the Romantic tradition even as her language delineates how problematic the Romantic aesthetic can be.

Tracing the ramifications of Tighe's strategic syntax turns the reader's seeming hardship into plenitude and can provide a comprehensive key to classroom discussion of all six cantos through one simple question. But the class must also address Tighe's use of source material, an issue raised by the second question I ask: What should readers know before they begin to read the poem? While students may not be able to identify the significance of Tighe's original verse translation of Apuleius's "Cupid and Psyche" into Spenserian stanzas, they do know the myth and what it says about relationships and female agency: my classes speak cogently to the myth's representation of female beauty, of competitive relations among women, of the essential imbalance between men and women in culture and romance, and of the female's limited role in accomplishing goals. As students detail the parameters of the myth, they see how perfectly it exemplifies the Romantic objectification of the female, and how effectively Tighe revises the myth, presenting Psyche's quest as an active pursuit, with Cupid in hand, of moral and psychological development. Moreover, my students view Tighe as participating in a tradition different from what we might assume when teaching other British Romantic poetry, in which we hope students will identify references to Homer, the Bible, Chaucer, Dante, Spenser, Shakespeare, or Milton; for my students Tighe anticipates the feminist revisionists they know from postmodernist reworkings of myths, fairy tales, and classic literary narratives, such as Anne Sexton's *Transformations*, Angela Carter's *The Bloody Chamber*, Marion Zimmer Bradley's *The Mists of Avalon*, and Jean Rhys's *Wide Sargasso Sea*. They appreciate Tighe's selection of the Psyche and Cupid myth as a starting point for reexamining the implications of beauty in feminist and masculinist texts as well as culture. And they appreciate that choice more keenly when I share with them that Tighe was known as a great beauty in her lifetime, that she was actually called "Psyche" by members of her literary circle (such as Thomas Moore, Matthew Lewis, and Lady Morgan), and that long after her death she continued to be invoked as the beautiful woman who produced a lovely poem, so that even the *Dictionary of National Biography* reports that she "was a very beautiful woman" (389).

This connection between the subject of Tighe's poem and Tighe's subjective experience becomes more and more interesting to my students as we continue through the second half of the semester and observe that *Psyche* can be considered a transition point between the first and second generation of male Romantic poets, as Lord Byron, Percy Shelley, and John Keats become concerned with and threatened by the prospective reciprocity of the Romantic aesthetic. Certainly Tighe has a powerful effect on later poets, as Keats acknowledges when he writes of "the blessings of Tighe" in his early lyric "To Some Ladies" and as he tellingly denies in a letter to George and Georgiana Keats (31 Dec. 1818), when he declares, "Mrs. Tighe and Beattie once delighted me— now I see through them and can find nothing in them—or weakness—and yet how many they still delight" (*Letters*). Surely more important to teaching the work of women poets in Romanticism courses, however, is Tighe's effect on Felicia Hemans and Letitia Elizabeth Landon, who further her influential exploration of the Romantic aesthetic's objectification of the female and whose engagement with that aesthetic is usefully complicated for students who have read Mary Tighe.

Men, Women, and "Fame":
Teaching Felicia Hemans

Susan J. Wolfson

I have confronted two problems teaching Felicia Hemans's poetry, one material and one aesthetic. The material problem had been the availability of texts, which the introduction to this volume addresses.[1] The aesthetic problem is the verbal texture of the poetry, which students may find disappointing compared to that of other (mostly male) writers. Even so, they respond to Hemans's engagement with issues of gender, a subject stimulating not only in itself but also for the way Hemans's conflicts complicate the language and organization of her poetry. These conflicts are reflected in formal and aesthetic asymmetries between her arguments (the palpable orthodoxies) and the images that Hemans uses to elaborate them, a critical effect that students can discover by devoting to her texts the sort of close attention they enjoy giving to texts by other writers in my course on Romantic-period writing.

I begin the unit on Hemans with the topic of Women and Fame, which I preface with texts by men meditating on fame. I start with a comment Lord Byron made in the wake of the overnight sensation of *Childe Harold's Pilgrimage, Cantos I–II* (1812), "I awoke one morning and found myself famous" (T. Moore 2: 137), and point out that he is one of the few writers of the nineteenth century to see his name become an adjective, *Byronic*, and a noun, *Byronism*. I then turn to a poet largely obscure in the same period, John Keats. We look at some early letters (written in the shadow of Byron's fame) in which he imagines *Endymion* as his own bid: "What a thing to be in the Mouth of Fame," he writes to fellow poet Leigh Hunt (*Letters* 1: 139). Thinking "of fame of poetry" is one of the few spurs for his work on *Hyperion* as he nurses his dying brother Tom (1: 369). The last letter we read is one Keats wrote to his beloved Fanny Brawne, while he was desperately ill:

> "If I should die," said I to myself, "I have left no immortal work behind me—nothing to make my friends proud of my memory." . . . Thoughts like these came very feebly whilst I was in health and every pulse beat for you—now you divide with this (may *I* say it?) "last infirmity of noble minds" all my reflection. *(Letters* 2: 263)

Students may recognize the quotation from Milton's meditation in *Lycidas* on "the spur" of fame (68–84); if not, they can read the verse paragraph that contains it. I ask them to pay attention both to the poet's ambivalence about fame and to his comparatively unambivalent language of gender. Milton represents lesser poetry as erotic play with women (sporting with Amaryllis and Neaera), and he casts the antagonists to fame in one's own time as female fates, the most dangerous of whom is the scissors-wielding "Fury." Correspondingly, the vindication of fame in the hereafter is promised by the male god of poetry, Phoebus, whose trust is in the most powerful male god of all, "all-judging Jove" (82).

Given this touchstone, students are ready to appreciate how "Fame," recognition by others, can be a sharply gendered issue. We turn to Keats's two sonnets on "Fame" (*Letters* 2: 104–05), which also use female gendering to disparage the love of fame (see Hofkosh, "Writer's Ravishment" 97–98; Wolfson, "Keats" 24–25). I ask students to consider how, like Byron, Keats registers the power of public opinion, but I note that Keats's celebrity was negative. His *Poems* (1817) and *Endymion* (1818) were abused in widely read reviews (*Blackwood's* [Z.], the *British Critic* [Rev. of *Endymion*], and the *Quarterly Review* [J. Croker]), and his self-esteem was challenged. Although in June 1819 Keats was claiming an "abatement of [his] love of fame" (*Letters* 2: 116), the two contemporaneous sonnets seemingly written in proof may constitute self-disciplining exercises rather than reflect a settled issue. In the context of our discussion, students can recognize what is at stake in the gendered configurations. In the first sonnet, "On Fame" ("How fever'd is that Man"), Keats represents his pure "name" as a virgin unspoiled by the world, and he urges "Man" to resist the self-degradation (a narcissistic self-molesting) entailed in the quest for fame. In the second, "Another on Fame" ("Fame, like a wayward girl"), Keats personifies "Fame" as a degraded woman, a promiscuous flirt: evoking the female readers whose influence on a poet's success Keats resents, she solicits a courtship that can only demean, even madden, any self-respecting (male) poet.

I remind students that in this marketplace even a famous poet such as Byron may find that celebrity is not without problems, compromising self-creation and masculine self-possession (Hofkosh, "Writer's Ravishment"; Manning). I then refine the issue, pointing out that for women writers in the age of Romanticism (and before)—notwithstanding the increase in published women writers and in female readers—the risk of fame is liability to judgment as un-feminine, immodest, and even (paradoxically) disreputable. A good item to introduce is Hannah More's caution in *Strictures on the Modern System of Female Education* (1799; much republished) that for a woman to exercise her talents "as instruments for the acquisition of fame" is "subversive of her delicacy as a woman" (2: 1). Our reading and class discussion are meant to define this risk and the way a famous poet such as Felicia Hemans represents it. We ponder the repeated theme, in poem after poem, of the tensed ratio of feminine delicacy, female fame, and woman's happiness (for related discussions, see Clarke; Leighton). The first case for close attention is her poem on *the* woman of national fame, "Joan of Arc, in Rheims," from Hemans's most popular volume, *Records Of Woman* (1828). We study the poem's epigraph (later to appear as the first stanza of Hemans's emblematically titled "Woman and Fame"): here a female poet, recognizing the temptation of Fame's "charmed cup" (1) cries, "Away! to me—a woman—bring / Sweet waters from affection's spring" (5–6). I ask students to examine the key metaphor and to compare the two drinks: true nurture is a naturally guaranteed resource of the heart, and the suspect, charmed drink is the intoxicant of a suspect woman, "Fame."

With this cue, we study how "Joan of Arc" organizes this lesson. What is Joan's fame at the historical moment of the poem, and why does Hemans stage this record at this point? Situating Joan at the dauphin's coronation (with honors to Joan for her role in bringing this about), Hemans recovers a feminine Joan and reestablishes the strong ties of Joan's domestic affections. I begin with Hemans's treatment of one of the chief signifiers of Joan's military career, her "helm" (20), asking students to note how the cathedral scene refigures it as a halo around "Woman"—not the warrior-woman but the virgin-devoted angel of the church:

> But who, alone
> And unapproach'd, beside the altar-stone,
> With the white banner, forth like sunshine streaming,
> And the gold helm, thro' clouds of fragrance gleaming,
> Silent and radiant stood?—the helm was rais'd,
> And the fair face reveal'd, that upward gaz'd,
>   Intensely worshipping:—a still, clear face,
> Youthful, but brightly solemn!—Woman's cheek
> And brow were there, in deep devotion meek,
>   Yet glorified with inspiration's trace
> On its pure paleness; while enthron'd above,
> The pictur'd virgin, with her smile of love,
> Seem'd bending o'er her votaress.—That slight form!
> Was that the leader thro' the battle storm?   (17–30)

Students see that Hemans offers the event as an occasion to celebrate the "power" of a woman—"Never before, and never since that hour, / Hath woman, mantled with victorious power, / Stood forth as *thou* beside the shrine didst stand" (35–37). I ask them to note as well how Hemans's language casts this power as spiritual rather than political, predicting how this "[d]aughter of victory" (46) will find herself more deeply a daughter of home. Hemans presents a competition between two kinds of nurture (recall the two drinks of the epigraph):

> . . . forth she came.—Then rose a nation's sound—
> Oh! what a power to bid the quick heart bound,
> The wind bears onward with the stormy cheer
> Man gives to glory on her high career!
> Is there indeed such power?—far deeper dwells
> In one kind household voice, to reach the cells
> Whence happiness flows forth!—The shouts that fill'd
> The hollow heaven tempestuously, were still'd
> One moment; and in that brief pause, the tone,
> As of a breeze that o'er her home had blown,
> Sank on the bright maid's heart.—"Joanne!"   (49–59)

I ask students to track the verbs, to see how the nation's honors—its stormy cheer for Joan's "power" and her leadership "thro' the battle storm"—are cast in terms of elevations ("rose," "high") but prove a "hollow heaven." We note that the "wind" of public acclaim yields to the "breeze" of home, the "deeper" dwelling of "one kind household voice," and that what sinks on the maid's heart is her domestic name, "Joanne," which patently contrasts with her title of fame, Joan of Arc. It is worth attending to the related verb *turn*: "Joanne," recognizing her father and brothers, "turn'd" (62), her physical reorientation anticipating a spiritual one in which she "saw the pomp no more" (71) as her "spirit turn'd" (77) to the visionary "*deep* repose" evoked by her childhood home (76; my emphasis).

I ask students to see how Hemans makes this movement a turn to an essential female self (domestic daughter) and so away from the glories of Joan's fame, "winning her back to nature" (81). What about *winning* (the true victory) and its dative, "to nature" (which essentializes the motive force)? Students are now prepared to grasp the key act: Joanne "unb[inds] / The helm of many battles from her head" to let "her bright locks" fall to "the ground" (81–83). If the students have read other poems by Hemans, they may refer the semiotic of hair to the gallery of rebellious Hemans women (Maimuna of "The Indian City," Eudora of "The Bride of the Greek Isle" [both in *Records*] and Stephania of "The Widow of Crescentius" [*Tales*]) in which unbound hair signals a violent emergence from customary restraints. Joan, by contrast, enacts the cliché (which students easily recognize) of a woman's unbinding her hair in a surrender to essential femininity. What rises? "Lifting her voice up" in a quasi prayer (84), the daughter of victory begs for paternal (domestic and divine) restoration in the language of a prodigal daughter (as students may recognize): "Bless me, my father, bless me! and with thee, / To the still cabin and the beechen-tree, / Let me return!" (85–87). What is the larger lesson?—the tragically irreversible economy of female fame, summed in the poet's final moral address to Joan, with class romance (peasant pastoral) reinforcing the lesson of gender: "too much of fame / Had shed its radiance on thy peasant-name" (89–90), for "fate allow[s] / The crown of glory unto woman's brow" (93–94) in a bad bargain. Its crown, however glorious, is hollow, "bought alone by gifts beyond all price" (91)—namely, "the paradise / Of home with all its loves" (92–93)—always a paradise forever lost in fame.

To help students grasp Hemans's self-reading in "Joan of Arc," I mention the assurance by Henry Chorley (her friend and later biographer) that Hemans "wears under all her robes of triumph, the pitying heart of a woman" (1: 27n), and a remark Hemans made at the height of her fame about her childhood homes: "How I look back upon [their] comparative peace and repose. . . . How have these things passed away from me, and how much more was I formed for their quiet happiness, than for the weary part of *femme célèbre*, which I am now enacting!" (Hughes 176). Students may sense the alienation signaled by the theatrical metaphor and the ironic intonation of the French term. It helps to compare this nostalgia with that of Wordsworth (whose poetry Hemans loved). While he too mourns the loss of childhood paradise (we refer to "Tintern Abbey," *The Prelude*, and the "Intimations" Ode), his sorrow is categorically that of adulthood in the world, not any particular consequence of having become famous (indeed, he often envied fellow writers' greater fame).

From "Joan" we turn to Hemans's self-mirroring stories of female artists, the most acute internalizings of her cultural lessons on what constitutes women's happiness. We begin with "Properzia Rossi" (*Records*)—the monologue of a famous artist who, dying of unrequited love, cries, "Worthless fame! / That in *his* bosom wins not for my name / Th' abiding place it ask'd" (81–83; the referent of the italics is an uncaring Roman Knight). I ask students to study how the poem's epigraph—"Tell me no more, no more / Of my soul's lofty gifts! Are they not vain / To quench its haunting thirst for happiness?"—keynotes this despair. When this same voice laments, "I depart, / Unknown, tho' Fame goes with me," students may observe a typical "Romantic" plight in this division of self into public "Fame" and a solitary "I." If they do, I ask them to consider what shape this plight takes for a famous female artist. A useful focus is Rossi's last resort, her enlistment of her art to serve her heart, embodying her "melancholy love" (14) in a proxy to the Knight (students may recall Tennyson's "The Lady of Shalott," written soon after [1831–32]):

> I would leave enshrined
> Something immortal of my heart and mind,
> That yet may speak to thee when I am gone,

> Shaking thine inmost bosom with a tone
> Of lost affection.   (9–13)

Students see that Rossi charges her art with the frustrated impulses of heart and nature. Examining the rest of the poem, we note that Rossi is always aware of the substitution, always conscious that she is inspired by what she lacks:

> It comes,—the power
> Within me born, flows back; my fruitless dower
> That could not win me love. Yet once again
> I greet it proudly, with its rushing train
> Of glorious images:—they throng—they press—
> A sudden joy lights up my loneliness,—
> I shall not perish all!   (25–31)

As habitual loneliness blights this momentary rush of glory, students grasp the significance of Hemans's rhyming of "power" and "fruitless dower." What is Rossi's final hope? Not to pursue her art but to collapse her "fame" into a "name" (another recurring rhyme) that may one day move the Knight to sad thoughts and a final recognition: *"'Twas her's who lov'd me well!"* (128).

What is the repeated story of gender? Fame without love is no satisfaction. We turn to the closing poem of *Records* and the most overtly self-referential of these allegories, "The Grave of a Poetess." When I ask students, "Who is this 'Poetess'?" they have to read the only clue, in Hemans's footnote: "author of Psyche"; most will still need to be told that this is Mary Tighe. When I ask, "What did this author accomplish as a poet?" they remark that Hemans's poem says precious little, beyond eulogizing the "light of song . . . shrined" in "woman's mind" (16, 14) and sounding a recurrent theme of "sorrow" (46). I ask them to consider the implication; a remark by Hemans on Tighe provides a cue: "her poetry has always touched me greatly from a similarity which I imagine I discover between her destiny and my own" (qtd. in Chorley 2: 212). We consider the overall agenda of Hemans's tribute—to cherish Tighe's delivery from the transient beauties and inevitable pains of life on "mortal ground" (49): "Now peace the woman's heart hath found, / And joy the poet's eye" (51–52). I ask students what is at stake in this divorce of "poet" from "woman," and I encourage them to see Hemans's sense of the inevitable determinations of "woman's heart." Visiting Tighe's tomb three years later, Hemans wrote, "my heart was envying the repose of her who slept there" (qtd. in Chorley 2: 211).

We are now prepared to study the epitome of this story, "Woman and Fame" (1829). But the preparation is somewhat untrustworthy, for I hope students will see how unstable a lesson this poem turns out to be. They grasp its argument right away: resist the intoxicant of fame for the deeper nurture of "home-born love." But what of Hemans's aesthetic elaborations?

> Thou hast a voice, whose thrilling tone
>   Can bid each life-pulse beat,
> As when a trumpet's note hath blown,
>   Calling the brave to meet:
> But mine, let mine—a woman's breast,
> By words of home-born love be blessed.
>   (13–18)

What is the effect of giving Fame a tone "thrilling" to the very pulse of life? It helps to refer to the analogous shock of Keats's idealization of the Grecian Urn's figures as enjoying a love that is "all *breathing* human passion far above" (28, my italics): "life-pulse beat" is as critical a fault line as Keats's "breathing," and although Hemans tries to shore up her cautionary lesson about Fame—"A hollow sound is in thy song, / A mockery in thine eye" (19–20)—I ask whether the woman seems to protest too much. Take the last stanza. It is the crescendo in the theme of rejecting "Fame," but it noticeably elides the reiterated alternative of home blessings:

> Fame, Fame! thou canst not be the stay
>   Unto the drooping reed,
> The cool fresh fountain, in the day
>   Of the soul's feverish need;
> Where must the lone one turn or flee?—
> Not unto thee, oh! not to thee!   (25–30)

"Not to thee" still leaves the question of where without a positive answer. The effect is a confession of a kind of no-woman's-land between the "record of one happy hour" (12) at home and the laurel wreath of fame that always seems a delusive charm.

Students begin to sense that the frequency with which Hemans has to write about "Woman" and "Fame" reports an unsettled lesson. At this point we may turn to other texts to explore the issue further, or I may give students an assignment on "Corinne at the Capitol." The assignment allows for a fruitful examination of these tensions because the poem's aesthetic elaborations pressure its frame of moralizing instruction. A good way to begin is by unpacking the poem's epigraph, from Mme de Staël (author of the wildly popular novel, *Corinne; or, Italy*, to which Hemans's title refers): "Les femmes doivent pense qu'il est dans cette carrière bien peu de sorts que puissent valoir la plus obscure vie d'une femme aimée et d'une mère heureuse" ("Women ought to realize that in this career [celebrity] there is very little equal to the worth of the most obscure life of a beloved wife and happy mother"). In addition to the obvious theme, it is important to point out the aptness of the synonymy in French of *woman* and *wife* (both designated by *femme*)—especially in relation to the sad fate of Staël's celebrated female artist, Corinne. When I ask students to assess the last stanza as part of this didactic frame, they recognize its second half, the epigraph of "Woman and Fame":

> Radiant daughter of the sun!
> Now thy living wreath is won.
> Crown'd of Rome!—Oh! art thou not
> Happy in that glorious lot?—
> Happy—happier far than thou,
> With the laurel on thy brow,
> She that makes the humblest hearth
> Lovely but to one on earth!   (41–48)

If the poem is the basis of an essay assignment, students might also read book 2 of *Corinne* (in translation), to which Hemans's poem refers. (For valuable discussions of this novel and women writers, see Moers; Leighton.) Or they might benefit from a summary of the key points, especially some crucial contrasts. For one, Staël's subtitle is critical, for in her story, Corinne's audience includes an Englishman who admits that, while at home he would have disdained her, "he did not apply any social conventions to Italy" (20). With him, we see Corinne for the first time, performing and celebrated in all her glorious genius. Staël elaborates the whole triumph, including the text of "Corinne's Improvisation at the Capitol" and concluding with a female apotheosis: "No longer a fearful woman, she was an inspired priestess, joyously devoting herself to the cult of genius" (32).

In Staël, Corinne appears in the gaze of a vacationing Englishman. What is the effect of Hemans's changing the bearer of this gaze to a seemingly enthusiastic English woman?

> Thou hast gained the summit now!
> Music hails thee from below;—
> Music, whose rich notes might stir
> Ashes of the sepulchre;
> Shaking with victorious notes
> All the bright air as it floats.
> Well may woman's heart beat high
> Unto that proud harmony!
> (17–24)

One possibility is that Hemans is working with the established popularity of *Corinne* among female readers, not only in England but also internationally. Having made this suggestion, I ask the students to assess the tone of "Well may . . .": is it an expression of a woman's pride in woman or a note of caution? It is useful to let the class know what follows in *Corinne*: Corinne falls in love with the Englishman, but he eventually abandons her to return to his proper English fiancée, and Corinne dies of a broken heart. I note that Corinne's abandonment and fatal despondency impressed Hemans far more than the novel's energetic opening did: "its close . . . has a power over me which is quite indescribable; some passages seem to give me back my own thoughts and feelings, my whole inner being" (qtd. in Chorley 1: 304).

Even so, how committed is Hemans's poem to the severe correction expressed in the last stanza and to its reminder of the melancholy conclusion of Staël's novel? What happens between the poem's admonishing headnote and its coda—that is, what kind of poetry does Hemans generate for Corinne's performance at the capitol in Rome? A line count is already an indicator: forty-two-and-a-half lines for Corinne's apotheosis, against the five-and-a-half-line moral coda. As students measure this disproportion and then note the radiantly excited poetry of the former group—"fires," "Joyously," "festal," "triumphs," "glory bright," "golden light," "ascending," "freedom," "proudly," "gemlike," "summit," "rich" "music," "victorious notes," "proud harmony," "thrilling power," "tide of rapture," "flush," "the joy of kindled thought / And the burning words of song"—they sense a disparity between the poem's aesthetic energies and its antithetical frame. By now, they can see this tension as an exemplary sign of the cultural contradictions with which women of genius had to contend in Hemans's historical moment. Indeed, Hemans never entirely resolves this tension, even through repeated enactments.

The class can then return its attention to "Properzia Rossi," particularly the headnote (which appears on the title page, before the epigraph):

> Properzia Rossi, a celebrated female sculptor of Bologna, possessed also of talents for poetry and music, died in consequence of an unrequited attachment.—A painting by Ducis, represents her showing her last work, a basso-relievo of Ariadne, to a Roman Knight, the object of her affection, who regards it with indifference.

Students easily apprehend the pathos of Rossi's fatally loveless celebrity; I try to get them to see how the embedded representation of Ducis's painting hints at a false calculus of loss: while Rossi despairs because the Knight is unmoved by her poignant self-imaging in Ariadne, Ducis's point may be to expose the Knight as a worthless dolt, not only indifferent to Rossi's affections and talents but also, as the painting's theme may imply, likely to betray her as Theseus did Ariadne (I ask students to research the allusion before class). We apply this double view of Rossi's plight to the concentration of Hemans's language, in the midst of Rossi's lament, on what *is* in this artist's possession: the independent joy of artistic talent and the emotional intensity of its creative power. Key metaphors of creation in this passage bear close attention. I remind students that Rossi's art is sculpture, and I ask them to locate terms that might apply to Hemans's art as well:

> The bright work grows
> Beneath my hand, unfolding, as a rose,

Leaf after leaf, to beauty; line by line,
I fix my thought, heart, soul, to burn, to shine,
Thro' the pale marble's veins. It grows—and now
I give my own life's history to thy brow,
Forsaken Ariadne! thou shalt wear
My form, my lineaments; but oh! more fair,
Touch'd into lovelier being by the glow
    Which in me dwells, as by the summer-light
All things are glorified.   (31–41)

Some of these terms—the work of the hand, the unfolding of leaf after leaf, the expression of self in form, in line after line—apply to poetic work, a sign both of Hemans's affiliation with Rossi's "talents for poetry" and, more particularly, of her sympathy with the way Rossi's art takes shape in self-doubling. Once again, Hemans has drawn a mirror image but doubled it: as Ariadne is to Rossi, so Rossi is to Hemans.

I finally suggest that the contradictions Hemans represents between the satisfactions of artistic creation and the culturally normative terms for women's self-esteem (being loved) were given to double measures—at once internalized by Hemans and her contemporaries as deeply personal conflicts, but also pressured into potentially critical insight. A compelling conclusion to this unit is Hemans's 28 June 1834 letter on the death of a friend and fellow writer, Maria Jane Jewsbury, in a cholera epidemic in India (where Jewsbury's new husband, a man she seemed to have married more out of desperation than love, had taken a position as a chaplain):

> How much deeper power seemed to lie *coiled up*, as it were, in the recesses of her mind, than was ever manifested to the world in her writings! . . . the full and finished harmony never drawn forth! Yet I would rather, a thousand times, that she should have perished thus, in the path of her chosen duties, than have seen her become the merely brilliant creature of London literary life, living upon those poor *succès de société*, which I think utterly ruinous to all that is lofty, and holy, and delicate in the nature of a highly-endowed woman.   (qtd. in Chorley 2: 313)

Having read "The Grave of a Poetess," students will grasp the curious consolation that Hemans seems to find in imagining Jewsbury's death as an escape from the worse fate of celebrity. To complicate the story, I ask them to contemplate the two emphasized phrases. My aim is to suggest that while Hemans pretends that the opposition is between the happy path of "duties" (as much "chosen" for a woman as by her) and shallow celebrity, this opposition competes with the incommensurability of being "a highly-endowed woman" of coiled-up energies whose only choice is self-sacrifice, either to chosen duties or to shallow *succès de société*. The patent excess of the "thousand times" Hemans would wish for life-unto-death as a dutiful wife, I suggest, is a hyperdiscipline that does not suppress her admiration and fascination regarding Jewsbury's "power" of mind and its coils of never-expressed creative energy (any more than the lesson of Corinne's misery eclipses the electric dazzle of her performance). In the perspective of this latency, the alternative to the fatal "path of . . . duties" is not hollow fame (which is too easily disparaged) but something Hemans could not yet, in the binds and blinds of her cultural moment, fully imagine for a brilliant woman.

NOTE

[1]All quotations of Hemans's poetry follow Kelly and Wolfson; the base texts are either lifetime volumes or (for posthumous publications) earliest posthumous editions.

Charlotte Smith's Lessons

Sarah M. Zimmerman

To begin a course in Romanticism with Charlotte Smith's poems is to recognize more clearly what many students came to study because of Smith's divergence from the students' expectations. Her sonnets' formal poetics, theatrical gestures, and persistent mournfulness often perplex students who anticipate a reprise of the canonical poets they have read in high school or in survey courses. Yet Smith's unfamiliarity is precisely what makes teaching her poetry so productive. Her work's sheer difference from the seeming naturalness of language and emotion that students generally expect of Romantic poets is conducive to a teaching approach that is conscious of how critics have traditionally defined the field. Her gender, popularity, and insistence on addressing social issues—often radical political ones—together make Smith a worthwhile foil for her canonical contemporaries and successors. In my courses I connect Smith with William Wordsworth to illuminate her relationship to poetic tradition, and I teach her with William Blake to situate her in the sphere of radical politics.

Smith and Literary Tradition

I employ Smith's unfamiliarity to contextualize and question claims that the canonical poets and some of their latter-day critics have made about Romantic poetry. Because her poetry is steeped in late-eighteenth-century cultural traditions and in radical politics, she helps ground and complicate subsequent claims by Wordsworth and others about a new poetics that breaks with past conventions. She thus enables students to study Romanticism in the light of critical arguments by, among others, Alan Bewell and Marilyn Butler, who view the period as one of continuities, not transitions. Smith's poetics and politics help students trace links between late-eighteenth- and early-nineteenth-century English literature, allowing teachers to focus both on the works' formal features and on their historical contexts. I have taught Smith at or near the beginning of undergraduate and graduate courses on Romanticism, but many of the topics and questions her poetry suggests could also arise in courses focusing on, for instance, women writers, late-eighteenth-century British literature, or poetry.

I begin by giving students enough information about Smith's life and social context to situate her historically and in relationship to writers with whom they are already familiar. Most students respond sympathetically to Smith; they are interested in the difficult circumstances in which she wrote (she wrote rapidly, to support her family), impressed by her immense productivity and her popularity, and curious about her subsequent obscurity. Why, they ask, haven't they heard of her before? This initial, inquisitive response is useful for setting up a series of questions about the cultural figure of the Romantic poet. I assign several poems from *Elegiac Sonnets*, published in 1784 and expanded in eight subsequent editions through 1800 (all quotations of Smith's works in this essay are taken from Stuart Curran's edition of Smith's *Poems*). I ask students how Smith fits— or does not fit—their conceptions of the Romantic poet, thus encouraging them to consider and articulate their notions of the Romantic artist. Students often recognize in Smith's poetry a handful of qualities they anticipate: solitude, alienation, an affinity with nature, and melancholy. Yet they also note discordant features: the sonnets' formal language and adherence to generic traditions, Smith's dramatic gestures (frequent sighs, lamentations, exclamations), and the intensity and duration of her sorrow. Her poet's theatricality upsets expectations of "low and rustic life" and "a plainer and more emphatic language" (W. Wordsworth, Preface 124). By her resemblance to and difference from the poet they expect, Smith enables students to rethink their assumptions about Romanticism.

Smith is particularly useful for teachers seeking to encourage students to examine Romanticism's debts to its literary past because she details her borrowings in her poems' copious explanatory notes. Yet her links to Romanticism are strong, since her influence was acknowledged by, among others, Wordsworth, Samuel Taylor Coleridge, and John Clare. Critics have suggested John Keats's debts to her; Jerome McGann has argued for her importance to Lord Byron ("Byron"); Bishop C. Hunt, Jr., details her influence on Wordsworth, who describes the debts owed to Smith in an explanatory note—written in 1835 and expanded in 1837—to "Stanzas Suggested in a Steam-boat off St. Bees' Heads." Wordsworth remembers her as "a lady to whom English verse is under greater obligations than are likely to be either acknowledged or remembered," who wrote with "true feeling for rural nature, at a time when nature was not much regarded by English Poets." Coleridge similarly helps situate Smith in the period. In his "Introduction to the Sonnets" (1796) he names Smith and William Lisle Bowles as "they who first made the Sonnet popular among the present English" (543). Coleridge's poem "The Nightingale" could be read alongside Smith's several sonnets on the bird and her representation of herself as a nightingale in the 1792 preface to the sixth edition of *Elegiac Sonnets*. As students draw lines of influence between Smith and more familiar figures, they gain valuable perspective on the canonical poets, whom they come to see within a literary and social context that includes lesser-known figures.

For example, Smith helps students assess Wordsworth's attempts to define a new kind of poetry, efforts upon which the conventional Romantic tenets of originality and of a revolutionary break with poetic conventions were built. I have students read Wordsworth's prose descriptions of his poetic strategies in the Preface (1800) and selections from the Essay, Supplementary to the Preface (1815). One central question comparisons of Smith and Wordsworth raise is how fully he manages to distance himself from his immediate literary predecessors. Usually some students argue that he succeeds, while others are more interested in the debts that he obscures. I often point to Smith's explanatory notes, which detail her many literary borrowings from, among others, Petrarch, Shakespeare, Milton, Pope, Edward Young, James Thomson, Rousseau, Thomas Gray, William Collins, Thomas Warton, and Goethe. Most useful for the classroom is Smith's acknowledgment of the influence of two poets from whom Wordsworth distances himself, Pope and Gray. Tracing this complex web of influence prompts the question of how—and why—certain features of her poetics might be excluded by or suppressed within canonical Romanticism. In particular, her pronounced sensibility and her popular success—both related to her gender—differentiate her poetry from the sort Wordsworth defines in his prose and poetry.

Students are usually able to formulate a basic understanding of a vocabulary of sensibility from the sonnets alone, although I provide supplementary information from Janet Todd's *Sensibility: An Introduction* and Butler's *Romantics, Rebels, and Reactionaries*. In the sonnets students often recognize as qualities of sensibility the poet's responsiveness to nature and to human suffering, her frequent sighs and exclamations, her elegiac tone, and her sustained appeals to readers' sympathy, all of which usually prompt discussion. The question of how far Wordsworth has shaped our responses to emotion in poetry usually generates debate among the students because this issue addresses their own reading practices.

Smith and Wordsworth provide different paradigms for appropriately responding not only to loss and sorrow but also to nature. I ask students to compare Smith's "To the Moon" (sonnet 4) or "To Night" (sonnet 39), a poem Wordsworth admired, with his poem "A Night-Piece." Students notice similarities in the speakers: their solitary reflectiveness, their affinity with a nocturnal landscape, and their contemplation of the heavens. But some students argue that Wordsworth, unlike Smith, distances himself from his literary past and insist that there are marked differences in how the two poets define the relation between speaker and nature and in what the speakers make of their nocturnal observations. Students have claimed that Wordsworth's speaker is more engaged with his natural surroundings because his responses seem more spontaneous than those of Smith's speakers. Other students have countered that the poems are equally prescriptive in modeling appropriate responses to nature.

Wordsworth's desire to distinguish his poems from those of the literature of sensibility raises another salient point of contrast between the two poets: her immense success. I ask students to consider Wordsworth's definitions of his new poetry in the Preface, focusing on his argument that poets must temper emotion with thought and reject the excesses of feeling he associates with popular literature. The Preface and the Essay, Supplementary to the Preface, exemplify Wordsworth's ambivalence about a popular audience. His comments —for instance his distinction, in the latter, between an ideal "People" and a much less desirable "Public"—contrast with Smith's evident need to reach a broad readership for a reason many students understand: self-support. This difference may take discussion in several directions: it may lead to Byron and, if the students are prepared, Byron's exclusion from influential accounts of the period such as M. H. Abrams's *Natural Supernaturalism*. The issue of popular success may in turn raise the topic of social hierarchies: How does Smith's urgent financial motivation for writing place her apart from the university-educated poets? Does her dependence on patrons, publishers, and readers group her with writers such as Felicia Hemans, Clare, and Keats?

Smith's solicitous courting of readers in her prefaces highlights another important difference from Wordsworth: how gender inflects their poetics. Smith's care to maintain a modest demeanor and her deliberate explanations of her motivations for entering the literary marketplace contrast with Wordsworth's assertions of serious purpose. Her comment at the end of the preface to the sixth edition of *Elegiac Sonnets* explicitly genders this conventional stance. She reassures her readers, "I am well aware that for a woman—'The Post of Honor is a Private Station'" (6). By comparing Smith's and Wordsworth's prefaces students may assess how gender circumscribes self-presentations of the period's poets. Students are able to gauge how gender, economic circumstances, and popular success work together to produce different versions of the cultural figure of the poet.

Through these cultural questions I focus attention on the use of conventions, encouraging students to consider how social expectations might gender a writer's poetics. Again, the economic motivation for seeking a sustained popularity influences Smith's poetic decisions. She seems, for instance, to cater to readers' expectations by frequently adhering to Shakespearean and Petrarchan sonnet forms. I ask students to think about how material circumstances might circumscribe a writer's ability to experiment. Her propriety in abiding by the rules of poetic tradition contrasts with Wordsworth's rhetoric of newness and his claim that his commitment to an experimental poetics has cost him "a large portion of phrases and figures of speech which from father to son have long been regarded as the common inheritance of Poets" (Preface 132). This comparison leads students to consider how Wordsworth's relative financial security and his surer claim to cultural authority as a male poet enabled him to undertake an ambitious poetic program. But the disparity between the two poets' relations to tradition may also prompt a closer look at their uses of form. Glossing several of Smith's sonnets reveals a persistent, if more understated, experimentation. She experiments with sonnet form in "To Spring" (sonnet 8) and "To Night," for instance, while she follows Shakespearean and Petrarchan patterns, respectively, in "To the Moon" and "To Melancholy" (sonnet 32).

The class can thematically address this relation between poetic convention and gender by discussing "On Being Cautioned against Walking on an Headland Overlooking the Sea, Because It Was Frequented by a Lunatic" (sonnet 70). I ask students to consider the poem's implicit comparison between the man's "hoarse, half-utter'd lamentation" and the speaker's precise, formal speech, which adheres roughly to Shakespearean sonnet form. The speaker ex-presses her "envy" of his freedom from *"nice felicities"* and from the rational understanding of sorrow. The differences between poet and "lunatic" are man-ifested in his incoherent ravings and her careful, rule-bound diction. Students often note that the distinction between madness and propriety is gendered. The man she watches is allowed to rave, while she seems constrained by her rhyme scheme. Yet asked why the poet does not assume his position, which she claims to envy, students recognize the price of his freedom, especially for a woman poet. The relationship between the two figures may be profitably explored fur-ther by consulting the engraved illustration to the sonnet, printed in several early editions. A male figure in the foreground wildly stares down to the sea from a cliff's edge, while a female figure watches him from the background. His garments, blown by the wind, barely cover him, while she, weighed down with fuller dress, maintains a cautious distance. The differences in their clothing lit-eralize his relative freedom and her hindrance by convention, a contrast that draws on a familiar eighteenth-century analogy between clothing and language.

Smith and Radical Politics

Smith's presence on a Romanticism syllabus helps ground her contemporaries and successors not only in literary and cultural traditions but also in the radi-cal politics of late-eighteenth-century England. Reading Smith and Blake to-gether sheds light on the poet's role in social events and the relation between the period's poetry and radical politics. Because some of Blake's best-known poems focus on specific events or circumstances as explicitly as Smith's do and because he experiments with eighteenth-century conventions of the pastoral, their early collections are easily paired. These volumes—Smith's *Elegiac Son-nets* and Blake's *Poetical Sketches* (1783), *Songs of Innocence and of Experi-ence* (1789–94)—also share a pervasive narrative of a fall from childhood innocence into an adult world of sorrows.

Again I lay a historical foundation for the comparison, briefly narrating the poets' biographical connections. I mention, for instance, their shared patron, William Hayley, who allowed his Sussex neighbor to dedicate *Elegiac Sonnets* to him less than a decade before inviting Blake to move to Felpham. Smith's son-nets and some of Blake's early poems participate in an eighteenth-century pas-toral tradition inherited in part from James Thomson's *The Seasons* (1726–30). Reading Blake's "To Spring," "To Summer," "To Autumn," and "To Winter" helps illuminate how Smith uses the seasons not only as a topic (e.g., in "Writ-ten at the Close of Spring" [sonnet 2], "To Spring," and "Written in October" [sonnet 87]) but also as an integral part of her tableaux of human emotions and natural scenes. When I ask students to compare the poets' uses of the seasons, they often observe that Blake's explicit eroticism—a sensuality made human by his personifications of the seasons—is absent from her poems. This distinction can lead to a discussion of how gender circumscribes poets' treatment of love and sexuality. To continue a gendered comparison of how Smith and Blake define the poet, I pair Smith's introductory sonnet, "The partial Muse has from my earliest hours" (sonnet 1), with Blake's "Introduction," in *Songs of Innocence*. Students often note that Smith's speaker, when chosen by a muse figure, takes care to assume the task modestly and even sorrowfully, while Blake's poet simply accepts his selection. But students also note important similarities—both poets find it important to define the speaker on opening the volume, and both emphasize the event of selection.

Reading *Elegiac Sonnets* and the *Songs* together draws attention to the collections' fall narratives and thus prompts discussion of the figure of the child and the representation of childhood. Smith depicts childhood more obliquely than Blake does; in her poems it is primarily a remembered time evoked to define the mature poet of experience—as exemplified in "To the South Downs" (sonnet 5). But she also includes a portrait of herself as a child playing with another girl on the banks of the Arun in "To Mrs. G." (sonnet 10), and she stands in Gray's place in the Eton Ode in "Sighing I see yon little troop at play" (sonnet 27). "The Glow-worm" (sonnet 58) tells a tale of a child's fall into adult knowledge that rivals Blake in graphic detail. The child, who captures a star-like insect to make "Fairy-lamps," awakes the next morning to discover "his lucid treasure, rayless as the dust" and "shudders to behold" it. Students will easily find differences between this child and Blake's children—especially the ironic, bitter figures of *Songs of Experience*. But there are important affinities in the poets' shared sense that childhood innocence is not just fragile but also narrowly circumscribed by a material world of sorrows that may intrude at any moment, as the boy with the glow-worm learns.

Smith's and Blake's treatments of childhood innocence lost are useful as thematic topics in themselves, but they may also lead to a discussion of the poems' social contexts. As David Erdman has argued, reading Blake's poems in historical context corrects a common perception of Blake as idiosyncratic, at home on neither eighteenth-century nor Romantic literature syllabi. Studying Smith's poetry helps situate Blake poetically and politically. Students reading Blake's treatments of the chimney sweepers' plight and of children at charity schools usually respond with interest and even fascination at witnessing a world they perceive to be historically far removed from their own. Selections from Smith's *Elegiac Sonnets*, *The Emigrants* (1793), Beachy Head, *Fables, and Other Poems* (1807), along with various poems in prose works, may be read alongside Blake's *Songs* to sketch a picture of some key issues in the period's radical politics: antiwar sentiment, poverty, and abolition.

For instance, in "The Sea View" (sonnet 83), "war-freighted ships" sail into the speaker's line of vision as she watches a shepherd reclining "on the soft turf." The scene quickly loses its pastoral aura as the ships "flash their destructive fire" and "the mangled dead / And dying victims then pollute the flood." "The Forest Boy" also expresses antiwar sentiments: it concludes with an address to "cold statesmen," who, "from pictured saloon, or the bright sculptured hearth, / Disperse desolation and death thro' the earth, / When ye let loose the demons of war." Her explanatory note demonstrates a frankness that rivals Blake's in wondering, "[W]ill mankind never be reasonable enough to understand that all the miseries which our condition subjects us to, are light in comparison of what we bring upon ourselves by indulging the folly and wickedness of those who make nations destroy each other for *their* diversion, or to administer to their senseless ambition" (111).

"The Dead Beggar" is "an elegy, addressed to a lady, who was affected at seeing the funeral of a nameless pauper." This poem works well in classroom discussions or as a paper topic in combination with William Wordsworth's "The Old Cumberland Beggar" and entries describing beggars in Dorothy Wordsworth's *Grasmere Journals* (1800–03). These works may be supplemented by brief passages in political writings like Mary Wollstonecraft's *A Vindication of the Rights of Men* (1790). I ask students to compare the writers' representations of beggars and to define the relationships established between speaker and beggar in each work. Smith's speaker gently rejects the lady's tears for a harsher irony: she tells the mourning woman to "rejoice, that tho' an outcast spurn'd by Fate," the beggar would be recompensed, since "Death vindicates the insulted rights of Man." Smith's vocabulary makes the poem's radical allusions clear. Her politics are even more explicit than her references to Wollstonecraft and Thomas Paine indicate. In the poem's explanatory note Smith acknowledges conservative responses to her poem and restates her argument: "It is surely not too much to say, that in a country like ours, where such immense sums are annually raised for the poor, there ought to be some regulation which should prevent any miserable deserted being from perishing through want, as too often happens to such objects as that on whose interment these stanzas were written" (96).

Smith's comments on slavery throughout her poetry and prose also help focus discussions of radical politics. Smith's *Conversations Introducing Poetry* (1804), which appeared three years before England abolished slave-trading, contains "To the Fire-fly of Jamaica." The poem depicts "the recent captive, who in vain, / Attempts to break his heavy chain, / And find his liberty in flight." These poems may be taught alongside the period's abolitionist writing, such as William Cowper's "Sweet Meat Has Sour Sauce," Ann Yearsley's *Poem on the Inhumanity of the Slave Trade*, Blake's "The Little Black Boy," and Anna Letitia Barbauld's "Epistle to William Wilberforce, Esq., on the Rejection of the Bill for Abolishing the Slave Trade."

The relationship between poetry and politics may also be addressed, from a less thematic angle in *The Emigrants*. Smith's speaker is a model of Romantic subjectivity: walking along the Sussex shore, observing her natural surroundings, she is reflective, recalling her own history even as she considers the plights of the émigrés. But in many ways she does not fit predominant models of Romantic lyricism. She is introspective but constantly engaged with her social surroundings, and she uses the conventional vehicle of the Romantic poet, memory, to recollect not only her own past but also the personal histories of several émigrés and thereby to record historical change. *The Emigrants* therefore allows the class to consider an issue central to recent studies of the period: the relation between Romantic poetry and contemporary historical events.

Smith's work is a rich resource for discussions of whether Romanticism is characterized by a denial or repression of its historical contexts, which are all but obliterated by the poet's introspectiveness, a quality manifested in the period's autobiographical and lyrical impulses. *The Emigrants* challenges this argument by featuring a lyric poet, recognizable as the autobiographical speaker of the sonnets, who reflects and recollects the social events of England, past and present, as well as her personal history. In discussion some students say that they find Smith's sympathetic identification with the émigrés convincing and rhetorically powerful and that the poem is a moving commentary on the events described. Others make an argument similar to one often made about Wordsworth: that, as the *Critical Review* notes, "Herself, and not the French emigrant, fills the foreground; begins and ends the piece; and the pity we should naturally feel for those overwhelming and uncommon distresses she describes, is lessened by their being brought into parallel with the inconveniences of a narrow income or a protracted lawsuit" (Rev. of *The Emigrants* 299–300). After such classroom debates, I tell students that their disagreement reiterates contemporary responses to Smith's cult of personality. Although many critics were sympathetic, others accused her of "egotism," a charge she answers in the 1797 preface to volume 2 of *Elegiac Sonnets*.

The resistances to Smith by her contemporaries and by students are pedagogically useful. If the figure of the Romantic poet inspires both enthusiasm and antipathy in students, then Smith complicates these responses. She makes clear the impact of the traditions of sensibility and radical politics and underscores the continued importance of the late eighteenth century throughout the period after her death in 1806, as exemplified in Percy Bysshe Shelley's radical politics; in Byron's sensibility; and in Keats's treatments of melancholy, the burdens of an oppressive consciousness, and the figure of the nightingale. Throughout classroom discussions of Smith's poetry, the gendered differences of her poetics help students better to examine the tenets of Romanticism, even as her poetry lays the foundation for a sustained consideration of the period's women writers. Her participation in the traditions of sensibility and radical politics provides a useful comparison with Mary Wollstonecraft, who warned against the dangers of sensibility to young women in *A Vindication of the Rights of Woman* (1792), while Smith's topicality and her social concern look forward to Dorothy Wordsworth's interest in domestic and local communities and to Felicia Hemans's explorations of the domestic and public realms.

Anna Seward, the Swan of Lichfield: Reading *Louisa*

Elizabeth Fay

Most students probably have not heard of Anna Seward or regard her scant representation in Romantic period anthologies as proof that her poetry is not worthy of study, given that only so much material can be covered in one course. But students succumb to her voice and subject once they are immersed in enough of her work to see that her concerns are identifiably Romantic, aesthetically consistent, and stylistically amenable to discussion and analysis. Because Seward is, like Felicia Hemans but unlike Mary Robinson and Joanna Baillie, first a poet, educated and trained as a poet, and aware of her place in poetic history, she provides a counter to the long-held beliefs that the Romantics were an elect group of male poets only and that women of the period wrote many novels and some fugitive verse but no poetry of the caliber of Samuel Taylor Coleridge's or Percy Shelley's. Seward's work provides students with larger perspectives on the Romantic period's time span (she published well before Wordsworth and Coleridge's *Lyrical Ballads* yet wrote within the aesthetic they reworked from sensibility into Romanticism in that volume) and on the Romantic poet's representation by gender, achievement, and genius. The work she considered her masterpiece, the poetic novel *Louisa* (1784), gives students a clear sense of Seward's relevance to British Romanticism.

In lectures on the Lake School poets, I explain that if they were idiosyncratic they were also purposeful, not merely provincial, in forming their fellowship outside the literary circles of London. The same is true of Seward. Following in the steps of earlier women poets such as Elizabeth Singer Rowe (the pastoral "Philomela"), Seward (the "Swan of Lichfield") understood that she could wield more power from her country seat than from the salons of London. She also understood the power politics of poetry: to be heard, she had to engage the masculine giants of the literary field, from Samuel Johnson and Erasmus Darwin (the two male literati of Lichfield) to the powerful London voice of *The Gentleman's Magazine*. Students gain a sense of Seward's acts of literary engagement by reading excerpts from Darwin's epic *Botanic Garden*—including the first section, which contains a contribution by Seward—alongside several of Seward's letters to *Gentleman's*. Seward knew from an early age in what field she would contend, and she made sure she would be heard there; despite parental pressure to give up the versifying that could make her unmarriageable, Seward formed herself into an astute literary player. It is helpful to students to understand how difficult this self-determination was for literary women who had to outmaneuver either marriage offers, as Jane Austen and Seward did, or proprietary husbands, as Robinson and Mary Tighe did. Perhaps because of this act of literary survival Seward chose ideal love or love loss as a theme for many of her poems. Her pursuit of a literary career also led her to direct her critical work toward dictating who should be in the canon and whose work should be castigated and toward defending those whom others wanted to eject. Her critical biography of Darwin, for instance, reveals her acute judgment and her sense of her own literary standing (*Memoir*).

It is important to read Seward from both a historical and a feminist perspective because she is an influential producer of poetry of sensibility, itself a largely female precursor to the High Romantic aesthetic, and because in order to create a space for her female-informed poetic sense she needed to manipulate and challenge literary and cultural norms. *Sensibility* described a new focus on the individual's emotions and subjective experience, especially as heightened by a meditative focus on the self, the experience of love, and the new nature aesthetic. Seward grew up within a highly literate circle of family and friends that initially encouraged her precocious poetic talents, and she matured when these factors were beginning to coalesce as a significant cultural force. She was still writing when Robinson, Mary Hays, and Mary Wollstonecraft were active, and she knew Johnson personally because her grandfather had taught him. Students examining Seward's texts in relation to her historical context should note that she took care to situate herself between the rational Johnsonian literary aesthetic and the literature of sensibility epitomized by the Della Cruscan movement, a group of writers headed by Robert Merry and encouraged by Seward's friend Hester Piozzi, who exchanged love poetry in the public medium of periodicals. Seward disliked Johnson's pronouncements and took umbrage at his dismissal of the Lichfield literary circle over which she presided, but she also disliked Della Cruscan sentimentality and believed that the group's first pseudonymous poems were actually all written by Merry, and somewhat badly, "strutting in such inflated defiance of everything like common sense, as the compositions of Della Crusca!" (*Letters* 2: 249). If Johnson was crass, inelegant, egotistical, and self-important, the Della Cruscans were crassly overornamental, inelegantly intruding their private effusions on the public and self-importantly confusing public and private poetic sentiments. Seward viewed Alexander Pope and Jean-Jacques Rousseau, in contrast, as the precursors to the sensibility she ultimately approved. Pope endowed his Eloisa (in "Eloisa to Abelard" [1717]) with a sensibility out of which Seward built her own; Rousseau's great masterpiece is his Julie, the new Eloisa (in *Julie, ou la nouvelle Héloïse* [1761]). From both man-made heroines Seward fashioned her own version of the sensible woman, Louisa, whose name clearly recalls Pope's and Rousseau's characters but more daringly also recalls the real medieval abbess Héloïse, whose brilliant intellect heightened her ability to feel passionately. However, where the real Héloïse could only write of her love to Abelard in terms that imply she must always prove her passion and love (Kauffman 64–89), Seward's Louisa is able to clarify her feelings by writing to a female friend who she clearly believes can read her heart and safeguard her private emotions from public display and interpretation.

To convincingly portray a truly new Héloïse, Seward had to go beyond creating a sympathetic female friend who could intervene in the plot—itself a significant interpolation of novel convention that students should note. She also had to experiment with genre. *Louisa, a Poetical Novel* (*Works* 2: 219–94) tells us in its title what Seward meant it to accomplish formally: to take the novel form as it had been applied to domestic romance (Langbauer 62–65) and turn it back into epic by way of pastoral love songs. This is an impossible feat according to genre traditions, but genre experimentation itself is a Romantic trademark. Even before Wordsworth and Coleridge's genre-mixing *Lyrical Ballads*, Charlotte Smith and Ann Radcliffe found the amalgam of prose and poetic forms congenial for the novel, although they emphasized and used verse more to bring a sensible flavor into their novel romances. In *Louisa* Seward chose to versify the domestic novel, a form that typically focuses on the heroine's love story at her crucial transition from adolescence into marriageability and that uses certain nonrealistic elements of the romance to bring about the desired end. Like both the novel and the epic, Seward's story is divided into epistolic chapters written by the characters to one another; the segments shape a continuous detailed story that flows beyond the boundaries of ordinary pastoral verse. Seward wove together poetic conventions for novel, epic, and pastoral verse to tell a tale that is both the national and cultural story of the epic and the deeply personal story of the domestic novel; this in turn becomes the allegorical story of the pastoral, replete with the figures Modesty, Grief, Hope, and Commerce that act as muse-like motivators of the narrative. To complicate things and further raise readerly interest, Seward brought in imaginative devices that would later become associated with Romanticism: orientalism, colonialism, brigands (romanticized by Schiller), capitalism, sentimentality, and interpolated stories of other lovers. This combination of approaches resulted in an irresistible format (*Louisa* was wildly popular), and out of that form Seward produced her own style of sensibility, which helped ground the High Romanticism soon to come. It is therefore interesting in courses on the Romantic period to read *Louisa* alongside works of High Romanticism, especially productions of the Lake School, to see how Seward's work foregrounds themes and attitudes that fascinate more frequently taught poets.

The four letters in *Louisa* carry the plot narrative of the story: Louisa relates events to her best friend, Emma, who has lived for four years in the East Indies and is due to return to England soon. Emma had previously lived an idyllic English rural life with Louisa and Eugenio. The letters negotiate the love relation of Louisa and Eugenio through Emma's readerly mediation. Louisa writes the first letter to Emma to say that the match between her and Eugenio is off; Eugenio broke the vow because he had to leave for a commercial venture to please his father, a merchant. But she has subsequently heard rumors that he has quickly married another woman. The second letter, from Eugenio to Emma, explains that on the same day he was to set sail he chanced to save a beautiful woman, Emira, from attacking rogues and conveyed her back to his family estate. Eugenio's father aids a match between his son and the new lady, who clearly desires Eugenio and who is the "splendid heiress of a vast domain" unlike Louisa, who will inherit little. Emira, "[t]hough frolic, insolent; though haughty, vain" (248), is the antithesis of the gentle pastoral characters Louisa and Emma, but when Eugenio's father goes bankrupt Eugenio has no choice but to marry the wrong woman. Good friend that she is, Emma sends Louisa this second letter between the acts, and the third letter is Louisa's response not to Eugenio but to Emma ("And my lov'd Emma's hand the vision shews" [265]), in which she makes peace with events and proves herself a true heroine through acceptance. Some time passes between this letter and the fourth, in which Louisa relates to Emma that Eugenio's father has begged her to visit Emira, who is dying from dissipation and frustrated love. He explains that his bankruptcy had forced Eugenio to wed Emira but that now his debt is repaid through the return of his "lucky sails" (279), while Emira has proved a bad mother, leaving her child at home to go to masked balls and operas and finally taking a lover. Aware that she is dying, Emira has asked for Louisa's visit, and when she sees Louisa she begs Louisa to raise her child for her. The novel ends with Louisa's apostrophe to her faithful friend—and not to her lover: "O come, my Emma! . . . / The Star of Joy relumes, and leads us on our way!" (293–94).

As an intermediary, Emma acts as the text's ideal reader, sympathetic but distanced; she provides a model for the actual reader because both Louisa and Eugenio expect her to respond in sensibility-laden ways to their letters. The similarity between her name and the siren Emira's reveals that the good and loyal Emma will know intuitively how to interpret her "other" and will understand the forces that the two lovers are up against. Emma will lead us "on our way" while Emira will stop the action for her own gain. An audience new to sensibility needed a model of how to read it, and since it was often joked that most readers could tell when to weep over the new poetry only by seeing which words were italicized, Seward's solution is a good one because it is educative. Readers should weep when the characters' plights make them ask for Emma's sympathy and emotive support. Conversely, Emira's overt desire, which she advances improperly, seeking a man at the expense of an already loved woman, warns readers of crass passions and abusive sentiments; she is the oriental serpent woman, a Lamia or "female Proteus in the wiles of love!" (252). Because three of the four letters are from Louisa to Emma and only one is from Eugenio to Emma, we can see that Seward was particularly interested in the woman-to-woman relation that often characterizes the emotional and aesthetic experience of sensibility. This sisterly rapport is explicitly opposed to the rivalry of Louisa and Emira. Louisa's love for Eugenio and the plot twists that frustrate her love are secondary; they provide the stimulus for passion but not the material of the text. The novel is about love loss and the distressing affective distance between love and its loss; the letters must not be between lovers, then, but must triangulate their emotions with a knowing third party who does not intrude narratively and so does not usurp the reader's right to emotional engagement. In focusing on the passing of information and plot development between two female friends and augmenting their letters with one from the lost lover to the friend, Seward attempts to give her new Héloïse the female subjective comprehension, "this sympathy of soul" (223) missing from the simpler female-to-male relation of Pope's and Rousseau's texts. And Emma's return to England means that Louisa as the new Héloïse has not been reduced to utter loss through Eugenio's desertion; rather, in gaining Emma she must surely regain Eugenio, who, we readers know, has never stopped loving Louisa. If the restoration necessitates the death of Eugenio's possessive wife, what is killed off is not so much another woman as an economic, industrial, and colonial threat that is the very vehicle by which Emma was separated from her friends for so long and the reason Eugenio originally leaves Louisa ("Attractive Commerce calls him to her tide / . . . His rising interests on the call attend, / For with a father's prosperous fate they blend" [232]). It is important to the plot that Eugenio's father refuses Louisa as a daughter-in-law because of her poor dowry and that he fails in business at the same time that Eugenio chances to save the life of the oriental Emira. Emira (rather than Emma in the East Indies) represents the colonizer, desiring new possessions and bartering for Eugenio, and her charms—like those of the allegorical and seductively beckoning Commerce—warn us that to insist on new wealth over already professed love is to ruin national interests.

When Eugenio writes to Emma, "The touching sweetness of Louisa's face; / Where from each feature beams, or mildly plays, / Refined intelligence, with varying rays," he is describing what Seward imagines the new Héloïse to look like. The passion of the medieval Héloïse is replaced by a melancholic, if not quite stoic, endurance that closely resembles the melancholic beauty, native "intelligence," and endurance of the English countryside itself. When falling in love, Emira is also temporarily influenced by this nature: "Thus the proud maid, of all her scorn disarmed, / By strange, and partial preference strongly charmed, / Feels a new Eden steal upon the bowers" (249). Louisa and the English countryside are closely allied, their brilliance a shared aspect: when economic intervention in the pastoral old order cuts Eugenio and Emma off from this brilliance, the emotional economy is disrupted. Both must be reconciled to it—Eugenio through finally marrying Louisa and Emma through returning to Britain—before the narrative can heal itself.

Wordsworth tackles the problem of commerce, pastoral beauty, and the emotional economies tied to these very British elements differently in his 1798 version of "The Ruined Cottage," a meditative poem in which the heroine, Margaret, loses her weaver husband during a widespread economic depression. The poem makes a useful contrast to *Louisa* because students readily grasp the similarities in the works, both of which retain echoes of the pastoral and the epic within their genre mix and both of which involve a third party who receives the narrative (Emma and Armytage). However, Wordsworth's fourth character, the poet-persona, intrudes a new and different dimension; he interprets events, instead of shaping them as Emira does, and he thus reveals Wordsworth's different purpose in telling a woman's love story. Because economics is privileged over love, Margaret is doomed beforehand; much more important than the effect of her love on her or on us, the readers, is the effect of her melancholy history on the poet-persona. We learn through his responses, rather than through the medium of Armytage; we feel his regret rather than Margaret's, and that distancing makes her into an object of sentimental sympathy. Margaret is not a heroine of sensibility as Louisa is, a being whose passions prevail over plot outcomes; Margaret is a real victim of real historical forces, and her emotions effect no change on her plot except to erase her literally from the land plot she and her family inhabit. The change in emphasis makes Margaret an object of pity for the affected poet-persona, but Louisa is her own subject because neither Emma nor Emira intervene between us and Louisa's emotional state. Students can see this difference more clearly when they notice that Margaret goes mad after her husband deserts her. Her madness objectifies her pain as a sentimental public display for us and her private feelings as a matter for our interpretation, but because we know only through Louisa's privileged correspondence with her sister-friend how she is able to accept and endure her desertion, she becomes a heroine we cheer for.

The pastoral connection of female and natural beauty produces a melancholic aspect of poetic vision for Wordsworth, but for Seward it *is* the new Héloïse. It is the beauty that draws the colonial exiles and the rejecting lovers back to the native center of poetic expression where Seward's own literariness is located and to the nature that will become the mainstay of Romanticism. By locating her story in the rural landscape, which offers a strongly subjective contrast to the industrialism and trade that pose economic threats to family unity and personal relationships, Seward firmly plants her conception of the new sensibility in the ground of emerging Romanticism.

Joanna Baillie's Poetic Aesthetic: Passion and "the Plain Order of Things"

Catherine B. Burroughs

Joanna Baillie is an important figure in the study of women's pre-twentieth-century theater theory. I say this immediately because, although I focus here on her poetry, I discuss it in the context of her generalizations and speculations about how plays should be written and produced on formal stages. This approach reveals that a poem like Baillie's "Lines to a Teapot" (*Works* 799–801) addresses a central concern of British Romantic theater theorists: what subjects constitute (or should constitute) the dramatic and the performable, and what kinds of spaces and performance modes are most conducive to enacting the drama of subjects that have been closeted away? These questions are significant not only to closet-drama revisionists. Students can also appreciate that Baillie's theory of theater suggests ways of healing the opposition between closet and stage, which has succeeded through the years in closeting Baillie and other Romantic theater artists (especially women) from critical view. Indeed, the elevation of poetry over playwriting in Romantic studies and the neglect of women's contributions to British Romantic theater are partially products of prejudice against closet drama.

I have elsewhere addressed how Baillie's theory of theater (and her dramaturgical practice) helps us redefine *closet drama*—from a play never intended to be performed (or simply never performed) on a public stage to a play that draws on actual closet space for its structure and subject matter. I suggest that discussing Baillie's poetry brings to light additional prejudices that apply to the classroom as well, prejudices encapsulated by the closet/stage dichotomy. Since many undergraduates regard the classroom as a closeted space supposedly lacking the kind of drama that they expect to encounter on the public stages of their social lives, it is often difficult to help them see why they might want to cultivate a more passionate relation to academic work in general and to literary criticism specifically. Baillie's interest in the closeted and the domestic provides a good opportunity to analyze how students' prejudices against the classroom strongly affect their pleasure, and their engagement, in reading and writing about literature.

To facilitate this discussion, which draws connections between what and how we study, I provide students with Baillie's "Introductory Discourse," the essay she attached to her first volume of plays, published anonymously in 1798, and with other prefatory remarks that she wrote between 1798 and 1851. Reading the preface to the second edition of *Miscellaneous Plays* (1805) enables students to begin to appreciate how Baillie's theory of theater and her poetic aesthetic intersect. Hardly anti- or untheatrical (as she has often been portrayed), Baillie stated that her highest ambition was "to leave behind in the world a few plays, some of which might have a chance of continuing to be acted even in our canvass theatres and barns" (*Works* 387). In the 1805 preface Baillie confesses:

> I have seldom seen any piece, not appearing to me to possess great merit (for such things I have seen), succeed upon the stage, without feeling inclined to say to myself, "don't despise this: very probably in attempting, even upon no higher grounds, such success as the present, and giving to it also the whole bent of your thoughts, you would find yourself miserably disappointed."   (*Works* 387)

Often she was. I mention this passage to students not to shift their focus to the performance history of Baillie's plays but rather to suggest that writing pure poetry (as opposed to poetic drama) may have consoled Baillie for what she perceived as her failed ambition.

Though it was clearly not the medium in which Baillie hoped to achieve recognition and enduring fame, she wrote poetry throughout her life. Eight years before her anonymous first volume of plays (1798), Baillie published a book of poems. A volume of narrative poetry, *Metrical Legends of Exalted Characters*, appeared in 1821, an edited volume of poetry appeared in 1823, her early poems were reissued in 1840, and a poem drawn from central Indian history, *Ahalya Baee*, was privately printed in 1849. Her collected works, published in 1851, end with nearly one hundred and fifty pages of poems.

Like William Wordsworth and Samuel Taylor Coleridge, with whom she is often compared (Curran, "Romantic Poetry: The 'I' Altered"; Ross, *Contours*; Brewer; Page; Yudin), Baillie urged poets and playwrights to turn their attention to "the plain order of things in this every-day world" (*Works* 6); good verse, she argues, focuses readers on human beings "engaged in the ordinary occurrences of life" (2). While Baillie set a number of her dramas in foreign countries and throughout her life expressed a missionary's interest in other cultures, her theater theory makes clear that some of these "ordinary occurrences" will be located in the closet—what Philippa Tristram calls "the innermost sanctum of them all" (250)—the physical feature of eighteenth-century English great houses in which, Baillie suggests, the progress of the soul can be traced as it etches its passions on the countenances of men and women during their most private moments. But because Baillie's aesthetic also values the construction of poems that are analogous to "some humble cottage" she brings into question the concept of what should or does constitute drama in the first place. Articulating a poetic aesthetic that takes as its subject matter "[n]either the descriptions of war, the sound of the trumpet, the clanging of arms, the combat of heroes, nor the death of the mighty"—in contrast to her dramaturgy—Baillie's theoretical discourse turns our attention to the drama inherent in "the fall of the feeble stranger, who simply expresses the anguish of his soul, at the thoughts of that far distant home which he must never return to again" (*Works* 6).

I try to help my students discover that Baillie best achieves her focus on the simple expression of human beings by resisting exotic, exaggerated, surreal, and unnatural language and themes. "I will even venture to say," Baillie writes,

> that were the grandest scenes which can enter into the imagination of man, presented to our view, and all reference to man completely shut out from our thoughts, the objects that composed it would convey to our minds little better than dry ideas of magnitude, colour, and form; and the remembrance of them would rest upon our minds like the measurement and distances of planets. (6)

Instead of writing romances, which she considers as remote from life as the "planets," Baillie aims with her poetry to animate people's "sympathetic propensity" (2) by teaching people to consider "beings like ourselves" (6). Or as she writes in the 1851 preface to *Fugitive Verses*:

> He who has been coursing through the air in a balloon, or ploughing the boundless ocean in the bark of some dauntless discover, or careering over the field on a warhorse, may be very well pleased after all to seat himself on a bench by his neighbour's door, and look at the meadows around him, or country people passing along the common from their daily work.
> (*Works* 771)

This attentiveness to the theatrical potential of lives that have been closeted away resonates in Baillie's poetic aesthetic, which valorizes the homely, the domestic, the unseen, the traditionally underappreciated accoutrements of private life housed in closet spaces, including a forgotten teapot.

Baillie's "Lines to a Teapot," like John Keats's "Ode on a Grecian Urn," presents a speaker meditating on an inanimate object and thereby asks questions about functionality, relevance, and use, recurring themes in Baillie's plays and poetry. In "A Mother to Her Waking Infant," for instance, the mother frets about how her baby's indiscriminate neediness might augur the grown child's indifference to the aging mother, as if the mother were an inanimate, irrelevant object herself:

> Thou'lt listen to my lengthen'd tale,
> And pity me when I am frail—
> But see, the sweepy spinning fly
> Upon the window takes thine eye.
> Go to thy little senseless play;
> Thou dost not heed my lay.   (*Works* 788)

In the teapot poem, Baillie's speaker peers into a "china closet" and addresses the teapot directly about the circumstances that have rendered it "a cheerless elf," sitting in "most ignoble uselessness," "[l]ike moody statesman in his rural den, / From power dismiss'd—." This action emphasizes that the domestic space allows for the theatricality of the voiced and dramatic mode: "And now thou'rt seen in Britain's polish'd land," the speaker says,

> Held up to public view in waving hand
> Of boastful auctioneer, whilst dames of pride
> In morning farthingals, scarce two yards wide,
> With collar'd lap-dogs snarling in their arms,
> Contend in rival keenness for thy charms.

Making an unmistakable comparison to slavery and slave ships, Baillie describes the teapot as having begun its odyssey to England "[p]ack'd in a chest with others of thy kind"; it is auctioned; its "parts [are] inspect[ed]"; and it is personified as feeling confused by the combination of fetishistic admiration and withering indifference it elicits. (I point out to my students that Baillie discusses slavery or has characters of African descent in dramas like *Rayner* [1804] and *The Alienated Manor* [1812] and poems like "School Rhymes for Negro Children" and "Devotional Song for a Negro Child.") Wrenched from its country of origin, where a "brown-skinn'd artist, with his unclothed waist / And girded loins" created it, the teapot comes to England, where it first is displayed prominently in a wealthy home and later, auctioned (a second time) to the owners of a "modern drawing-room."

The portrayal of the teapot also suggests similarities between the slave trade and the marriage market. As a central instrument of eighteenth-century upper-class social customs and, by 1800, an important signifier of social achievement among the proliferating middle classes, the teapot represents certain women who served as orchestrators or directors of semiprivate social ceremonies. Feminist scholarship has encouraged fuller appreciation of the traditionally feminine domestic activities—child rearing, tea-table talk, the organization of myriad social interactions—and some feminist scholars have regarded certain of these activities as a kind of improvisational theater. Indeed, Baillie's speaker would have us infer how this seemingly useless object in the china closet has been instrumental both to women's animation and to their "no-use," to cite a phrase from Baillie's friend Mary Berry (2: 318). It has contributed to the former by providing the locus for what Sue-Ellen Case calls "the dialogue of present time" (46)—the kinds of interchanges that occur in the "personal theaters" (Case's term) of women throughout history. This dialogue, cultivated in the private gatherings of female social actors trained to conduct their lives in modes we might view as highly theatrical (since self-consciously ritualized and performative), is "built on mutuality and intersubjectivity" and "operates not by mimesis but by enactment"—that is, through present-tense embodiment; it is "an engaged dialogue, rooted in everyday life" (47). According to Case, women's efforts in different historical periods to construct interactive rituals in the domestic spaces of their houses—as in the salon—may be viewed as positive efforts to make theater in spite of the difficulties of doing so:

> The women who ran the salons played all the parts involved in theatrical production: the playwright (in conversation), the director (in casting the production by creating the guest list, helping create the scenes by making the introductions, setting the pace by actively keeping the conversation going), the actor, the set-designer (in decorating the home, deciding the menu, choosing the room for the evening) and the costume-designer (in setting the fashion and formality of the dress code). Though the guests were co-producers in many of these functions, the hostess defined the parameters of the occasion. (47)

In describing the teapot's female handler the speaker of Baillie's poem celebrates the way her exertion also empowers the teapot to realize its function fully:

> But O! when beauty's hand thy weight sustain'd,
> The climax of thy glory was attain'd!
> Back from her elevated elbow fell
> Its three-tired ruffle, and display'd the swell
> And gentle rounding of her lily arm,
> The eyes of wistful sage or beau to charm—
> A sight at other times but dimly seen
> Through veiling folds of point or colberteen.
> With pleasing toil, red glow'd her dimpled cheek,
> Bright glanced her eyes beneath her forehead sleek,
> And as she pour'd the beverage, through the room
> Was spread its fleeting, delicate perfume.
> Then did bright wit and cheerful fancy play
> With all the passing topics of the day.

"So delicate, so varied, and so free" is this conversation "inspired" by the woman's interaction with the teapot "[t]hat goblet, bowl, or flask could boast no power / Of high excitement, in their reigning hour, / Compared to thine;—red wildfire of the fen, / To summer moonshine of some fairy glen."

Yet though it is the centerpiece of the highly stylized rituals of domestic theater, by poem's end the teapot sits in "ignoble uselessness" after another auction in which "sober connoisseurs, with wrinkled brow / And spectacles on nose, thy parts inspect, / And by grave rules approve thee or reject." The teapot's destiny reminds us that even though middle- to upper-class women performed a number of domestic activities energetically, they could easily find themselves rendered useless and obsolete over time.

This is a dreary message. But it is important to remind students that the speaker's apostrophe to the teapot turns on the belief that this domestic object

—though now powerless and nonfunctional—has a dramatic history, which the speaker implies is clearly worth telling. Prerequisite to tracing this tale is the discovery of the teapot in its closet hiding space. This action—going into closets to uncover interesting stories, stories that may have been ignored because of their associations with domesticity and the private sphere—is crucial to Baillie's theater theory, and it informs her poetic aesthetic. The instructor should also remind students that this particular domestic object is not indigenous to Britain: it resides in the closet spaces of English domiciles but it has traveled in the world's theater. The teapot's movement between cultures and between the public and private settings of English society can therefore be seen as analogous to the dynamic Baillie advocates in her theory of theater and dramaturgy, a dynamic of fluid and flexible navigation that values equally the public and private spheres (Mellor, "Joanna Baillie").

From this demonstration it is but a short step to a discussion of how students can learn to defamiliarize "the plain order of things" in the classroom, which may be viewed as a closet theater for the rehearsal of reading and writing about the experiences of both the familiar and the foreign. Talking about Baillie's poem in the context of her theater theory helps students home in on the very customariness they may have come to devalue in the course of an education that too rarely raises their self-consciousness about what they are doing with their educational lives. A discussion of Baillie's teapot poem also helps them consider why the classroom is so often bounded off from the social histrionics equated with passionate living. When students start to see how they devalue the spaces in which literary criticism is forged because they associate these spaces with "no-use" or "no-drama," they begin to question what their culture does and does not consider dramatic—and why the functions of the classroom often seem irrelevant to them as they contemplate the nonacademic world. We learn to find passion in "the plain order of things" when we approach Baillie's poetic aesthetic through her theater theory, which directs us to look into closet space for a drama previously unseen or underappreciated.

NOTE

I am grateful to Fredric V. Bogel for his careful reading of this essay and for the numerous discussions he and I have shared on the topics raised here.

The Milkmaid's Voice: Ann Yearsley and the Romantic Notion of the Poet

Madeleine Kahn

When I studied the Romantic poets in graduate school, I learned about the great poems of the canonical six. I learned to appreciate how the most successful Romantic poems do in fact, as Wordsworth theorized, elevate the commonplace and suspend—and so give significance to—"spots of time" (*Prelude* 12.208). Poems such as Coleridge's "Frost at Midnight" and Wordsworth's "Tintern Abbey" (both as didactic in their way as the eighteenth-century poems against which the Romantics claimed to rebel) teach the reader to experience what the poet experienced: along with the lyric "I" of the poem, we submit to the healing power of nature, which provides an arena for the poet's self-conscious contemplation. The poet's art is to use that contemplation to transform past experience into poetry. The subject of the poem is the poet's consciousness; the process is the incorporation of significant objects into that consciousness.

Thus I learned about the poetry of the canonical six rather as they might have taught it themselves; though I did not realize it at the time, I learned about Romantic poetry through the lens of Romantic ideology. Romantic ideology is so thoroughly embedded in the culture and school system of the United States that it is difficult to recognize it as an ideology. Even now, if our students have any assumptions (as I did, however vague) about what makes a real poet or real poetry, the assumptions are handed down from the Romantics: the poet is a lone man struggling to impress his sense of value on the world. To do so he tries to escape from the corrupting influence of civilization, and he welcomes (often in nature, sometimes in a garret) the overflow of feelings that comes with his efforts to make a universal aesthetic out of his personal history. Good poetry is about the poet's individual consciousness, and the most perfect poetic form is the lyric. By these standards, of course, the poetry of Wordsworth, Keats, and others looks like the apogee of great poetry. By pointing this out I do not mean to deny that much of it is great poetry. When I suggest, as I do below, that we change our courses on the Romantics to complicate both our conventional notions about the period and the enduring Romantic image of poetry itself, I am not suggesting that we knock the glories of Shelley or Keats or Wordsworth out of the canon. On the contrary, I propose a model of teaching that eschews the hierarchical scheme that requires us to judge one poet against another and to make room only for the best.

I propose that we can complicate our notions of Romanticism and of poetry and adumbrate a new model of relationships among poets from the past by beginning a course on Romantic poetry with the poems of Ann Yearsley, the "Bristol Milkwoman." Although Yearsley (1756–1806), who sold milk door to door in Bristol, was essentially self-educated, she managed to write poetry that prompted Hannah More to praise her "perfect" ear ("Prefatory Letter" vii) and

Elizabeth Montagu her "force of imagination [and] harmony of numbers" (qtd. in Roberts 206). At one point Yearsley and her family were so destitute that they nearly starved to death. They were rescued, but not in time to save her mother, who had been living with them. Yearsley's bitter despair and grief are reflected in her first book of poems, *Poems on Several Occasions*, published with More's help in 1786. She later broke with More and went on to publish several more works (including *Poems on Various Subjects*, 1787, and *A Poem on the Inhumanity of the Slave-Trade*, 1788). All these experiences find their way into her poems: her poverty and despair, her hard labor as a milkwoman, her friendship and later feud with More, her reawakening as a poet, her feelings about being a mother and a daughter, and her fierce sense of the respect due to her as a human being.

Once known primarily as a historical oddity for her dispute with her erstwhile patron, Yearsley has come to attract considerable critical attention, and selections of her poems are now routinely included in anthologies of eighteenth-century and Romantic British poets. She plays an unsettling role in such anthologies, for she is both like and startlingly unlike most of the other poets anthologized. This superficial likeness and deep difference from the more familiar poets is what makes her so useful in a course on Romantic poetry. It allows us to set up a dialogue between Yearsley's poems and, for example, Wordsworth's, showing how two poets from the same era, working with much of the same material, can promulgate two very different notions of the poet and of the function of poetry. This approach not only enriches our understanding of the Romantic period but also reminds us that even such a familiar (and therefore seemingly natural) poetic ideology as that of the more canonical Romantics was (and is) only one of many competing ideologies.

Wordsworth is the most familiar promulgator of the Romantic ideology, and my students use him as a touchstone long before we consider any of his poems in class. Almost the first thing anyone says about Yearsley's poetry, for example, is how similar it is to Wordsworth's. Like Wordsworth, Yearsley writes about the commonplace and the ugly, about madness and despair, about physical labor, and about the redemptive powers of the natural landscape. Her narratives, like his, are often about being rescued from despair and restored to a celebration of life by poetry. These observations allow me to point out that both poets are rooted in eighteenth-century poetic traditions and that, while Yearsley often uses the classical allusions and personifications that Wordsworth decries in his Preface to *Lyrical Ballads* (1798), they share the typical late-eighteenth-century longing for the natural and distaste for the artificial. In their search for the natural, both give voice to experience that had been traditionally excluded from poetry. Thus early in discussion we establish a context for reading the canonical Romantics in relation to other poets, and we begin to consider both what they were attempting to express and what they were attempting to exclude. Such a context, in which we read poets in dialogue with each other, keeps even the most familiar poetry alive for the students.

For example, many students are familiar with Wordsworth's "Resolution and Independence" (1807), or at least with Lewis Carroll's scathing parody of it in "The White Knight's Song." In Wordsworth's poem, the poet uses the first person to relate his escape from "fears and fancies [that] thick upon me came; / Dim sadness — and blind thoughts, I knew not, nor could name" (27–28)—through his encounter with the leech gatherer, who becomes for him "my help and stay secure" (139), even though the poet doesn't actually listen to what "the oldest man . . . that ever wore grey hairs" has to say (56). The poet's restoration to equanimity becomes considerably less assured, however, when we read the poem next to the depiction of bitter struggle in Yearsley's poetry.

Like Wordsworth, Yearsley is searching for a "supporter" of what she calls "my infant mind" ("Night: To Stella" 87 [in *Poems on Several Occasions*]). Even when she finds one, though, the poet seems always in danger of slipping back into the "despondency and madness" that Wordsworth also fears ("Resolution and Independence" 49). Although "Night: To Stella" is about being converted from despair by More (Stella), who has "tun'd / My rusting powers to the bright strain of joy" (209–10) and freed Yearsley to be a poet, she describes herself as "[c]heerless and pensive o'er the wilds of life" (81) and as

> Uncouth, unciviliz'd, and rudely rough,
> Unpolish'd, as the form thrown by by Heaven,
> Nor worth completion, or the Artist's hand,
> To add a something more.   (137–40)

And in another poem in the same collection, "To Mr. R—, on His Benevolent Scheme for Rescuing Poor Children from Vice and Misery, by Promoting Sunday Schools," Yearsley describes the nearly inescapable fate of those (like herself when she was destitute) whom poverty deprives of the luxury of sensibility:

> The poor illiterate, chill'd by freezing want,
> Within whose walls pale Penury still sits,
> With icy hand impressing every meal,
> Cannot divide his slender, hard-earn'd mite
> Betwixt his bodily and mental wants;
> The soul must go — for hunger loudly pleads,
> And Nature will be answer'd.   (125–31)

This description is a powerful one; it lingers and colors Yearsley's praise for "the hope to save a ruin'd world" (11), just as her description of herself as "[u]ncouth, unciviliz'd, and rudely rough" shades the newly acquired optimism of the poet's persona in "Night: To Stella." As my students note, the details of poverty and misery are never quite transformed, even by the healing powers of nature, kindness, and poetry. Instead, as one of my students said, they interrupt the narrative of the poem like large boulders left in the road. While Wordsworth's poetic persona seems always, by the end of the poem, to be striding forward toward healing (the episodic structure of *The Prelude* offers a wonderful example), Yearsley's poetic persona seems always to be in danger of sliding backward toward madness or despair. Reading them together brings into question the Romantic notion of the healing power of poetry. It does so in the most immediate way: my students often complain that Yearsley is depressing and that her poems never achieve a conclusion.

When I ask students what makes Yearsley's poetry so depressing, they usually point to an aspect that they at first think is too simple to be important. As one student put it, "She's not standing in the same place as Wordsworth." As I would put it, the different positions from which these two poets write have far-reaching implications for the claims their poetry makes and for the way we read those poems. In "Resolution and Independence," for example, Wordsworth describes the leech gatherer as an object, a "huge stone," a "sea-beast," a "thing endued with sense" (57, 62, 61). And although the leech gatherer is a man of "Choice word and measured phrase, above the reach / Of ordinary men" (95–96), he is not privy to the meaning that his existence has for the poet. His "whole body" is "apt admonishment" (109, 112) to the poet in his despair, but the leech gatherer himself is "cheerful," "kind," and "stately" (135, 136), apparently untroubled even in his fierce poverty by the despair that wracks those of finer sensibilities. Moreover, he has no agency; he doesn't offer help to the poet. Rather, he functions as raw material for the poet to interpret for his own purposes.

For Wordsworth, the poet's position, then, is a superior one. His poetic sensibility allows him to assign meaning to whatever is inarticulate in the landscape—natural objects, the poor, or women. As the description of the leech gatherer shows, the poet often equates poor individuals with inarticulate natural objects. Women are often similarly passive, nearly natural objects made significant through the poet's use of them. (For a striking example of a woman used as if she were an inarticulate object, note how Wordsworth's sister Dorothy functions as a repository of unreflective, un-self-conscious feeling in "Tintern Abbey" [1798], where the poet "read[s] / My former pleasures in the shooting lights / Of thy wild eyes" [117–19].)

In contrast, Yearsley's portrait of fierce poverty and misery does not participate in this hierarchy. The most obvious reason is that she often writes of her own experience of poverty. She calls herself "rudely rough" and "not worth completion"; nonetheless, she has written the poem we are reading. Yearsley thus occupies a double position, as the mind that needs illuminating—the "soul [that] wants firm support" ("Night: To Stella" 158)—and as the poet who can, with Stella as muse, "paint the tremors of the soul / In Sorrow's deepest tints" (25–26).

Students discover this seemingly simple difference from Wordsworth and most of the other Romantics through a close reading of Yearsley's poems. That same close reading can also lead them to recognize the complex implications of this difference. For in the ideology of the canonical Romantics, the poet writes to reveal the glories of the commonplace to the reader. But in Yearsley's poetry the commonplace glorifies itself. In her poetry the experience of a laboring woman—and, more important, the meaning of that experience—is not mediated by the male poet; she claims poetic authority for herself. If such a laboring woman can glorify her own experience and reveal its multiple meanings herself, then her poetry proposes a revision to the typical Romantic relation between the poet and the object of contemplation. In that relation (see, e.g., "Resolution and Independence" and "Tintern Abbey") the male poet always remains the subject of the poem, but he reveals his growing consciousness to himself and to the reader by writing about an object or an other that he incorporates. The reader, then, functions as a kind of apprentice poet in the poem. With the poet as our guide, we follow in his footsteps and experience vicariously the "growth of a poet's mind" (as the subtitle to *The Prelude* reminds us). The hierarchy extends downward from the poet, who gives meaning to what he sees, through the reader, who can be led to apprehend that meaning, to the other, who, at the bottom of the hierarchy, never suspects that such meaning might be made out of his or her experience or existence.

In Yearsley's version of the relation, the poet does not simply confer meaning. At times it seems meaning is already inherent in the experience—the poet's or others'—that the poet contemplates. Indeed, the poet may be inadequate to the task of expressing that meaning, even when it is the mingling of the "Tragic Tale" and the "grateful rapture" of her own experience ("Night: To Stella" 23, 149). The poet converses with the material instead of mastering it, even when that material is her own experience. This conversational model, in contrast to Wordsworth's hierarchy, accounts in part for the seeming lack of resolution in many of Yearsley's poems and for the different demands her poems make on us and on our students. Often we are drawn into the conversation; almost always we are asked to give up our comfortable distance from the conflict within the poem (which might be conflict between the poet's past and present selves, between her and Hannah More, or between her hopes for poetry and her knowledge of its limitations). My students at first find Yearsley's poems unsatisfactory because they lack the transcendent conclusions students have come to expect from Romantic poetry. As we question that expectation in class, however, many students engage so fully with Yearsley's poetry that they come to feel like her collaborators.

As the description of the "poor illiterate" from "To Mr. R—" shows, even when Yearsley is describing someone else's misery from her relatively lofty position as a poet, that description is not what we would now call, and not by accident, romanticized. Unlike the leech gatherer, whose extreme poverty somehow bestows on him an unconscious simple nobility (which the poet is denied because of the plenty and leisure in his life), Yearsley's "poor illiterate" is brought down by "freezing want," so that he forfeits his soul and ends up "envelop'd, groping, s[u]nk in vulgar toils; / To eat and sleep includes the soul's best wish" (132–33). Yet Yearsley's poem does not just offer a contradiction to Wordsworth's interpretation of the effects of poverty on the soul. For this description is part of a poem that otherwise sounds much like Wordsworth. "To Mr. R——" includes praise for the "Benevolent Scheme for rescuing Poor Children from Vice and Misery" as well as the assertion that "Jehovah['s] . . . voice / . . . sounds / From Misery's lowest shed" (164–66), thus ennobling the impoverished and their patrons alike. Unlike Wordsworth, however, Yearsley heightens our awareness of multiple, even contradictory, meanings in the experience of poverty. Rather than choose one meaning or resolve any contradictions, she offers us instead the poem as an attempt at achieving a balance between those possible meanings. As readers we participate in creating that balance in the poem. In the process we experience in miniature the inclusive alternative to the Romantic worldview that Yearsley's poetry as a whole has to offer.

Whereas Wordsworth struggles to make his experience universal and to determine the meaning, however ambivalent, of each thing he encounters, Yearsley refuses both the universal and the absolute. We can see this refusal in her use of a conversational rather than hierarchical model; in her insistence on multiple meanings; in her foregrounding of her double, and unstable, position as poet and apparently inarticulate laboring woman; and in her challenging, sometimes aggressive, relationship to the reader. She is fully aware of how unusual it is for her to write from her position, which poetry ignored until the canonical Romantics appropriated it, and she dares us to be unsympathetic. When she warns, "[B]ut never talk of aid / For miseries like mine, which mock relief" ("Night: To Stella" 189–90), or "For mine's a stubborn and a savage will" ("To the Same [Stella]; On Her Accusing the Author of Flattery" 8), she claims poetic authority *as a milkwoman*. By writing of her experience at the margins of society in the language of the mainstream, she is refusing the double bind in which the traditional poetic hierarchy would place her, as either a poet or an inarticulate female laborer. In refusing this double bind, she attempts to use her skill as a poet to articulate the experience of the inarticulate female other who, like Dorothy with her "wild eyes" in "Tintern Abbey," would seem to be only the object of poetry, not its subject or its author. Thus Yearsley lays claim to both sides of what became the traditional Romantic divide between the poet and the silent other whom the poet uses to achieve transcendence. She occupies both positions in the poem: William Wordsworth's and the wild-eyed Dorothy Wordsworth's or William Wordsworth's and the leech gatherer's. This balancing, this refusal to give over one perspective entirely in favor of the other or to offer her readers a comfortable hierarchy, makes Yearsley's poetry more than simply an addition or correction to the Romantic poetic ideology. Her poems present an alternative to the Romantic project, which is to universalize individual experience and to encompass all experience within a single poetic vision.

Yearsley's poetry, then, allows us to open up the way we teach the Romantics. Most obviously she shows that women and laborers wrote poetry in this period. That this is surprising reveals just how thoroughly gender and class assumptions shape the canonical Romantic notion of the poet. But Yearsley, writing in the same critical and historical moment as the canonical Romantics, also offers another powerful alternative to the Romantic notion of the poet and the function of poetry. In place of the poet as maker or even god, she offers us the poet as contradictory subject, striving to make room for the conflicting elements of experience. Thus, beginning our consideration of the Romantics with a figure like Ann Yearsley helps us establish a model that includes conflicting views instead of ranking them. We can extend that model from Yearsley's poems to the whole of the literary tradition. Yearsley gives us the occasion, the vocabulary, and the specific perspectives to show our students that the Romantic ideology is not uncontested or absolute and does not need to be so to be valuable.

Yearsley's poetry violates and so questions the Romantic poets' conception of the place of laborers and women in poetry, providing an alternative to silent, naturalized others, like Dorothy and the leech gatherer. Yearsley thus allows us to teach our students to think about how the poetic persona is constructed and how the poet uses that persona to seduce readers into affirming the worldview of the poem. In particular, her poetry offers us a way to help our students grow aware of the critical assumptions we inherited from the Romantics. When we show our students that, for example, the Romantic claim to universality is based on assumptions that can be questioned, we reveal that such claims always influence the kinds of experience and ideas that get expressed and legitimized in poetry and in literary criticism. This critical awareness can in turn lead the class to develop together multiple readings of a given poem, including readings that acknowledge the material and social situations of both reader and poet.

Such multiple readings also allow us to show our students how every interpretation is produced by a productive interplay between a literary text and the theories or assumptions we bring to it. Thus, William Wordsworth's poetry looks different if we read it through the lens Ann Yearsley offers us from how it does if we read it through the literary-critical assertions of the Preface to *Lyrical Ballads*. Taking both approaches in the same course on the Romantics allows our students to gain a cautionary sense of the limits of any one critical approach and an appreciation of the value of a mosaic of approaches. They will also gain a sense of the capaciousness of the Romantic period, with its many unresolved and fruitful contradictions. To Dorothy's apparently silent acquiescence to William's efforts to "behold in thee what I was once" ("Tintern Abbey" 120) "and read / My former pleasures in the shooting lights / Of thy wild eyes" (117–19), we can now add Ann Yearsley's "stubborn and . . . savage will" and her "dar[ing], in Fancy's boundless walk, / [To] invoke thy Muse, and hail thy song sublime" ("Night: To Stella" 13–14).

Teaching with Annotated Editions

Stephen C. Behrendt

We are all familiar with the frustration of trying to teach the British women poets of the Romantic period effectively when there are few good secondary materials—even when we are fortunate enough to have access to decent primary texts. But I have used this problem as the basis of a profitable class exercise for undergraduates and graduates. While our students have used anthologies for years, they have seldom given much thought to the considerations that go into the volumes' construction and annotation. Therefore I like to have students prepare an annotated edition of a poem by a little-known woman writer. Doing so gives them direct, hands-on experience with a variety of research tools and methodologies and engages them actively in the process of recovery that has spurred the renewed interest in women writers of the period. Moreover, the project illustrates the sort of pragmatic, nuts-and-bolts decisions editors and anthologizers actually make in preparing texts for a variety of readers and scholars. Finally, because the assignment is a group project, my students learn useful lessons about interpersonal negotiation as they define and assign tasks and responsibilities. Often students find this project the most interesting aspect of the course, even though they usually approach it at first with a mixture of anxiety, confusion, and plain ignorance. So while the project affords students direct experience with the sort of scholarship familiar to all of us who teach noncanonical or lesser-known writers, it also engages them—sometimes addictively—in aspects of historical, social, and philological research they might otherwise be loath to undertake.

I most frequently use annotated edition projects in Romantic Poetry, an upper-level, sixteen-week semester course that has no prerequisites (our curriculum has none) and that typically attracts seventy to eighty percent English majors among its target enrollment of thirty. Of these, fewer than a quarter or as many as half may be graduate students (both MA and PhD). Given these class demographics, I prepare four or five annotated edition packets, and once I have become acquainted with the students and have a sense of their personalities and their ability (or inability) to work together, I ask for volunteers to form project groups. Because I make the assignment about four weeks into the term, students have had time to get to know one another, and so they often do some initial grouping on their own. Typically the graduates and undergraduates prefer to avoid one another (mutual suspicion, mutual contempt, mutual anxiety), and so I make a point of distributing the graduates about equally among the groups (this step almost always defuses the antipathy between the groups, as the undergraduates find to their pleasure that they fare well and the graduates discover that undergraduates do indeed know things—often surprisingly many things).

For the assignment I draw on a substantial number of texts by little-known authors that I have accumulated over the years (from archival research, interlibrary loans, and electronic sources). While many of these texts (and their authors) may be of fairly limited importance even in the grand scheme of a revisited British Romanticism, the poems I select all have aspects that make them well worth group study. Most recently, for instance, I chose Elizabeth Moody's "Thoughts on War and Peace" (from *Poetic Trifles*, 1798), Eliza Daye's "Lancaster Castle, by Moonlight" (from *Poems, on Various Subjects*, 1798), Ann Candler's "Reflections on My Own Situation, Written in T-tt-ngst-ne House of Industry, February 1802" (from *Poetical Attempts*, 1803), and Margaret Sarah Croker's *A Monody on the Lamented Death of Her Royal Highness the Princess Charlotte-Augusta of Wales and of Saxe Cobourg Saalfield* (1817). I prepare copies of the title page of each volume, the table of contents (if the volume includes more than one work), and the text of the poem, including any annotations. The student group is to prepare an annotated edition that glosses the poem's language and any significant literary, historical, or topical references and allusions and to provide a brief background on the poet and the poem's historical context, along the lines of a biographical and critical headnote in a substantial textbook anthology. Finally, I suggest that the groups write brief essays exploring the poem's relation to others we are studying and tentatively assessing it as a literary work of art. I carefully avoid using words like *good* or *value*, leaving the students to wrestle with issues of quality and valuation just as we do in our class discussions of other texts, canonical or not.

The first stage of the project involves getting to know the poem at the surface level: students identify words, images, and allusions for which they will need to provide explanatory notes. If they don't arrive at their own system for making the decisions, I suggest that as they read the poem they simply note any word, image, or reference they don't understand on first reading. They can then compare lists, divide up the unknowns, and head to the library to examine sources like the *OED* and the *DNB*, which I describe in class. So much for the easy part.

For most students, however sophisticated, a project of this complexity requires extra motivation. Like many instructors, I face students whose knowledge of history and cultures—not to mention the arts—is sketchy at best. To make the project work I must get students involved in an almost archaeological sense with the day-to-day historical and cultural realities to which the project points. I stress that most of the authors they are annotating are no longer known to us, and I ask them to contemplate how and why persons come to be famous or to disappear. What are the particular, local cultural causes? And who were the authors themselves? What can we learn about them and about how cultures are structured—and how literary history is written—by exploring the recoverable details of daily life? I find that students become much more actively engaged in the project when they begin to connect with their findings about lives that unfolded some two centuries ago. For many students, the first details are like the end of a string; they become almost compulsive about winding the string into a ball, and given reasonable guidance and a good deal of encouragement they tend to do an excellent job. Indeed, they often surprise themselves.

The annotated edition project, as it has evolved, reflects my concern that the poems I select should lead my students to examine broader issues of social, political, economic, intellectual, and of course literary context. When I assign Moody's "Thoughts on War and Peace," I hope students discover the poet's relation to the Radical movement in the aftermath of the French Revolution. Moody was sufficiently involved in antiwar publication during the 1790s that one of her poems, "Anna's Complaint; or, The Miseries of War" (1794) was included in the pamphlet *War a System of Madness and Irreligion* (1796), published by the humanitarian George Miller under the pseudonym Humanitas. Encountering two footnotes that are quotations in French, with only short title indicated, the students learn a useful lesson about bibliographic research—not to mention the value of second-language training. Moreover, studying the poem's dense web of historical allusion, they come to greater insight about both the extent of Moody's education and her willingness to enter into public political discourse.

Daye's "Lancaster Castle" also yields several useful leads. Like Moody's poem, it was published in 1798, the year of *Lyrical Ballads*. Its stanzaic form and its subject matter interestingly anticipate William Wordsworth's "Elegiac Stanzas," on Peele Castle. The placement of Daye's poem at the end of the volume recalls the placement of "Tintern Abbey," a comparably weighty and philosophical conclusion. Finally, its warm praise of John Howard leads the students to Howard's efforts on behalf of penal reform in England, an important subject that leads in other productive directions, including William Godwin's *Caleb Williams* and the historical situation of prisoners from hardened criminals to unfortunate debtors and their families. Moreover, the poem's strong historical bent draws students into the useful task of identifying and tracing Daye's allusions to historical persons, places, and events.

Candler's "Reflections on My Own Situation" works analogously, leading students to examine the late-eighteenth-century workhouse and its effect both on society and on the unfortunate people confined there, many of whom had little hope of leaving. There is a good deal of literature on this subject, it turns out, including even accessible documents dealing with the workhouses around Ipswich, where Candler lived. Furthermore, since Candler is described on the title page and elsewhere as an "Ipswich cottager," the poem offers students a useful opportunity to examine the work of "unlettered" poets as part of what became something of a minicult of "rustic genius." Here students can consider yet another alternative to both the privileged male poet of the Romantic stereotype and the working-class woman poet whom Donna Landry examines in *The Muses of Resistance*. It is helpful to give ambitious student groups copies of Candler's "On Perusing the History of Jacob, after I Had Left T-ttngst-ne House of Industry." This poem, which concludes *Poetical Attempts* and makes a good companion piece to "Reflections," provides both closure and a poignant indication of how the unfortunate and indigent were customarily encouraged to suffer silently and even to be grateful for the adversity that brought opportunities for virtuous perseverance.

Finally, Croker's *Monody* takes up the death in childbirth in 1817 of the Princess Charlotte Augusta of Wales, daughter of the prince regent and hence key to the royal succession. Her death and that of her infant son were widely mourned in an extraordinary national outpouring of grief, some of which was surely staged to make the dead princess into a commodity and turn a quick pound or two for the opportunistic publisher. Through their research students discover a good deal about the volatile social and political climate of the later Regency and why so many citizens had invested such hope in the young princess, as well as about the way popular culture functioned then as today to create popular mythologies around persons and events of compelling public interest—or curiosity. Examining the context of this poem, students learn about the hundreds of poems produced and published on the occasion, as well as the sermons, songs, engraved prints, memorial cards, ceramic pieces, metalware, and textiles that document the extraordinary public orgy of memorializing. And they may be surprised to find that the unnumbered stanzas of Croker's poem, which are printed one to a page, are sonnet stanzas and that the poem is in fact an articulated sonnet sequence, a discovery that may lead to further thought about the revival of the sonnet in the Romantic period and the Romantic sonnet sequence as a form.

These are only a few of the possibilities that annotated edition projects present. The finished products are always a surprise, and I always arrange to have them duplicated for all the class members. Even when, as in my department, there are no funds for the copying, a copy shop can usually prepare good copies of all the projects for only a dollar or so each, and the students are almost all eager to have the copies, even if they must pay for them. Sometimes the projects take unexpected and exciting turns. One technologically savvy group prepared their text in a hypertext format, offering it to their classmates for the price of a floppy disk. Continued development of computer resources like the Internet will make it increasingly easy—and useful—for students to share their work with student scholars elsewhere.

Such research projects have extraordinary benefits for students, who learn a great deal precisely because they are engaged on their own in the very sort of activities their instructors frequently pursue. I try to make that point often, because I think it is more important than ever that we cultivate a sense of the real excitement of discovery that attends our efforts to recover previously unenfranchised writers. And I am always gratified to observe that the annotated edition projects help students become not only better close readers of primary texts but also more sophisticated literary and cultural historians as they situate the poems for themselves and within the poems' historical contexts.

Introducing Felicia Hemans
in the First-Year Course

Deborah Kennedy

Students in a first-year college or university course in English literature can benefit in a number of ways by studying Felicia Hemans during the survey of the major Romantic poets. A comparative approach helps students locate writers chronologically and sometimes ideologically, developing their sense of literary history. In this particular case, students will also become keenly aware of the difference that Hemans's female perspective makes to their reading of the other poets. I recommend beginning with a lecture that outlines Hemans's life and career, since it provides valuable contextual information. It will quickly spark the interest of the class, not only because of Hemans's impressive publishing successes but also because many students are fascinated by the story of her life as a working and writing mother who became one of Britain's best-loved poets. Given her wide-ranging subject matter and vast knowledge of world history (see Sweet), Hemans should be presented as a cosmopolitan writer, whose facility in more than five languages and epigraphs from such writers as Wordsworth, Byron, and Goethe show that she was very conscious of writing in the company of the best poets of her day. A distinguishing feature of her work is her examination of how historical events—or imaginary ones—might have affected women and the family (see Ross, *Contours* 267–316, and Mellor, *Romanticism and Gender* 135–43). This preoccupation is evident in the short poem "The Effigies," which makes an excellent starting point and contains what should become one of Hemans's best-known quotations: "Woman! . . . What was *thy* tale? . . . What bard has sung of *thee*?" (25–32). (Except where otherwise noted, quotations from Hemans are taken from the Lippincott edition of *Poetical Works*.) If the class has already studied other female writers—such as Anne Finch—then examining Hemans's career can demonstrate how her success changed the status of the female writer. Her fame established a new model for the writing woman; previously, women writers often published anonymously, or their reputations died with them.

Only one of a dozen first-year literature anthologies I read in 1995 includes Hemans's work: *The Norton Anthology of English Literature*, volume 2 (Abrams). Since some readers might use this text, I would like to discuss briefly its selections: "England's Dead," "The Landing of the Pilgrim Fathers," and "Casabianca," all famous examples of Hemans's patriotic verse. "England's Dead" boasts of England's imperial glory by listing places around the globe where English soldiers and travelers have died. The poem not only demonstrates Hemans's expert control of stanzaic pattern but also invites students to debate the tone of the speaker, because the overt nationalism seems undercut by an implicit criticism of the violent martyrdom of masculine culture. "The Landing of the Pilgrim Fathers," a tribute to Puritan families seeking freedom from religious persecution, can help students understand "Casabianca" because the pilgrims risked their lives emigrating to New England. In other words, their actions demonstrate, as do Casabianca's, that there are certain values and beliefs worth risking one's comfort and one's life. The boy Casabianca perished serving in the Battle of the Nile because he remained at his post on a burning ship, not having received orders to leave. His actions, whether viewed as foolhardy or saintly, can lead the class to reconsider today's notions of heroism. While the patriotic subject matter of these three poems links them coherently, instructors should supplement them with another poem or two, such as "The Effigies" or those discussed below, to ensure that students understand the broad range of Hemans's subjects and personae.

It is most fruitful to introduce Hemans's poetry to first-year students together with certain canonical Romantic texts. My first example, "The Wings of the Dove" (*Complete Works*), composed of eleven quatrains, can be taught effectively in combination with John Keats's "Ode to a Nightingale." "The Wings of the Dove" is one of Hemans's many poems that articulate a desire for freedom, though instead of the imagery of chains, found in several of her texts, this poem expresses the conventional human desire for the freedom of a bird's flight. Students can easily come up with examples of this conventional trope from movies, music videos, posters, cards, and religious iconography. Discussion can focus on how Hemans's treatment of a conventional subject is memorable for both its Christian context and its female perspective.

Teaching this poem allows for a discussion of the Bible's importance as a literary source. The title and the epigraph come from Psalms 55.6: "Oh that I might have the wings of a dove, that I might flee away and be at rest." The dove serves as a Christian symbol in the gospel story of Christ's baptism: "he saw the Spirit of God descending like a dove, and lighting upon him" (Matt. 3.16). Hemans calls the dove the "holiest bird" (6), and she imagines it finding in the forest a holy resting place that breathes "a spirit o'er the solitude" (16). She describes the dove in intellectual and spiritual terms, unlike the sensual imagery of Keats's ode.

The second point to emphasize is that the first-person speaker is female, and gender accounts for some of the differences in how the two poets represent the desire for freedom. In Keats's opening stanzas, the speaker feels as if he has drunk hemlock or "emptied some dull opiate to the drains" (3), and he imagines a beaker full of wine, that he "might drink" his way "into the forest dim" (19, 20). The genteel Felicia Hemans could not exactly write about opium and wine approvingly, but Keats (and De Quincey) certainly could. However, Hemans shares with Keats a desire to escape what he calls "the weariness, the fever, and the fret" (23). She wistfully notes that the dove carries none of humankind's "dark" remembrances (20), and her "wild wish" (33) is expressed in one stanza that is especially Keatsian in its diction, tone, and imagery:

> Oh! to some cool recess
> Take, take me with thee on the summer wind,

> Leaving the weariness
> And all the fever of this life behind.
>   (25–28)

Soon afterward the comparison to Keats ends when the speaker reveals her sex, describing her pain as "burning woman's tears" (39). Moreover, she departs from Keats in her conclusion, describing the loving home she will return to, unlike his "Forlorn" world (71):

> *Had* I thy wings, thou dove!
> High midst the gorgeous Isles of Cloud to soar,
> Soon the strong cords of love
> Would draw me earthwards—homewards—yet once more.
>   (41–44)

The speaker's insistence on choosing the cords of love, not an escape from them, seems the antithesis of the typical Romantic quest, and it may disappoint those who prefer the seductive ending of Keats's poem. However, some students might value Hemans's draw "homewards," because it offers the possibility of love and companionship while acknowledging the responsibilities of domestic life. These poems allow the class to explore the attraction of freedom, the difference that gender makes, and the appeal and the drawbacks of the two contrasting endings.

Another canonical poem often taught in first-year courses, Percy Shelley's famous sonnet "Ozymandias," works well with Hemans's "The Image in Lava." Both poems are concerned with relics of former civilizations—Shelley's with the remains of King Ozymandias's statue and Hemans's with the remains of a woman embracing her child, found at the site of the first-century eruption of Mount Vesuvius. Students are quick to notice the contrast in gender between the relics: Shelley's poem tells of how a man boasted about his kingdom and immortal fame but only a broken statue and a desert remain to mock him, while Hemans's poem venerates an image preserved in lava of a nameless mother and child who nonetheless became great as a symbol of mother love. Ironically, it is the image not of a king but of a mother and a child that has endured (see A. Harding). Moreover, Shelley's sonnet ends with a bleak image of nothingness—"the lone and level sands stretch far away" (14)—but Hemans concludes by viewing the image in lava as an affirmation of the power of love.

Studying the two poems together can also help students learn about tone and emotional register in poetry. After encountering the cool and rational (in fact, rather un-Shelley-like) tone in "Ozymandias," students might be dizzied by Hemans's emotionally wrought poem with its twelve exclamation points. Angela Leighton offers an analysis of the characteristic theatricality of Hemans's verse that attracted and roused her female readers (13). Undeterred by the exclamation marks, my students have been enthralled by the story of the image in lava and have empathized with Hemans's sense of excitement. Female students in particular are often moved by and appreciative of the woman's voice and the mother love in Hemans's poetry, perhaps finding in Hemans a part of their world that they do not find in Keats or Shelley. Female and male students in a first-year class can expand their understanding of women writers, of poetry, and of literary history through this comparative approach, in which they read the once-famous Hemans in conjunction with the work of her more frequently taught peers.

The Appeal of the Domestic in the First-Year Course: Susanna Blamire

Becky Lewis

My first-year English composition and literature students groan when I mention poetry. Most come from high schools that have traditional English curricula, which stress canonized poetry, praised for its aesthetic qualities rather than for its accessibility. Students expect to be frustrated, befuddled, and eventually thwarted by poetry. In the limited amount of time I have to market my wares, therefore, I try to teach poetry that is student-friendly, that builds on a literary tradition including both men and women, and that expands students' conceptions of poetry. Because my students come to me with a general idea about Romanticism and already recognize William Blake, William Wordsworth, Samuel Taylor Coleridge, Percy Bysshe Shelley, and John Keats, I have no qualms about introducing the work of Romantic women poets in the hope of broadening their horizons and their notions of poetry and Romanticism. I take two seventy-five-minute periods to do this. I assign poetry by men but I center my discussion on the domestic in poetry by women.

Stuart Curran, in his groundbreaking essay "Romantic Poetry: The 'I' Altered," points to the prominence of women novelists, playwrights, and poets during the Romantic period and suggests that it is important to revalue the quotidian in assessing the unique contributions of women writers. As Wordsworth attempted to write his poetry in "the real language of men," Curran observes, women poets wrote in "the language of women" (194–95). Many Romantic women writers addressed the domestic world in which they lived and worked. It is this concern with the everyday that makes the work of poets such as Susanna Blamire, Anna Letitia Barbauld, and Jane Taylor accessible to first-year students. I photocopy poems to supplement the assigned readings in a standard introduction-to-literature text—the anthologized favorites such as Blake's "London," Keats's odes, and Wordsworth's "My Heart Leaps Up." I give biographical sketches of the poets, which allow me to describe the domestic and political spheres and the context and constraints under which women and men wrote. The invaluable work of Roger Lonsdale and Paula Feldman provides background information on the women writers. When possible, I show portraits and early editions of their work.

I like to begin with a very early poet, Susanna Blamire (1747–94). Students may be reluctant to think of her as a Romantic because of her birth and death dates. However, her sympathy with the natural world, the commonplace, and the common folk exemplifies important tenets that we associate with Romanticism. I usually begin with one of her shorter poems, such as "The Siller Croun," which offers a good example of the Scottish influence on her poetry. Blamire's poem *Stoklewath; or, The Cumbrian Village*, at 1,156 lines is too long for the available time, and so I generally assign the first 300 lines. Extending and augmenting the traditional portrayal of the eighteenth-century village represented in James Thomson's *The Seasons* (1744), Oliver Goldsmith's *The Deserted Village* (1770), and Thomas Crabbe's *The Village* (1782), *Stoklewath* explores a day of village life, showing the time by describing the sun, the sky, and their varying colors. In the first ten lines I point out the new value placed during Blamire's time on escape to the rural and the idealization of the rural life. Blake's "London" provides a useful counterpoint.

I note that in Blamire's attempt to negotiate with the heroic couplet (the meter expected for serious poetry) her expressive voice is rendered uneven and not nearly so natural as the voice in some of her shorter poems and songs, such as "The Siller Croun." This observation can lead us to talk about the differences in education between men and women and among the classes during the late eighteenth and early nineteenth centuries. We examine some of the reasons women and the lower class were deprived of the classical education in which upper-class men learned to write in the supposedly more acceptable forms of poetry. I mention that *Stoklewath* was never published in Blamire's lifetime but that a fair copy was found after her death, revealing Blamire's serious intent (Lonsdale 279).

What makes *Stoklewath* striking and memorable is Blamire's unaffected celebration of the simple domestic life of the rural villagers. She introduces her experience as a woman by focusing on the centrality of women to the home and by extension to the entire community. A major theme is the home as the source of nurture, cure, and redemption for those who suffer the tragedies and frustrations of life. I ask the students to consider how Blamire illustrates these qualities as she details the morning chores of women. We point out the cozy language that describes the cottage gardens and predicts the cheerful times that the harvest will make (all following quotations are from the Feldman anthology): "many an apple . . . with nice care is lock'd in oaken chest, / Till Christmas comes, and tarts draw out the feast"; "carrots and turnips Sunday-feasts supply"; "blest potatoes meet the thankful eye" (27–30, 41, 42). Her account is a lush catalog of what women do to care for families and friends, tending the cottage gardens, harvesting the bounty, and carefully putting it away for the winter.

I remind the students that during Blamire's time there was no aspirin or penicillin, or any other miracle cure, and that the cottage gardens served as household medicine cabinets, providing herbs such as "balm, and sage, and hyssop [that] physic yield" (37). Modern herb books tell us that balm reduces fever; sage makes a good gargle for sore throat, tonsillitis, and canker sores; hyssop alleviates colds and the sting of insect bites. Thus in surveying the herb gardens Blamire also alludes to the curative influence of the home.

As the day proceeds, women bustle around completing errands, sweeping floors, scalding bowls, buying cheese when a "failing cow" does not supply, preparing for the noonday meal (93). The cheering smells of "fried rasher" and "savoury pancakes" greet the tired men as they return home for a meal and rest

(124). We consider how Blamire adds to the store of poetic diction as she weaves one domestic detail after another into her description of this important event. She effectively and creatively combines allegory and classical allusion with domestic imagery: "Smoking potatoes meet their thankful eyes, / And hunger wafts the grateful sacrifice; / To her libations of sweet milk are pour'd / And Peace and Plenty watch around the board" (124–27). Her procedure reminds us of what Barbauld does for a more immediately humorous purpose in "Washing Day." In *Stoklewath* members of the family circle come together almost like celebrants in an archaic rite whereby the gods must be appeased. For her, food sustains not only the body but also the spirit. The instructor can fruitfully compare Blamire's use of classical imagery in the poem with Keats's in "Ode on a Grecian Urn."

Children appear frequently in Romantic verse, of course, and Blamire does not forget the children in the Stoklewath school at lunchtime. Some join their families at home, while others bring lunches "safely infolded by a mother's care" (143). Blamire describes these lunches: "bread and cheese" (145), "butter oaten-cakes" (147), "new milk, which seem / Best to demand the name of good thick cream" (148–49). After a nourishing lunch, the adults rest but the children play various games: chase or "the hounded-hare" (152); the boys, a rough game of "foot-ball" (156); the girls "form a smiling circle on the green, / Where chuckstones, dolls, and totums, all are seen" (162-63). I remind students that while Wordsworth is sometimes called the poet of childhood, he has difficulty rendering the childhood experience when he describes the tic-tac-toe game in *The Prelude*: "We schemed and puzzled, head opposed to head / In strife too humble to be named in verse" (1.512–13). Blamire names the humble trivialities of childhood easily and naturally. Other children in poems by Wordsworth, Coleridge, and Blake can be used for further comparison.

Inside the school the school-dame is the nurturing figure, and Blamire alludes to the dark underside of the domestic in her portrait of this woman earning a living in one of the few jobs then available to women. She has spent her lunchtime dealing with a child who called her a "clucking hen" and "a wrinkl'd witch" (171, 175). As she calls her unruly brood in after recess, her voice is described as "tremulous" (186), a small detail that expresses Blamire's empathy for the woman's lonely life.

Students can find other examples of Blamire's insight into domestic frustrations, such as the story of little Peggy, who can't get wheat bread because the baker has no yeast and who is kicked by the cow she milks. However, Peggy's frustrations are soothed by the nurturing effect of the home. Nevertheless, Blamire raises concern about the fate of the home amid political and industrial change through the conversation of two old women at their spinning wheels bemoaning the loss of old values. Their spinning wheels have been superseded by cloth mills, and their fear that "the world's turned upside down" accurately prefigures the traumatic changes that will alter the domestic fabric of life (270).

In the interest of time, I generally summarize the latter part of the poem, which details the men's world in Stoklewath as the scene shifts to the village pub, "The Hounds and Hare," whose name echoes the children's game of hounded-hare, a connection underscored when the poet describes the "wondrous sign" (454): "The sportive scene tempts many a wight to stay, / As to the school he drags th' unwilling way" (460–61). The men's world may be beset by war, tragedy, and loss, but it is always redeemed by the home. In literature and life we are taught to dismiss the domestic as trivial, but throughout the poem Blamire stresses the power and importance of the women's sphere, the domestic, and the feminine in providing redeeming nurture and cure. Her unique, holistic, and feminine way of setting everyday frustrations and pain as well as tragedy in the nurturing context of the home lends a strong Romantic element to the poetic vision of village life in the later eighteenth century. Her astute observations of the feminine domain and its underside of frustration, alienation, and tragedy are distinctive, Romantic, and (as my students' response indicates) readily accessible.

Gendering Subjectivity:
Women Romantics in a Poetry Survey Course
Donelle R. Ruwe

For several semesters, I have taught an elective poetry survey (cross-listed in English and gender studies) that I designed for non-English majors fulfilling a humanities requirement. The class learns about the writing and reading of poetry about self-identity: who we are and how we establish ourselves in relation to gender, literature, and the world around us. Students read meditative, confessional, and autobiographical poems beginning with the Romantics and concluding with Sharon Olds, using the debates about subjectivity and what it meant to be a poet in the Romantic era as a foundation for the survey. I move from traditional readings of canonical texts about the poet to feminist critiques of these traditional readings to the alternative subjectivities posed by women writers. As my students explore past and current debates surrounding the different definitions of the poet, they learn what is at stake politically and poetically—who and what are excluded each time the poet is defined.

My course begins with a five-week session on the Romantics. I first give an introductory historical lecture adapted from Stuart Curran's "Romantic Poetry: Why and Wherefore?" emphasizing the Romantic preoccupations with inner growth and creativity and the development of poetry as a privileged discourse restricted by class, education, and gender. Then I guide my students through traditional interpretations of the Romantic ideology of the self in canonical texts: William Blake's prophetic identity in "Introduction" ("Hear the voice of the Bard"); William Wordsworth's isolated self in "Tintern Abbey" and his education as a poet in *The Prelude* (selections from books 1, 5, and 6); and Samuel Taylor Coleridge's concern with the workings of the creative imagination in "The Eolian Harp" and his definition of imagination and fancy in chapter 13 of *Biographia Literaria*. I have found it helpful to use as an interpretative guide to poetics "The Self," a brief definition essay by Christian La Cassagnere that outlines the critical assumptions and crises involved in canonical interpretations of texts about the self. Through reading questions and in lengthy class discussions, I help my students uncover the inherent contradictions in masculine versions of subjectivity and in the positioning of the feminine as object or other. Discussion often focuses on the solipsism of masculine Romanticism, the ways in which a godlike imagination—one that Coleridge calls "the eternal act of creation in the infinite I AM" (*Biographia* 304)—is potentially sacrilegious and is defined in masculine terms. I draw attention to the silencing of the feminine as nature and object in contrast to the masculinized speaking poet and subject. Students quickly grasp that Dorothy is spoken to but does not speak in "Tintern Abbey"; that her wild eyes merge with nature; that she is to Wordsworth what he was before he became a writer; that *The Prelude* idealizes the poet as one who is chosen by nature and who has the leisure to study; that Coleridge's Sara is presented as a reality check, an unimaginative mind acting as a foil for his creative mind. To prevent my students from adopting an overly simplistic binary model of a masculine and a feminine Romanticism, I suggest that, in this age of sensibility, even the "masculine" participates in the feminine. I recommend Susan Wolfson's essays "Feminizing Keats" and "Keats and the Manhood of the Poet," Anne Mellor's discussion of Keats in *Romanticism and Gender*, and Alicia Ostriker's discussion of Blake in "The Road of Excess."

Once we have a baseline understanding about canonical poetic subjectivity and how it colonizes, excludes, or objectifies the feminine, we read Romantic women writers whose texts both participate in this subjectivity and provide alternative representations of the self. When shifting from canonical writers to women poets, we first examine tracts about female education because they were the main forum for discussion of women's literary, social, and political status. We analyze excerpts from Mary Wollstonecraft's *A Vindication of the Rights of Woman*, Maria Edgeworth's "Letters to Literary Ladies," and Hannah More's *Strictures on the Modern System of Female Education*. To foster discussion I have asked students to collect quotes indicating each author's position on women's biological or cultural nature; to list problems in the education system and each woman's suggested reforms; and to describe how each writer presents the potential dangers or benefits of differing types of female education. I also provide a copy of William Upton's illustrated books of children's verse *The School-Boy* and *The School-Girl* (1820). In a verse pattern modeled after Jane Taylor's "My Mother," Upton uncritically depicts the active life of schoolboys ("Just Breeched" and "At College") and the domestic enclosure of schoolgirls ("Needlework," "Quitting School," and "Learning to Draw"). Upton's rhymes and accompanying pictures spark a lively, concrete debate about education, for Upton idealizes the gender inequities that Wollstonecraft and others protest: while boys are taught the classics and the sciences and constantly play outdoors, the girls, as one of my students notes, "are rarely allowed outside, and when their daintiness is thrown to the wolves of oxygen, they wear bonnets like horse blinders to shield them from the sun." We brainstorm a list of ways this gendered education might affect women who want to be poets.

Thus far I have given my students an uncomplicated overview of the nineteenth-century ideology of separate feminine and masculine spheres. I have also explained that nineteenth-century critics were constructing poetry as a genre by categorizing popular texts as nonpoetry and high art as real poetry. I now want my students to realize that it is at this historical moment—when the canon is being created and poetry defined as a masculine art form in a closing of ranks response against the incursion of women's texts—that various writers, male and female, assert with renewed vigor the rights of women as educable, moral beings. Integral to this debate is the children's literature that we critics have too easily dismissed, even as the early creators of the canon did. Anna Letitia Barbauld, Ann and Jane Taylor, Hannah More, Lucy Aiken, Mary Wollstonecraft,

Sarah Trimmer, Maria Edgeworth, and many other prominent women writers were notable children's authors. These women could partly evade the censure that haunted them as public figures by writing as mothers, governesses, or moral instructors for an audience traditionally within the feminine province— children. But most important, these children's texts are surprisingly contemporary in their presentations of strong mothers and female teachers; in their demands of educational, literary, and social respect for women; and in their critiques of gender in poetics. My class studies Mary and Charles Lamb's poetry for children, which questions gender roles, and Charlotte Smith's *Conversations Introducing Poetry: Chiefly on Subjects of Natural History: For the Use of Children and Young Persons*, in which a powerful mother teaches her daughter to become a poet not in a sentimental mode but in the classical tradition.

Before I ask students to select a children's poem for close reading, I walk them through my interpretation of Mary Lamb's "What Sort of Thing Is Fancy?," which links literary authority, imagination, and gender. Here, two siblings write three-line stanzas to each other. As they struggle for power within the game's parameters, they exchange a pen. I like to dramatize this poem by having a male and a female student read aloud the brother's and sister's lines as they pass a pen back and forth. The sister first holds the pen and initiates the rules of a friendly interactive game. By the poem's conclusion, the aggressive brother takes control of the pen and "acts the universal knower who thinks that there is a single valid meaning and that he owns it" (M. Myers, "Reading" 66). The sign of the victor is possession of the pen—the phallic object in metaliterary texts. This shift of control over the pen(is) is enacted over the definition of the imagination as the brother takes over the game and forces the sister to guess his definition of *fancy*, deriding her as a dunce. I return to this poem later, when my students discuss Coleridge's definition of creative imagination in reference to texts on the imagination by women: Barbauld's "To Mr. S. T. C[oleridge]" and "The Origin of Song Writing" and Smith's *Elegiac Sonnets* numbers 47, 48, and 70 (Curran, *Poems*).

My students write solid and creative essays on children's poetry, for its accessible diction encourages them to move beyond surface meaning to explore the poems' broader implications. I have received strong responses to several poems by the Lambs: "The First Tooth," in which an elder sister envies the attention a younger brother receives; "The Sister's Expostulation on the Brother's Learning Latin," in which a sister begs a condescending brother for an education; "Written in the First Leaf of a Child's Memorandum Book," which shows a child's concern about beautiful handwriting over the content of her diary; "The Two Boys," which describes a poor boy who can read but can't afford books and a second boy who can eat but can't afford food; "Choosing a Profession," in which a boy thinks about a career; and "To a Young Lady, on Being Too Fond of Music," in which a little girl spends too much energy on her music, neglecting her books.

I copy "Conversation the Tenth" from volume 2 of Charlotte Smith's *Conversations* (159–91): a mother, Mrs. Talbot, criticizes the British education system for encouraging boys to read "heathen mythology; and Ovid, the most fanciful, and by no means the most proper among the Roman poets" (161). Mrs. Talbot requires her son to write his sister a long poem, "Flora," in which he turns garden plants into mythological beings, for the mother wishes to teach her daughter (and her son by extension) that mythology can be learned and taught with propriety if kept within the moral restraints of the domestic space. I ask my students to prepare to contextualize Smith's *Conversations* in the poetic and pedagogical debate of the Romantic era. I initiate discussion by focusing on how Smith's prose sets up her poetry by providing advance information to guide her audience. Alan Richardson's *Literature, Education, and Romanticism* supplies crucial background information on the pedagogical debate and its implications for poetry. When students express interest in writing papers on Smith, I suggest linking *Conversations* to Wollstonecraft's *Original Stories from Real Life: With Conversations Calculated to Regulate the Affections* (illustrated by William Blake) as well as to other children's texts that present strong female mentors. Mitzi Myers's essay on the heroic mother figure, "Impeccable Governesses, Rational Dames, and Moral Mothers" is an excellent bibliographic source for such texts.

My purpose in teaching a survey focused on the construction of the poet is to transmit a sense of poetry as a vibrant, challenged as well as challenging, genre. By discussing how particular writers create identities that valorize their ideals of the poet and poetry, I dispel the off-putting conception of a monolithic, unchanging tradition of masters whose works have risen naturally to the top by intrinsic merit. Instead, my students learn how gender, culture, education, and literature together define the role of a poet and determine who is entitled to fill that role. The exclusionary practices behind subjectivity continue to inform our readings as we move on to later works about the self such as Elizabeth Barrett Browning's *Aurora Leigh*, Walt Whitman's *Song of Myself*, and HD's poems on becoming a poet, "The Master" and "The Dancer." Once my students go beyond asking what a poem says to examine why and how the poem says it, they have acquired a valuable tool for critiquing the conditions of subjectivity as they appear in poetry and other discourses as well. My intention is not only to teach information about poetry and poetics but to provide my students the sophistication to see and critique the power struggles in other contexts and in other claims to subjectivity.

Justification Strategies in the Writings of Joanna Southcott: Teaching Radical Women Poets in Conservative Institutions

Kevin Binfield

Teaching poetry by women of the British Romantic period poses challenges in any setting, given the period's domination by male authors, but in institutions where curricular and pedagogical innovation may be regarded with suspicion, the task is especially formidable. In some schools, revisionist faculty members face classrooms heavily populated by conservative students frequently skeptical of canonical (in both the literary and religious senses) innovations. When I first taught the prophetic works of Joanna Southcott in second- and third-year period surveys at a conservative, church-affiliated college, I found myself justifying the text selection. Eventually, however, I learned to deflect classroom issues of justification away from pedagogy and toward the justification strategies that Southcott and other noncanonical writers used.

Justification is itself an ethical matter: that is, it involves constructing an ethos that evinces values the audience acknowledges. Southcott's task is made difficult by her writing at the convergence of two masculinized public structures—poetry and religion. Sidonie Smith describes the problems facing a woman who, like Southcott, assumes a public role through her writing:

> If she presumes to claim a fully human identity by seeking a place in the public arena . . . she challenges cultural conceptions of the nature of woman and thereby invites public censure for her efforts. If she bows to the discursive pressure for anonymity, however, she denies her desire for a voice of her own. (7–8)

In conservative classrooms, Christian or otherwise, Southcott encounters some of the same pressures and obstacles she did in her day, both as a prophet employing a patriarchal discourse and as a poet writing during a masculinized literary period. The double resistance complicates Southcott's work, but it also presents an opportunity to teachers introducing her work to contemporary students who may initially contest her work, her voice, and her rhetorical self-positioning. Engaging present-day resistances to her *prophetic* claims makes it possible for students to appreciate the resistance that Romantic-period women encounter as *poets* and to recognize the strategies they employed to legitimate their writing.

My students rarely question works by Joanna Baillie and Mary Robinson, mainly because the students typically are less interested in the relation between gender and poetics than in that between gender and religion, but the verses dictated to Southcott by God almost always elicit challenges to her authorial standing—not merely her theological positions or her interpretations of the

Bible but also her right to write on such issues at all. Most of the students bring with them acquired attitudes that regard the idea of a preaching woman as objectionable on its face; this is the discursive pressure they most readily notice. Examining their objections and their sense of women's proper religious roles, then, provides a convenient contextual link to the early nineteenth century.

Establishing a context requires sampling opinions on the place of women in religious life, from essays collected in Joyce Irwin's *Womanhood in Radical Protestantism, 1525–1675* to twentieth-century clerical publications in the misogynist tradition, such as John Rice's *Bobbed Hair, Bossy Wives, and Women Preachers*. Reading within this tradition, students are able to survey an entire self-supporting structure of scriptural objections to women's assuming primary roles as spiritual teachers. The objections that fuel this resistance system are readily forthcoming in classroom discussion. Paul, for example, ascribes to women a moral weakness that demands regulation: "Adam was not deceived but the woman being deceived was in transgression" (1 Tim. 2.14, King James Version). He also limits women's pastoral and prophetic roles— "Let your women keep silence in the churches: for it is not permitted unto them to speak; but they are commanded to be under obedience, as also saith the law" (1 Cor. 14.34)—and advocates familial constraint (Eph. 5.22).

The appearance of systematicity—weakness, limitation, and control—solidifies these objections. Citing contrary Bible passages often avails nothing; it is most practical for the instructor to confront the entire misogynist system rhetorically, appealing to students' values (Bizzell 195, 200). In Margaret Fell's *Women's Speaking Justified, Proved, and Allowed by the Scriptures* and Mary Wollstonecraft's *Vindication of the Rights of Woman*, students find a nascent feminism that claims a space for itself without entirely abrogating traditional Christian and English mores: Wollstonecraft, for example, argues for education that will produce "affectionate wives and rational mothers" (79 [Penguin, 1985]).

Dealing well with the question of tradition is critical. In one class experimenting with marginal epistemic privilege, I found that my direct questions regarding Southcott's special perspective on tradition fell flat. The failure of such questions indicated what should have been obvious—that centrality rather than marginality is the basis of legitimation for students who do not routinely admit epistemic privilege in positions outside fundamental Christianity. Upon reconsideration, I found that in any event the marginal-central dichotomy is inadequate to understanding Southcott's appeal; her position may be marginal, but her justifications depend upon centrality.

In an essay on Phillis Wheatley, Helen Burke recognizes that traditional appeals afford an alternative to justification through marginal privilege (33–34). Like Wollstonecraft and Fell, Southcott must appropriate tradition while creating a place for herself. In much of her writing she directly confronts traditional objections with contrary Bible passages. Most of my students know the Bible well enough to recall a passage or two that a woman might (in the words of one student) "misconstrue as allowing her preaching." In *A Word to the*

Wise, Southcott follows Fell in noting legitimating passages—Joel 2.28–29, Acts 2.17, Galatians 3.28, and 1 Thessalonians 5.19–20. However, countercitation alone fails to undermine the self-supporting misogynist structure. The rest of the lesson involves identifying more systematic strategies of justification.

The pattern that prophetic legitimation follows resembles the poetic equivalent that Burke describes: "To establish a literary identity, to earn the title 'poet,' one had to insert oneself into this tradition, recognizing the tradition, even while asserting one's own right to speak" (34). Southcott's problem is that her tradition prohibits her from championing it. I have my class consider whether it would be better for Southcott to reject the tradition altogether or to embrace it. Asking students to write exegetical essays on passages in Revelation serves well at this point. I intend the assignment in part to generate students' confidence in their authority by allowing them to devise their own justification strategies. The strategies usually fall into identifiable categories: some students affiliate themselves with an existing, supporting discourse; others oppose their own writing to an objectionable text or a text by an objectionable author; some disregard other texts altogether, confident in the effectiveness of their very confidence. After some discussion, they write two different prefaces to Southcott's *The Strange Effects of Faith* (one of her primary prophetic texts)—one rejecting tradition and the other embracing it. The difficulty the students have in rejecting the tradition to which most of them subscribe and its gender-determining forms, even for rhetorical purposes, suggests Southcott's predicament to them. More important, discussing their strategies turns their attention from religion to rhetoric, allowing a more productive investigation to begin.

Southcott inserts herself into a patriarchal tradition by embracing the foundation of Pauline objections to women's preaching—Eve's moral weakness. The continuity of ideas has a stylistic counterpart in the transitions between Southcott's voice and the voice of the inspiring spirit for which, justified by Joel 2.28–29, she claims to be the vehicle. The prefatory remarks of a humble dairymaid give way to verses issuing from the spirit itself. The transitions are abrupt, seldom set apart by any excuse that God is speaking through her. One exemplary passage moves from Southcott's own prose discussion of one follower's salvation to God's verse voice:

> [S]o hereby ye are to know, that Mr. Bruce is brought forth unto the world an heir of God . . . and the promise made to the woman fulfilled.

> So now see clear the shadow's here,
>   She's clothed with the son,
> For all his clothing she does wear,
>   And the tenth year is come.   (*Continuation* 50)

Southcott seems to be commandeered by a divine (male) discourse with a legitimacy of its own. She makes no apologies for her role or for the shift from willfulness to inspiration; a defensive transition would diminish the force of the prophecy by implying a self-aware willfulness.

The uninterrupted transition from Southcott's prose to the spirit's verse reveals a systematicity, continuous with Scripture, that fundamentalist students particularly appreciate. Gaining this hold, Southcott goes on to define her prophecies within a system contradicting systems advocated by male writers. She does not oppose a monolithic patriarchal discourse in her prophecies; rather, she rejects the ideas of particular men, theistic conservatives and deistic Radicals alike, creating in the same movement the potential for both male error and female truth.

Southcott downplays her claims to truth by employing a strategy of self-deprecation similar to the one that Burke describes in Phillis Wheatley (34), but with a variation. Part of Southcott's traditional claim is a comparative yet ironic self-deprecation by which she distinguishes between herself and the learned, the conservators of tradition, so that she might discredit the reproofs of an arrogant "University Religion" removed from the spiritual needs of her working-class audiences (Balleine x):

> And what a proud, conceited fool must I be, to say of myself, I have more knowledge than the learned, and can tell them better than they know from my own wisdom. . . . Shall I say I had the spirit of wisdom given me, when I never had any talents to boast of in my life, and was considered by all my worthy wise brothers and sisters the simplest of my father's house? And I always deemed myself the same; but the Lord hath chosen the weak foolish things of this world, to confound the great and mighty.
> (*Strange Effects* 69)

Through self-deprecation, Southcott inoculates herself against charges of arrogance in rebutting her (male) clerical detractors, such as Jeremiah Garrett. Southcott writes, in her own voice, "I have never ascribed anything to my own self, but this vain man, has ascribed Honor and Power to himself, wisdom and understanding above the race of mankind." The spirit joins Southcott, remarking on the large portrait in the front of Garrett's book that depicts Garrett surrounded by the paraphernalia of faith:

> So from his picture I'll begin,
>   See how he 'th placed it there,
> Upon his head the Cross do stand,
>   Then let him now take care;
> Though over it, he 'th plac'd the crown
>   That ne'er was plac'd by ME
>
> . . . .

> But if he knew my perfect word
> He'd tremble at my rod.   (*Answer to Garrett* 8)

Aspiring to a grand style (familiar to students who regularly read and write religious poetry), the verse balances her self-deprecation by formally corroborat-
ing what her comparative references to Garrett imply—that she, despite
objections, is a worthy vehicle for God's message.

Southcott opposes not only male representatives of tradition but also those
who threaten tradition. Extracts from Thomas Paine's *Age of Reason* provoke
most students into faulting his scientific materialism, his deism, and his attacks
on conventional Christianity, making it possible to see Southcott as a moderate
of sorts, especially in *An Answer to Thomas Paine's Third Part of* The Age of
Reason.

Situating her writings between extremes, Southcott claims a central position
from which she can utilize her most refined strategy—the fulfillment trope.
Fulfillment refers to patterns of completion and inversion. Southcottian and
biblical prophecies raise the expectation (held by fundamentalist students) that
the weak and humble have a place in a divinely mandated whole. Like Fell,
Southcott posits a woman's spiritual role that is defined by the enmity between
her seed and the serpent's (Fell 677–78; *Word* 16). The woman, through her
special place, becomes champion of a system that previously had excluded her;
however, her new centrality is only the place from which she must redeem herself and a world whose fall she wrought. A millenarian fulfillment can occur
only through a metaphysical undoing, "the Woman's" redemption against "her
Foe," Satan: " 'Twas by a woman, *first the deed was done*; / Because she did the
serpent first obey, / To bring it back must turn the other way" (*Word* 27).

By treating strategies of justification as Southcott does, as negotiations over
values rather than as marginal assaults upon a traditional system, it is possible
to situate her prophetic verses within a tradition that pretends to exclude them.
Southcott is able to embrace the very premises that bar her prophecies, trans-
forming marginality into centrality when she writes, "[T]he woman must be ar-
rayed in the glory of My Spirit, before Man that is born of a woman can be
redeemed" (*Word* 31). By its claims to legitimacy in both position and practice,
her writing is not merely justified; it is necessary and systematic in a way that
students can come more fully to appreciate, no matter what their religious or
ideological orientation.

Sight, Sound, and Sense:
L. E. L.'s Multimedia Productions

Glenn T. Dibert-Himes

Of the more than thirteen hundred works that Letitia Elizabeth Landon (L. E. L.) published between 1820 and her untimely death in 1839, she considered her work in the British literary annuals her best. Her contributions—usually poetic responses to engravings printed with the text—offered what we might call an early-nineteenth-century multimedia presentation involving verbal and visual components. Occasionally the publisher provided a musical score to accompany a poem. In this essay I use "Cottage Courtship," from the 1835 edition of *Fisher's Drawing-Room Scrapbook*, as a representative example.

L. E. L.'s interdisciplinary art offers a wonderful opportunity to the instructor devising and teaching an introductory community-college literature course. One of my courses, Modern Literature, presents a multicultural perspective on literary production to beginning students; the instructor decides which writers to include and how to mix and measure them. I structure my syllabus around modules; we study L. E. L. in the module Nineteenth Century Literature—Romanticism to Realism.

Since L. E. L. is not in our anthology, I photocopy a handout from *Fisher's*. In addition, using a high-resolution flatbed scanner I prepare versions of several of L. E. L.'s texts, which I store on a CD-ROM; I then can project the engravings that accompany many of the texts onto a large screen during discussion. (Because of the rapid evolution of digital technology and the availability of many useful software programs and peripherals, I describe technical requirements here in general terms.) The projection equipment I use allows us to zoom in and expand sections of the engravings in order to discuss even minute details. Because one can use commonly available technology such as DAT recorders and digital-editing software to record sound directly to the CD-ROM for easy playback, I could incorporate into this interdisciplinary teaching package a recording of the musical version of "Cottage Courtship" composed by Henry Russell, which a graduate student performed for me. I use the handouts and multimedia materials in several ways. First we discuss nineteenth-century British "coffee-table books"; I usually bring an annual to class, so that students can handle an important cultural artifact—a staple of any fashionable British drawing room. Second, the contemporary popularity of the annuals can prompt broader discussion about popular culture and literature, eliciting questions that allow me to introduce students to other British women writers of the Romantic period who created widely popular works.

Third, teaching "Cottage Courtship" allows us to explore the intricate dynamics of L. E. L.'s work. When the students receive the printouts, they are initially drawn especially to the engraving, which sets up certain natural expectations about what the verbal text will contain. However, in the next class, after the students have studied the poem, they often express surprise at the in-congruities between the engraving and the poem. Their comments open a dis-cussion of reader response and of how the author manipulates the reader's perception to create a certain effect. Noting the contrasts and the occasional outright contradictions in "Cottage Courtship," we can consider how L. E. L. and other Romantic writers invited a synthetic response to the two components. The engraving for the poem at hand sets up expectations that the verbal text un-dermines, while the audio (musical) text complicates matters further still.

For the late Romantic reader as for the modern student, the physical setting in "Cottage Courtship" was established through the engraving, in which an ap-parent suitor dutifully visits the cottage home of a young woman. Also at the cottage is the young woman's family, which includes father and mother, chil-dren, and even the family cat. The setting is innocuous, but the expressions on the faces of the family members are anything but tranquil. The father and mother, eyes barely raised, glance sheepishly toward the expectant young man. One child turns to the old man to be picked up, and the little one in front leans back in apparent alarm. During the session in which we first begin to consider L. E. L.'s poem, and before I hand out the poem itself or play the music, I ask the students to write out their responses to the engraving and then to read some of the responses aloud. The exercise usually produces a spontaneous dis-cussion, since the students typically are excited by the variety in their re-sponses. Often they focus on the young man who is saluting the family, many students commenting on his quaint and, in their view, archaic responsibility to face the family. However, L. E. L. focuses not on him but on the young woman, creating a dramatic monologue that moves behind the surface drama of the vi-sual image and into the young woman's mind.

As we begin discussing the poem, I first zoom in on the young woman's face in the projection of the engraving. I point out that since the poem was written in response to the engraving, we might assume that the speaker is the young woman. Her countenance in the engraving is, interestingly, none too happy. Somewhat stooped and seemingly uncomfortable, her eyes downcast, she seems more resigned to what is happening than excited or flattered. I read the poem to the class and suggest that we inquire whether various sections of the poem might indicate unexpected inner responses of the speaker to the scene.

The first stanza, for instance, might lead us to suspect that the speaker's strategy is to be preemptive. Certainly we can see from the image that she is not smiling, yet the first line speaks of someone who is. The reference is to the young man, whose expectant countenance she acknowledges even as she com-mits herself to seldom smiling, so that her future mate will not hold her smiles in too light esteem. In other words, the young woman may have adopted a strategy to avoid being taken for granted.

In the second stanza the young woman further reveals her resistance to dom-ination, insisting, "'Tis not kindness keeps a lover / He must feel the chain he wears" (9–10). Apparently, she is looking ahead to a time when the romantic enchantment of courtship is over and she becomes dependent and thus vulnerable. I point out that women's vulnerability to men was a persistent theme in L. E. L.'s poetry and that as a consequence of being bound to a lover, the woman in her poems is almost always destroyed and often ends up dead. In "Cottage Courtship" the speaker suggests a possible defense: maintaining a distance between herself and her lover, so that her husband becomes dependent instead of her. I like to hand out copies of Andrew Marvell's "To My Coy Mistress," so that we can discuss the very different perspective of the male speaker toward his lover's strategy. Not surprisingly, an animated debate on gender roles and gender relations often ensues.

Eventually, we move on to the third stanza of L. E. L.'s poem, in which the speaker expresses a fairly open suspicion of men and their motives in marriages. She ends with this advice to her female audience: "Their torment is your gain; / Would you keep your own heart scathless, / Be the one to give the pain" (22–24). That women constituted the primary audiences for the annuals, as I remind students, lends weight to the speaker's admonition.

Once we work through the poem, students discover that it completely recasts the situation presented in the engraving. I then introduce Russell's score and a recording of it to contextualize yet another recasting of L. E. L.'s theme. I again remind the students of the annuals' social role in the British parlor, where they were placed so as to invite one to page through them when conversation waned or while one waited for the host. I also point out that British sitting rooms were often equipped with pianos and that people might spend many evenings around the piano enjoying popular songs. L. E. L. targeted just such gatherings by including musical scores (there are three in the *Fisher's* containing "Cottage Courtship"), ensuring that her poetry could be sung as well as read. The score's unexpectedly light and airy sound yields yet another paradoxical contrast to the poem's harsh tone. When I play the recording, I usually ask the class to picture a nineteenth-century woman standing next to the piano in a lavishly furnished parlor singing the song and to consider the irony of pairing that image with the text. Things are frequently not what they might seem in "Young Ladies' Verses" of the early nineteenth century.

Students in my classes get caught up in this early-nineteenth-century multimedia art. Though response usually follows the scenario I describe above, students often move the discussions in different directions, which frequently involve aspects of modern interdisciplinary popular culture and art. Regardless, presenting L. E. L.'s work in the multidisciplinary fashion she intended presents many opportunities to contextualize nineteenth-century literature and its interdisciplinary aspects. "Cottage Courtship" has proved an effective vehicle for introducing some of the major themes and phenomena that the class goes on to explore further in connection with later works. Given L. E. L.'s historical position at the intersection of the Romantic and Victorian periods, her work holds equally broad promise for courses limited to the nineteenth century.

By including multimedia materials in my courses I hope to provide ways for my students to contextualize the literature we discuss. The sensory elements that multimedia applications allow me to bring into the classroom enhance instruction in a way that traditional methods cannot. The digital images I collect for my course, such as reproductions of rare nineteenth-century texts, constitute a permanent resource and give students access to important cultural artifacts not held by many libraries. The interactive experience I present in multimedia class sessions allows students to structure their own learning experiences—to explore material at their own paces, to sample material in any order, and to pause to take notes or repeat sequences.

I usually ask students for short feedback essays after a multimedia session. I estimate that at least ninety percent of the students ask for more material, which I find encouraging. Students ask me to add more of the audio commentaries that I record and include on the CD-ROMs; many ask for more music and visual art from the time. Because the sessions energize our subsequent discussions and our more traditional classroom activities, I place them strategically throughout the semester (one every two to three weeks); we mine these peak instructional moments through writing miniresearch projects (often team projects involving class presentations) and discussions.

I develop multimedia teaching tools to use in two teaching situations. In the first I project a presentation in front of the class while lecturing or holding spontaneous class discussions of the presented material. Most liquid-crystal-display front-projection systems allow for computer-generated graphics, sound, and video. The second presentation environment, and the one I prefer, is the multistation electronic classroom, which allows students truly to interact with the material. Each student is equipped with a computer, headphones, and the interactive program. During the session I move around the classroom and talk with students. The students not talking to me continue with the program, so that the class is not placed on hold while I address one student's concerns. Since I can project the components of these applications in front of the class or even place them on reserve in the library, I prepare all the packages as fully integrated multimedia applications.

I should point out—probably to the relief of some readers—that I am by no means a computer whiz. Yet I have very much enjoyed developing multimedia materials for my students, using wonderful software for the nonspecialist. The software allows users to diagram presentations automatically simply by dropping icons that represent preprogrammed functions onto a flow line. For example, the program might contain icons for adding and using audio or video files, graphics, or text. A selection menu shows the icons for the available functions. Having established the sequence of functions, the instructor imports the desired content—that is, copies the files into the proper points in the flow line—and the program does the rest. Many of these programs also contain ready-to-use flow lines, which allow the author to create a multimedia package without designing it from scratch. A consultant at one of the New Media Centers belonging to the

New Media Center Consortium can provide more information about user-friendly software systems. (The New Media Center Consortium is a group of college and university New Media Centers that are working in conjunction with software and hardware companies to provide faculty members support in developing multimedia instructional materials. As of this writing nearly one hundred New Media Centers nationwide participate in the consortium.)

After determining what I want to do and the kind of software I need, I work up a rough storyboard, a hard-copy layout resembling the structure of a World Wide Web site: my students can follow hyperlinks in the finished package as if browsing on the Web. I can allow the same sort of browsing if I am using the application for front projection, as in the "Cottage Courtship" presentation. I can work with the class interactively, and we do not need to examine material in a rigid linear order. When I draw up the storyboard, I try to link the sections to one another so as to allow users to explore all the material by choosing a number of possible routes. The links appear in the finished applications as on-screen devices including icons, "hot spots," "return buttons," and "click-on objects."

Once I have finished the storyboard, I use scanners to digitize images and to include texts. I always scan images at very high resolutions because one can print good-quality hard copy from high-resolution files and can use the files for digital applications. Then I create scripts for any audio commentary I might wish to include (I find that students like one- to three-minute clips), edit music I might need, and finally record video segments. I convert all these materials into digital files that I can import. I always try to leave plenty of time to polish the application. Once the package is running smoothly, I copy it to a CD-ROM. It is now ready for use; it can be run from the disk at a computer, copied to a server for multiple users on a network, or projected onto a screen.

NOTES ON CONTRIBUTORS

Stephen C. Behrendt is George Holmes Distinguished Professor of English at the University of Nebraska, Lincoln, and author of *Shelley and His Audiences* (1989), *Reading William Blake* (1992), and *Royal Mourning and Regency Culture: Elegies and Memorials of Princess Charlotte* (1997). He edited *Approaches to Teaching Shelley's Frankenstein* (1990). He is currently working on a book about British women writers and radicalism in the Romantic period.

Kevin Binfield is assistant professor of English at Murray State University, where his teaching includes courses in British Romanticism, literary theory, and rhetoric. In addition to his research on nineteenth-century British working-class and radical authors, he is editing a collection of Luddite writings and an edition of the works of Joanna Southcott.

Catherine B. Burroughs, associate professor of English at Cornell College, is interested in English Romantic theater and women's theater theory. She has published widely on Joanna Baillie and on Romantic theater and is the author of *Closet Stages: Joanna Baillie and the Theater Theory of British Romantic Women Writers* (1997).

Kay K. Cook is associate professor and associate chair of language and literature at Southern Utah University, where her teaching includes courses in British Romanticism, women's studies, autobiography, and playwriting. She has published numerous studies on autobiographical writing. Among her current projects is a book on Dorothy Wordsworth's *Grasmere Journals*.

Stuart Curran is Vartan Gregorian Professor of English and director of the Center for Italian Studies at the University of Pennsylvania. In addition to books on Percy Bysshe Shelley, he is the author of *Poetic Form and British Romanticism* (1986) and editor of *The Poems of Charlotte Smith* (1993) and *The Cambridge Companion to British Romanticism* (1993). Among his current projects is a hypertext CD-ROM edition of *Frankenstein*.

Glenn T. Dibert-Himes is a research fellow of the British Royal Academy. He is at Sheffield Hallam University, England, where he is studying the Edition Corvey, a Romantic-era library in Germany. He has published on L. E. L. and is working on multimedia projects about her and a book about British publishing in her contemporary period.

Julie Ellison is professor of English and associate vice president for research at the University of Michigan, Ann Arbor. Her interests encompass British and American literature of the eighteenth and nineteenth centuries. She is the author of *Emerson's Romantic Style* (1984) and *Delicate Subjects: Romanticism, Gender, and the Ethics of Understanding* (1990) and is working on a book-length study of politics and emotion in eighteenth-century Anglo-American writing.

Mary A. Favret, associate professor of English at Indiana University, Bloomington, is the author of *Romantic Correspondence: Women, Politics, and the Fiction of Letters* (1993) and the coeditor of *At the Limits of Romanticism* (1994). Her teaching and research interests in British Romanticism include gender and genre. She is working on a book about violence in Romanticism.

Elizabeth Fay, associate professor of English at the University of Massachusetts, Boston, is the author of *Feminist Introduction to Romanticism* (forthcoming). Her other books include *Becoming Wordsworthian: A Performative Aesthetics* (1995) and *Eminent Rhetoric: Language, Gender, and Cultural Tropes* (1994).

Paula R. Feldman, professor of English at the University of South Carolina, Columbia, is coeditor of *The Journals of Mary Shelley* (1987) and *Romantic Women Writers: Voices and Countervoices* (1995). She has also edited *British Women Poets of the Romantic Era: An Anthology* (1997). Among her ongoing projects is an edition of Felicia Hemans's *Records of Woman*.

Joel Haefner teaches at Illinois State University, where he serves as a coordinator of academic computing. He has published on various aspects of women writers of the Romantic period and is the coeditor of *Re-visioning Romanticism: British Women Writers, 1776–1837* (1994).

Madeleine Kahn is associate professor of English at Mills College, where her teaching includes eighteenth-century literature, feminist theory and pedagogy, and gender studies. Her publications include *Narrative Transvestitism: Rhetoric and Gender in the Eighteenth-Century English Novel* (1991) and articles on nineteenth-century topics. She is at work on a book on teaching at a women's college.

Deborah Kennedy is assistant professor of English at Saint Mary's University in Nova Scotia. Her research has appeared in *Philological Quarterly*, *Victorian Poetry*, and *Women's Writing*. She is completing a book on Helen Maria Williams.

Jane King is a graduate student at the University of California, Davis, where she is completing her dissertation on women Romantic poets' intertextuality and female bonding, particularly in poems that explore solitude and abandonment.

Greg Kucich, associate professor at the University of Notre Dame, is coeditor of *Nineteenth-Century Contexts*. In addition to *Keats, Shelley, and Romantic Spenserianism* (1991), he has published articles on Romanticism, gender, and historical invention. His current projects include a book on Romanticism and the gendering of history.

Becky Lewis, coprincipal of Preston College, University of South Carolina, Columbia, numbers among her research and teaching interests nineteenth-century British women writers, illustration, periodicals, and publishing history. She is currently writing on illustrations of women in British periodicals of the 1890s.

Harriet Kramer Linkin is associate professor of English at New Mexico State University, Las Cruces, where she teaches courses in Romanticism and gender, women writers, and gender and language. She has published on William Blake, on gender issues, and on Romanticism and pedagogy. She is completing a book on Mary Tighe.

Kari Lokke is associate professor of English and comparative literature at the University of California, Davis, where she does research in areas including French, German, and English Romanticism, as well as women writers and aesthetics. She has published

Gérard de Nerval: The Poet as Social Visionary and is working on a book on transcendence in novels by Germaine de Staël, Mary Shelley, Bettine von Arnim, and George Sand.

Anne K. Mellor is professor of English at the University of California, Los Angeles. She has written *Mary Shelley: Her Life, Her Fiction, Her Monsters* (1988) and *Romanticism and Gender* (1993) and coedited *British Literature, 1780–1830* (1996). Her research and teaching emphases include Romantic literature and gender, feminist theory, and women writers and the public sphere.

Judith Pascoe is assistant professor of English at the University of Iowa, where her research and teaching centers on late-eighteenth- and early-nineteenth-century British literature and culture. She is the author of *Romantic Theatricality: Gender, Poetry, and Spectatorship* (1997).

Alan Richardson, professor of English at Boston College, works broadly in all areas of British Romantic writing, including children's literature, gender studies, and colonial discourse. His most recent book is *Literature, Education, and Romanticism: Reading as Social Practice, 1780–1832*. His projects include a study of the relation of Romantic-era psychology to the unconscious, sensibility, and the brain.

Donelle R. Ruwe is assistant professor of English at Fitchburg State College. Her research and teaching interests include nineteenth-century British women poets and creative writing. A member of the governing board of the Eighteenth- and Nineteenth-Century British Women Writers Association, she has published, in addition to her own poetry, studies of Native American literature and women's poetry.

Scott Simpkins is associate professor of English at the University of North Texas. He is the editor of *Studies in the Novel*, and he has published widely on Romanticism, modern literature, and semiotics. He is working on book-length studies of the Romantics' subversion of the book and their literary representations of stigma.

Nanora Sweet is senior lecturer at the University of Missouri, St. Louis, where she teaches courses in British Romanticism and feminist criticism. Her articles on Hemans and international Romanticism are appearing in *At the Limits of Romanticism*, *The Lessons of Romanticism*, *European Romantic Review*, and elsewhere. She is coediting a volume of essays on Hemans with Julie Melnyk.

Carol Shiner Wilson has taught literature and women's studies at Muhlenberg College, where she is dean of the College for Academic Life. She is the coeditor of *Re-visioning Romanticism: British Women Writers, 1776–1837* (1994) and is the editor of *The Galesia Trilogy and Selected Poems by Jane Barker* (1997). She is working on a study of needlework in Anglo-American literature and culture.

Susan J. Wolfson is professor of English at Princeton University. Her most recent books include *Formal Charges: The Shaping of Poetic Form in British Romanticism* (1996) and *Figures on the Margin: The Language of Gender in British Romanticism* (1998). In addition to coediting two anthologies of Romantic literature currently in preparation, she continues her research in poetic form, aesthetic ideology, and gender in Romantic writing.

Sarah M. Zimmerman is assistant professor of English at the University of Wisconsin, Madison, where she teaches courses in late-eighteenth-century and Romantic poetry and prose and in critical theory. She has published on Charlotte Smith, Percy Bysshe Shelley, and John Clare and is completing a study entitled *Romanticism, Lyricism, and History*.

SURVEY PARTICIPANTS

The following scholars and teachers generously agreed to participate in the survey of approaches to teaching British women poets of the Romantic period that preceded the preparation of this volume. Many responded in great detail, and even those who reported only that their own courses do not routinely include any of these authors made welcome contributions. To all these good colleagues we extend our gratitude. Without their assistance, their support, and their many suggestions, this volume would not have been possible.

M. H. Abrams, *Cornell University*
John M. Anderson, *Boston University*
Isobel Armstrong, *University of London*
Timothy R. Austin, *Loyola University, Chicago*
Kevin Binfield, *Murray State University*
Diana Bowstead, *Hunter College, City University of New York*
William D. Brewer, *Appalachian State University*
Catherine B. Burroughs, *Cornell College*
Kay K. Cook, *Southern Utah University*
Stuart Curran, *University of Pennsylvania*
Glenn T. Dibert-Himes, *Sheffield Hallam University*
Julie Ellison, *University of Michigan, Ann Arbor*
Mary A. Favret, *Indiana University, Bloomington*
Elizabeth Fay, *University of Massachusetts, Boston*
Paula R. Feldman, *University of South Carolina, Columbia*
Michael Ferber, *University of New Hampshire, Durham*
Joel Haefner, *Illinois State University*
Kathleen Hickok, *Iowa State University*
Sonia Hofkosh, *Tufts University*
Frank Jordan, *Miami University, Ohio*
Madeleine Kahn, *Mills College*
Deborah Kennedy, *Saint Mary's University*
Jane King, *University of California, Davis*
Katharine Kittredge, *Ithaca College*
Greg Kucich, *University of Notre Dame*
Becky Lewis, *University of South Carolina, Columbia*
Kari Lokke, *University of California, Davis*
Marlene Longenecker, *Ohio State University, Columbus*
Jerome J. McGann, *University of Virginia*
Anne K. Mellor, *University of California, Los Angeles*
Margaret M. Morlier, *Auburn University*
Judith Pascoe, *University of Iowa*
Linda H. Peterson, *Yale University*
John G. Pipkin, *Rice University*
Alan Richardson, *Boston College*

Susan J. Rosowski, *University of Nebraska, Lincoln*
Marlon Ross, *University of Michigan, Ann Arbor*
Donelle R. Ruwe, *Fitchburg State College*
Richard C. Sha, *American University*
Scott Simpkins, *University of North Texas*
Nanora Sweet, *University of Missouri, St. Louis*
Leonard Trawick, *Cleveland State University*
Herbert Tucker, *University of Virginia*
Heidi Van de Veire, *Victoria University*
Constance Walker, *Carlton College*
Keith Welsh, *Webster University*
Carol Shiner Wilson, *Muhlenberg College*
Susan J. Wolfson, *Princeton University*
Sarah M. Zimmerman, *University of Wisconsin, Madison*

WORKS CITED

Aaron, Jane. *A Double Singleness: Gender and the Writings of Charles and Mary Lamb.* New York: Oxford UP, 1991.

———. "'On Needle-work': Protest and Contradiction in Mary Lamb's Essay." Mellor, *Romanticism and Feminism* 167–84.

———. "The Way above the World: Religion and Gender in Welsh and Anglo-Welsh Women's Writing, 1780–1830." Wilson and Haefner 111–27.

Abrams, Meyer H. "English Romanticism: The Spirit of the Age." *Romanticism Reconsidered: Selected Papers from the English Institute.* Ed. Northrop Frye. New York: Columbia UP, 1963. 26–72.

———. *Natural Supernaturalism.* New York: Norton, 1971.

———, ed. *The Norton Anthology of English Literature.* 6th ed. Vol. 2. New York: Norton, 1993.

Adburgham, Alison. *Women in Print: Writing Women and Women's Magazines from the Restoration to the Accession of Victoria.* London: Allen, 1972.

Agress, Lynne. *The Feminine Irony: Women on Women in Early Nineteenth-Century English Literature.* Madison: Fairleigh Dickinson UP, 1978.

Aiken, Lucy. *Epistles on Women, Exemplifying Their Character and Condition in Various Ages and Nations.* London: Johnson, 1810.

Alexander, Meena. "Dorothy Wordsworth: The Grounds of Writing." *Women's Studies* 14 (1988): 195–210.

———. *Women in Romanticism: Mary Wollstonecraft, Dorothy Wordsworth, and Mary Shelley.* New York: Barnes, 1989.

Alston, R. C. *A Checklist of Women Writers, 1801–1900: Fiction, Verse, Drama.* London: British Lib., 1990.

Altick, Richard D. *The English Common Reader: A Social History of the Mass Reading Public, 1800–1900.* Chicago: U of Chicago P, 1957.

Anderson, John M. "'The First Fire': Barbauld Rewrites the Greater Romantic Lyric." *SEL* 34 (1994): 719–38.

Arac, Jonathan. *Critical Genealogies: Historical Situations for Postmodern Literary Studies.* New York: Columbia UP, 1989.

Armstrong, Isobel. "The Gush of the Feminine: How Can We Read Women's Poetry of the Romantic Period?" Feldman and Kelley 13–32.

———. *Victorian Poetry: Poetry, Poetics, and Politics.* New York: Routledge, 1993.

Armstrong, Nancy. *Desire and Domestic Fiction: A Political History of the Novel.* New York: Oxford UP, 1987.

Ashfield, Andrew, ed. *Women Romantic Poets, 1770–1838.* New York: St. Martin's, 1995.

Astell, Mary. *The Christian Religion.* London: Wilkin, 1705.

Auerbach, Nina. *Communities of Women: An Idea in Fiction.* Cambridge: Harvard UP, 1987.

————. *Romantic Imprisonment: Women and Other Glorified Outcasts*. New York: Columbia UP, 1985.

Austen, Jane. *The History of England*. London: British Lib., 1993.

————. *Northanger Abbey*. London: Penguin, 1985.

Baillie, Joanna. *The Dramatic and Poetical Works*. 1851. Hildesheim, Ger.: Olms, 1976.

————. *A Series of Plays: In Which It Is Attempted to Delineate the Stronger Passions of the Mind*. 3 vols. London: Longman, 1821.

Balleine, G. R. *Past Finding Out: The Tragic Story of Joanna Southcott and Her Successors*. New York: Macmillan, 1956.

Barbauld, Anna. *The Works, with a Memoir by Lucy Aikin*. Vol. 1. Ed. Lucy Aikin. London: Longman, 1825.

Barker-Benfield, G. J. *The Culture of Sensibility: Sex and Society in Eighteenth-Century Britain*. Chicago: U of Chicago P, 1992.

Barrell, John. *English Literature in History, 1730–80: An Equal, Wide Survey*. New York: St. Martin's, 1983.

Bath, Elizabeth. *Poems, on Various Occasions*. Bristol: Desmond, 1806.

Behrendt, Stephen C. "Anthologizing British Women Poets of the Romantic Period: The Scene Today." *Critical Matrix: The Princeton Journal of Women, Gender, and Culture* 9.1 (1995): 95–105.

————. "Mary Shelley, *Frankenstein*, and the Woman Writer's Fate." Feldman and Kelley 69–87.

————. "Questioning the Romantic Novel." *Studies in the Novel* 26 (1994): 5–25.

Belenky, Mary Field, Blythe McVicker Clinchy, Nancy Rule Goldberger, and Jill Mattuck Tarule. *Women's Ways of Knowing: The Development of Self, Voice, and Mind*. New York: Basic, 1986.

Bennett, Betty T., ed. *British War Poetry in the Age of Romanticism: 1793–1815*. New York: Garland, 1976.

Benstock, Shari, ed. *Feminist Issues in Literary Scholarship*. Bloomington: Indiana UP, 1987.

Berry, Mary. *Extracts of the Journals and Correspondence of Miss Berry, from the Year 1783 to 1852*. Ed. Lady Theresa Lewis. Vol. 2. London: Longmans, 1865. 6 vols.

Betham, Mary Matilda. *A Biographical Dictionary of the Celebrated Women of Every Age and Country*. London: Crosby, 1804.

Bethune, George W. *The Female Poets: With Biographical and Critical Notices*. Philadelphia: Lindsay, 1848.

Bewell, Alan. *Wordsworth and the Enlightenment*. New Haven: Yale UP, 1989.

Bizzell, Patricia. "The Teacher's Authority: Negotiating Difference in the Classroom." *Changing Classroom Practices: Resources for Literary and Cultural Studies*. Ed. David B. Downing. Urbana: NCTE, 1994. 194–201.

Blain, Virginia, Patricia Clements, and Isobel Grundy, eds. *The Feminist Companion to Literature in English: Women Writers from the Middle Ages to the Present*. London: Batsford, 1990.

Blake, William. *The Marriage of Heaven and Hell*. *The Complete Poetry and Prose of William Blake*. Ed. David V. Erdman. Garden City: Anchor, 1982. 33–45.

————. *William Blake's Poetry and Designs*. Ed. Mary Lynn Johnson and John E. Grant. New York: Norton, 1979.

Blamire, Susanna. *The Poetical Works of Miss Susanna Blamire, "The Muse of Cumberland."* Comp. Henry Lonsdale. Preface, memoir, and notes by Patrick Maxwell. Edinburgh: Menzies, 1842.

Blanchard, Laman. *The Life and Literary Remains of L. E. L.* 2 vols. Philadelphia: Lea, 1841.

Bolter, Jay David. *Writing Space: The Computer, Hypertext, and the History of Writing*. Hillsdale: Erlbaum, 1991.

Boyle, Andrew. *An Index to the Annuals*. Worcester: Boyle, 1967.

Breen, Jennifer, ed. *Women Romantic Poets: 1785–1832*. London: Dent, 1992, 1994.

Brewer, William D. "The Prefaces of Joanna Baillie and William Wordsworth." *The Friend: Comments on Romanticism* 1.2 (1991): 34–47.

Browne [Hemans], Felicia Dorothea. *Poems*. Liverpool: Cadell, 1808.

Buck, Claire, ed. *The Bloomsbury Guide to Women's Literature*. New York: Prentice, 1992.

Burke, Edmund. *Reflections on the Revolution in France*. Ed. William B. Todd. 1790. New York: Rinehart, 1959.

Burke, Helen. "The Rhetoric and Politics of Marginality: The Subject of Phillis Wheatley." *Tulsa Studies in Women's Literature* 10 (1991): 31–45.

Burns, Robert. *The Works of Robert Burns*. Ed. John Wilson. Glasgow: Fullarton, 1852.

Burroughs, Catherine B. "The English Romantic Closet: Women Theatre Artists, Joanna Baillie, and *Basil*." *Nineteenth-Century Contexts* 19 (1995): 125–49.

————. "English Romantic Women Writers and Theatre Theory: Joanna Baillie's Prefaces to the *Plays on the Passions*." Wilson and Haefner 274–96.

Bush, Vannevar. "As We May Think." *Atlantic Monthly* July 1945: 101–08.

Butler, Judith. *Gender Trouble: Feminism and the Subversion of Identity*. New York: Routledge, 1990.

Butler, Marilyn. *Maria Edgeworth: A Literary Biography*. Oxford: Oxford UP, 1972.

————. *Romantics, Rebels, and Reactionaries: English Literature and Its Background*. Oxford: Oxford UP, 1981.

Byron, Lord. *The Complete Poetical Works*. Ed. Jerome J. McGann and Barry Weller. Vol. 2. New York: Oxford UP, 1980. 6 vols. to date. 1980– .

Calliope; or, The Musical Miscellany: A Select Collection of the Most Approved English, Scots, and Irish Songs Set to Music. London: Elliot, 1788.

Candler, Ann. *Poetical Attempts, by Ann Candler, a Suffolk Cottager, with a Short Narrative of Her Life*. Ipswich: Raw, 1803.

Cantor, Paul. "Stoning the Romance: The Ideological Critique of Nineteenth-Century Literature." *South Atlantic Quarterly* 88 (1989): 705–20.

Carhart, Margaret S. *The Life and Work of Joanna Baillie*. Yale Studies in English 64. Ed. Albert S. Cook. New Haven: Yale UP, 1923.

Carlson, Julie. *In the Theatre of Romanticism: Coleridge, Nationalism, Women*. Cambridge: Cambridge UP, 1994.

"Carolina, Baroness Nairne." *DNB*. 1968.

Case, Sue-Ellen. *Feminism and Theatre*. New York: Methuen, 1988.

Chambers, Robert, ed. *Cyclopaedia of English Literature*. 2 vols. Boston: Gould, 1853.

Chambers, William, and Robert Chambers. *Chambers' Edinburgh Journal* 11 (1842): 238–39.

Charney, Davida. "The Effect of Hypertext on Processes of Reading and Writing." Selfe and Hilligoss 238–63.

Chodorow, Nancy. *The Reproduction of Mothering: Psychoanalysis and the Sociology of Gender*. Berkeley: U of California P, 1978.

Chorley, Henry F. *Memorials of Mrs. Hemans, with Illustrations of Her Literary Character from Her Private Correspondence*. 2 vols. London: Saunders, 1836.

Cixous, Hélène. "The Laugh of the Medusa." *The Rhetorical Tradition: Readings from Classical Times to the Present*. Ed. Patricia Bizzell and Bruce Herzberg. Boston: Bedford–St. Martin's, 1990. 1232–45.

Claridge, Laura, and Elizabeth Langland, eds. *Out of Bounds: Male Writers and Gender(ed) Criticism*. Amherst: U of Massachusetts P, 1990.

Clarke, Norma. *Ambitious Heights: Writing, Friendship, Love: The Jewsbury Sisters, Felicia Hemans, and Jane Welsh Carlyle*. New York: Routledge, 1990.

Clive, John. *Scotch Reviewers: The Edinburgh Review, 1802–1815*. Cambridge: Harvard UP, 1957.

Cole, Lucinda, and Richard G. Swartz. "'Why Should I Wish for Words?': Literacy, Articulation, and the Borders of Literary Culture." Favret and Watson 143–69.

Coleridge, Samuel Taylor. *Biographia Literaria*. Ed. James Engell and Walter Jackson Bate. Vol. 1. Princeton: Princeton UP, 1983.

———. *The Complete Poetical and Dramatic Works*. Ed. James Dykes Campbell. London: Macmillan, 1938.

———. "Introduction to the Sonnets." 1796. Rpt. in Coleridge, *Works* 542–44.

Colley, Linda. *Britons: Forging the Nation, 1707–1807*. New Haven: Yale UP, 1992.

Cook, Albert. *Canons and Wisdom*. Philadelphia: U of Pennsylvania P, 1993.

Cook, Kay. "Immersion." *A/B: Auto/Biography Studies* 10 (1995): 66–80.

———. "'I Will Not Quarrel with Myself'": Dorothy Wordsworth, Subjectivity, and Romantic Autobiography." Diss. U of Colorado, Boulder, 1992.

———. "Self-Neglect in the Canon: Why Don't We Talk about Romantic Autobiography?" *A/B: Auto/Biography Studies* 5 (1990): 88–98.

Copley, Stephen, and John Whale, eds. *Beyond Romanticism: New Approaches to Texts and Contexts, 1780–1832*. Syracuse: Syracuse UP, 1991.

Courtney, Janet E. *The Adventurous Thirties: A Chapter in the Women's Movement*. 1933. Freeport: Books for Lib., 1967.

Cowper, William. *The Poems of William Cowper*. Ed. John D. Baird and Charles Ryskamp. Vol. 3. Oxford: Clarendon, 1995.

Cox, Jeffrey N., ed. *Seven Gothic Dramas, 1789–1825*. Athens: Ohio UP, 1992.

Cristall, Ann Batten. *Poetical Sketches*. London: Johnson, 1795.

[Croker, John Wilson]. Rev. of *Endymion*, by John Keats. *Quarterly Review* 19 (1818): 204–08.

Croker, M. S. *A Monody on the Lamented Death of Her Royal Highness the Princess Charlotte-Augusta of Wales and of Saxe Cobourg Saalfield*. London: Lloyd, 1817.

Crosby, Christina. *The Ends of History*. New York: Routledge, 1991.

Curran, Stuart, ed. *The Cambridge Companion to British Romanticism*. Cambridge: Cambridge UP, 1993.

———. "Charlotte Smith and British Romanticism." *South Central Review* 11.2 (1994): 66–78.

———. "Mary Robinson's *Lyrical Tales* in Context." Wilson and Haefner 17–35.

———, ed. *The Poems of Charlotte Smith*. New York: Oxford UP, 1993.

———. *Poetic Form and British Romanticism*. New York: Oxford UP, 1986.

———. "Romantic Poetry: The 'I' Altered." Mellor, *Romanticism and Feminism* 185–207.

———. "Romantic Poetry: Why and Wherefore?" Curran, *Cambridge Companion* 216–35.

———. *A Textbase of Women's Writing in English, 1330–1830*. Bibliography of British Women Poets, 1760–1830. Brown U Women Writers Project.

———. "Women Readers, Women Writers." Curran, *Cambridge Companion* 177–95.

Dabundo, Laura, ed. *Encyclopedia of Romanticism: Culture in Britain, 1780s–1830s*. New York: Garland, 1992.

Davidoff, Leonore. "The Family in Britain." *People and Their Environment*. Vol. 2 of *The Cambridge History of Britain, 1750–1950*. Ed. F. M. L. Thompson. Cambridge: Cambridge UP, 1990. 71–129.

Davidoff, Leonore, and Catherine Hall. *Family Fortunes: Men and Women of the English Middle Class, 1780–1850*. Chicago: U of Chicago P, 1987.

Davidson, Mary V. "What We've Missed: Female Romantic Poets and the American Nature Writing Tradition." *CEA Critic* 54.1 (1991): 110–18.

Davis, Gwenn, and Beverly A. Joyce, eds. *Poetry by Women to 1900: A Bibliography of American and British Writers*. Toronto: U of Toronto P, 1991.

Daye, Eliza. *Poems, on Various Subjects*. Liverpool: M'Creery, 1798.

Dekker, George. *Coleridge and the Literature of Sensibility*. New York: Barnes, 1978.

Deleuze, Gilles, and Félix Guattari. *Kafka: Toward a Minor Literature*. Trans. Dana Polan. Minneapolis: U of Minnesota P, 1986.

Dictionary of Literary Biography. Detroit: Gale.

Dictionary of National Biography. London: Smith, 1885–1906.

Doane, Mary Ann. *Femmes Fatales: Feminism, Film Theory, Psychoanalysis*. New York: Routledge, 1991.

Donovan, Josephine. "Toward a Women's Poetics." Benstock 98–109.

Drabble, Margaret, ed. *The Oxford Companion to English Literature*. Oxford: Oxford UP, 1985.

Dyce, Alexander. *Specimens of British Poetesses*. London: Rodd, 1827.

Edgeworth, Maria. *Castle Rackrent*. Ed. George Watson. Oxford: Oxford UP, 1980.

Eichner, Hans. "The Rise of Modern Science and the Genesis of Romanticism." *PMLA* 97 (1982): 8–30.

Ellison, Julie. *Delicate Subjects: Romanticism, Gender, and the Ethics of Understanding*. Ithaca: Cornell UP, 1990.

———. "The Politics of Fancy in the Age of Sensibility." Wilson and Haefner 228–55.

Elwood, Anne Katharine. *Memoirs of the Literary Ladies of England, from the Commencement of the Last Century*. 2 vols. London: Colburn, 1843. New York: AMS, 1973.

Rev. of *The Emigrants*, by Charlotte Smith. *Critical Review* 9 (1793): 299–302.

Rev. of *Endymion*, by John Keats. *British Critic* ns 9 (1818): 649–54.

Erdman, David. *Blake: Prophet against Empire*. 3rd ed. New York: Dover, 1991.

Evance, Susan. *Poems*. London: Longman, 1808.

Ezell, Margaret J. M. *Writing Women's Literary History*. Baltimore: Johns Hopkins UP, 1993.

Faderman, Lillian. *Surpassing the Love of Men: Romantic Friendship and Love between Women from the Renaissance to the Present*. New York: Morrow, 1981.

"Family History." *Blackwood's Edinburgh Magazine* 80 (1856): 466.

Fanshawe, Catherine Maria. "A Riddle." *A Collection of Poems, Chiefly Manuscript, from Living Authors*. Ed. Joanna Baillie. London: Longman, 1823. 71.

Favret, Mary A. *Romantic Correspondence: Women, Politics, and the Fiction of Letters*. Cambridge: Cambridge UP, 1993.

———. "Spectatrice as Spectacle: Helen Maria Williams at Home in the Revolution." *Studies in Romanticism* 32 (1993): 273–95.

———. "Telling Tales about Genre: Poetry in the Romantic Novel." *Studies in the Novel* 26 (1994): 153–72.

Favret, Mary A., and Nicola Watson, eds. *At the Limits of Romanticism: Essays in Cultural, Feminist, and Materialist Criticism*. Bloomington: Indiana UP, 1994.

Faxon, Frederick W. *Literary Annuals and Gift Books: A Bibliography, 1823–1903*. Middlesex: PLA, 1973.

Feldman, Paula R., ed. *British Women Poets of the Romantic Era: An Anthology*. Baltimore: Johns Hopkins UP, 1997.

———, ed. *The Poems of Felicia Hemans*. Baltimore: Johns Hopkins UP, forthcoming.

Feldman, Paula R., and Theresa M. Kelley, eds. *Romantic Women Writers: Voices and Countervoices*. Hanover: UP of New England, 1995.

Fell, Margaret. *Women's Speaking Justified, Proved, and Allowed by the Scriptures*. 1667. *The Rhetorical Tradition: Readings from Classical Times to the Present*. Ed. Patricia Bizzell and Bruce Herzberg. Boston: Bedford–St. Martin's, 1990. 677–85.

Fergus, Jan, and Janice Farrar Thaddeus. "Women, Publishers, and Money, 1790–1820." *Studies in Eighteenth-Century Culture* 17 (1987): 191–207.

Ferguson, Frances. "On the Numbers of Romanticisms." *ELH* 58 (1991): 471–98.

Ferguson, Moira. *Eighteenth-Century Women Poets: Nation, Class, and Gender*. Albany: SU of New York P, 1995.

———, ed. *First Feminists: British Women Writers, 1578–1799*. Bloomington: Indiana UP, 1985.

———. "Resistance and Power in the Life and Writings of Ann Yearsley." *Eighteenth Century* 27 (1986): 247–68.

————. *Subject to Others: British Women Writers and Colonial Slavery, 1670–1834.* New York: Routledge, 1992.

Ferris, Ina. *The Achievement of Literary Authority: Gender, History, and the Waverly Novels.* Ithaca: Cornell UP, 1991.

Fliegelman, Jay. *Declaring Independence: Jefferson, Natural Language, and the Culture of Performance.* Stanford: Stanford UP, 1993.

Franklin, Caroline, ed. *The Romantics: Women Poets of the Romantic Period, 1770–1830.* 12 vols. New York: Routledge, 1996.

Freneau, Philip. *The Poems of Philip Freneau.* Ed. Fred Lewis Pattee. 2 vols. New York: Russell, 1963.

Furniss, Tom. "Nasty Tricks and Tropes: Sexuality and Language in Mary Wollstonecraft's *Rights of Woman.*" *Studies in Romanticism* 32 (1993): 177–209.

Fussell, Paul. *Poetic Meter and Poetic Form.* New York: Random, 1965.

Gaull, Marilyn. *English Romanticism: The Human Context.* New York: Norton, 1988.

Gelpi, Barbara Charlesworth. *Shelley's Goddess: Maternity, Language, Subjectivity.* New York: Oxford UP, 1992.

George, M. Dorothy. *London Life in the Eighteenth Century.* London: Kegan, 1925.

Gilbert, Sandra M., and Susan Gubar. "'But Oh! That Deep Romantic Chasm': The Engendering of Periodization." *Kenyon Review* 13:3 (1991): 74–81.

————. *The Madwoman in the Attic: The Woman Writer and the Nineteenth-Century Literary Imagination.* New Haven: Yale UP, 1979.

————, eds. *The Norton Anthology of Literature by Women: The Tradition in English.* New York: Norton, 1985.

Gilligan, Carol. *In a Different Voice: Psychological Theory and Women's Development.* Cambridge: Harvard UP, 1982.

Glaspell, Susan. *Trifles.* Boston: Baker, 1924.

Gorak, Jan. *The Making of the Modern Canon: Genesis and Crisis of a Literary Idea.* London: Athlone, 1990.

Goslee, Nancy Moore. "Hemans's 'Red Indians': Reading Stereotypes." Richardson and Hofkosh 237–61.

Graff, Gerald. *Professing Literature: An Institutional History.* Chicago: U of Chicago P, 1987.

Greer, Germaine. "The Tulsa Center for the Study of Women's Literature: What We Are Doing and Why We Are Doing It." *Tulsa Studies in Women's Literature* 1.1 (1982): 5–26.

Grier, Roosevelt. *Rosey Grier's Needlepoint for Men.* New York: Walker, 1973.

Guest, Harriet. "The Wanton Muse: Politics and Gender in Gothic Theory after 1760." Copley and Whale 118–39.

Haefner, Joel. "(De)Forming the Romantic Canon: The Case of Women Writers." *College Literature* 20.2 (1993): 44–57.

————. "The Romantic Scene(s) of Writing." Wilson and Haefner 256–73.

Hale, Sarah Josepha. *Woman's Record; or, Sketches of All Distinguished Women, from Creation to AD 1854.* 1855. New York: Source Book, 1970.

Harding, Anthony John. "Felicia Hemans and the Effacement of Woman." Feldman and Kelley 138–49.

Harding, Sandra. "Rethinking Standpoint Epistemology: What Is 'Strong Objectivity'?" *Feminist Epistemologies*. Ed. Linda Alcoff and Elizabeth Potter. New York: Routledge, 1992. 49–82.

Hayden, John O. *The Romantic Reviewers, 1802–1824*. Chicago: U of Chicago P, 1968.

Hays, Mary. *Female Biography; or, Memoirs of Illustrious and Celebrated Women of All Ages and Countries*. 6 vols. London: Phillips, 1803.

Hazlitt, William. *The Collected Works of William Hazlitt*. Ed. A. R. Waller and Arnold Glover. 12 vols. London: Dent, 1902.

———. *Lectures on the English Poets*. 2nd ed. London: Taylor, 1819.

Hearts and Hands: The Influence of Women and Quilts on American Society. Videotape. San Francisco: Hearts and Hands, 1988.

Heinzelman, Kurt. "The Cult of Domesticity: Dorothy and William Wordsworth at Grasmere." Mellor, *Romanticism and Feminism* 52–78.

Hemans, Felicia. *The Complete Works of Mrs. Hemans*. 2 vols. New York: Appleton, 1861.

———. *Felicia Hemans, an Anthology*. Ed. Gary Kelly and Susan J. Wolfson. Peterborough, ON: Broadview, forthcoming.

———. *The Poetical Works of Felicia Dorothea Hemans*. Oxford: Oxford UP, 1914.

———. *The Poetical Works of Mrs. Felicia Hemans*. New ed. Philadelphia: Grigg, 1835.

———. *The Poetical Works of Mrs. Felicia Hemans*. Philadelphia: Lippincott, 1855.

———. *The Poetical Works of Mrs. Hemans* (Albion Edition). London: Warne, 1900.

———. *"Records of Woman," with Other Poems*. Edinburgh: Blackwood; London: Cadell, 1828.

———. *Tales, and Historic Scenes, in Verse*. London: Murray, 1819.

Hickok, Kathleen. *Representations of Women: Nineteenth-Century British Women's Poetry*. Westport: Greenwood, 1984.

Hilbish, Florence. *Charlotte Smith, Poet and Novelist (1749–1806)*. Philadelphia: U of Pennsylvania, 1941.

Hodgson, John. "Sympathy and Imagination: Wordsworth and English Romantic Poetry." *Approaches to Teaching Wordsworth's Poetry*. Ed. Spencer Hall and Jonathan Ramsey. New York: MLA, 1986. 130–36.

Hoeveler, Diane Long. *Romantic Androgyny: The Women Within*. University Park: Pennsylvania State UP, 1990.

Hofkosh, Sonia. "Sexual Politics and Literary History: William Hazlitt's Keswick Escapade and Sarah Hazlitt's *Journal*." Favret and Watson 125–42.

———. "A Woman's Profession: Sexual Difference and the Romance of Authorship." *Studies in Romanticism* 32 (1993): 245–72.

———. "The Writer's Ravishment: Women and the Romantic Author—The Example of Byron." Mellor, *Romanticism and Feminism* 93–114.

Holford, Margaret. *Margaret of Anjou: A Poem*. London: Murray, 1816.

Homans, Margaret. *Bearing the Word: Language and Female Experience in Nineteenth-Century Women's Writing*. Chicago: U of Chicago P, 1986.

———. "Keats Reading Women, Women Reading Keats." *Studies in Romanticism* 29 (1990): 341–70.

———. *Women Writers and Poetic Identity*. Princeton: Princeton UP, 1980.

Howell, T. B., ed. *Cobbett's Complete Collection of State Trials*. 34 vols. London: Bagshaw, 1809–26.

[Hughes, Harriett Mary Browne]. *Memoir of the Life and Writings of Felicia Hemans: By Her Sister; with an Essay on her Genius: By Mrs. Sigourney*. New York: Francis, 1845. Rpt. of vol. 1 of *The Works of Mrs. Hemans*. 6 vols. London: Cadell; Edinburgh: Blackwood, 1839.

Humanitas [George Miller of Dunbar]. *War a System of Madness and Irreligion. To Which Is Subjoined by Way of a Conclusion, The Dawn of Universal Peace, Wrote on the Late Fast Day, 1796*. N.p.: n.p., 1796.

Hunt, Bishop C., Jr. "Wordsworth and Charlotte Smith." *Wordsworth Circle* 1 (1970): 85–103.

Hunt, Leigh. "Specimens of British Poetesses." *Men, Women, and Books: A Selection of Sketches, Essays, and Critical Memoirs from His Uncollected Prose Writings*. 1847. London: Smith, 1891. 257–86.

Hunt, Lynn. *Politics, Culture, and Class in the French Revolution*. Berkeley: U of California P, 1984.

Hunter, Mrs. John. *Poems*. London: Payne, 1802.

Irwin, Joyce, ed. *Womanhood in Radical Protestantism, 1525–1675*. New York: Mellen, 1979.

Jackson, J. R. de J. *Annals of English Verse, 1770–1835: A Preliminary Survey of the Volumes Published*. New York: Garland, 1985.

———, ed. *Romantic Poetry by Women: A Bibliography, 1770–1835*. New York: Oxford UP, 1993.

Jameson, Anna. *Characteristics of Women: Moral, Political, and Historical*. Vol. 1. London: n.p., 1832. 2 vols.

Johnson, James. *The Scots Musical Museum: Originally Published by James Johnson with Illustrations of the Lyric Poetry and Music of Scotland by William Stenhouse*. Fwd. Henry George Farmer. Hatboro: Folklore Assoc., 1962.

Johnson-Eilola, Johndan. "Reading and Writing in Hypertext: Vertigo and Euphoria." Selfe and Hilligoss 195–219.

Jones, Ann Rosalind. *The Currency of Eros: Women's Love Lyric in Europe, 1540–1620*. Bloomington: Indiana UP, 1990.

Jones, Chris. "Helen Maria Williams and Radical Sensibility." *Prose Studies* 12 (1989): 3–24.

Jones, Vivien. "'The Coquetry of Nature': Politics and the Picturesque in Women's Fiction." *The Politics of the Picturesque: Literature, Landscapes, and Aesthetics since 1770*. Ed. Stephen Copley and Peter Garside. Cambridge: Cambridge UP, 1994. 120–44.

———. "Women Writing Revolution: Narratives of History and Sexuality in Wollstonecraft and Williams." Copley and Whale 178–99.

Jordan, Winthrop D. *White over Black: American Attitudes toward the Negro, 1500–1812*. Chapel Hill: U of North Carolina P, 1968.

Kaplan, Cora. "Wild Nights: Pleasure/Sexuality/Feminism." *Sea Changes: Essays on Culture and Feminism.* London: Verso, 1986. 31–56.

Kauffman, Linda S. *Discourses of Desire: Gender, Genre, and Epistolary Fictions.* Ithaca: Cornell UP, 1986.

Keats, John. *The Complete Poems.* Ed. John Barnard. Harmondsworth: Penguin, 1977.

———. *The Letters of John Keats.* Ed. Hyder E. Rollins. 2 vols. Cambridge: Harvard UP, 1958.

———. *Poems by John Keats.* London: Ollier, 1817.

Kelly, Gary. *Women, Writing, and Revolution, 1790–1827.* New York: Oxford UP, 1993.

Kelly, Gary, and Susan Wolfson, eds. *Felicia Hemans: Selected Poems.* Peterborough, ON: Broadview, 1997.

Kennedy, Deborah. "Revolutionary Tales: Helen Maria Williams's *Letters from France* and William Wordsworth's 'Vaudracour and Julia.'" *Wordsworth Circle* 21 (1990): 109–14.

———. "Storms of Sorrow: The Poetry of Helen Maria Williams." *Man and Nature* 10 (1991): 72–92.

———. "Thorns and Roses: The Sonnets of Charlotte Smith." *Women's Writing* 2 (1995): 1–11.

Klancher, Jon. *The Making of English Reading Audiences, 1789–1832.* Madison: U of Wisconsin P, 1987.

Knapp, Samuel L. *Female Biography: Containing Notices of Distinguished Women, in Different Nations and Ages.* New York: Carpenter, 1834.

Kowaleski-Wallace, Elizabeth. *Their Fathers' Daughters: Hannah More, Maria Edgeworth, and Patriarchal Complicity.* New York: Oxford UP, 1991.

Kreissman, Bernard, ed. *The Early Victorian Period, 1840–1869.* Pt. 2 of *The University of California, Davis, Minor British Poets.* Davis: U Lib., 1985.

———, ed. *The Romantic Period, 1789–1839.* Pt. 1 of *The University of California, Davis, Minor British Poets.* Davis: U Lib., 1983.

Kristeva, Julia. *Revolution in Poetic Language.* New York: Columbia UP, 1984.

———. "Women's Time." *The Kristeva Reader.* Ed. Toril Moi. New York: Columbia UP, 1986.

Krueger, Christine L. *The Reader's Repentance: Preachers, Women Writers, and Nineteenth-Century Social Discourse.* Chicago: U of Chicago P, 1992.

Kuist, James M. *The Nichols File of the* Gentleman's Magazine: *Attributions of Authorship and Other Documentation in Editorial Papers at the Folger Library.* Madison: U of Wisconsin P, 1982.

La Cassagnere, Christian. "The Self." *A Handbook to English Romanticism.* Ed. Jean Raimond and J. R. Watson. New York: St. Martin's, 1992. 237–42.

Lamb, Charles, and Mary Lamb. *The Works of Charles and Mary Lamb.* Ed. E. V. Lucas. 5 vols. London: Methuen, 1903–05. New York: AMS, 1968.

Landon, Letitia Elizabeth. "Cottage Courtship." *Fisher's Drawing-Room Scrapbook, with Poetical Illustrations by L. E. L.* London: Fisher, 1835. 40.

Landow, George P. "Hypertext, Metatext, and the Electronic Canon." *Literacy Online:*

The Promise (and Peril) of Reading and Writing with Computers. Ed. Myron C. Tuman. Pittsburgh: U of Pittsburgh P, 1992. 67–94.

———. *Hypertext: The Convergence of Contemporary Critical Theory and Technology*. Baltimore: Johns Hopkins UP, 1992.

Landry, Donna. *The Muses of Resistance: Laboring-Class Women's Poetry in Britain, 1739–1796*. Cambridge: Cambridge UP, 1990.

Langbauer, Laurie. *Women and Romance: The Consolations of Gender in the English Novel*. Ithaca: Cornell UP, 1990.

Lanham, Richard A. *The Electronic Word: Democracy, Technology, and the Arts*. Chicago: U of Chicago P, 1993.

Laqueur, Thomas. "Representing Sex." *Making Sex: Body and Gender from the Greeks to Freud*. Ed. Laqueur. Cambridge: Harvard UP, 1990. 160–87.

Lee, Anna Maria. *Memoirs of Eminent Female Writers*. Philadelphia: Grigg, 1827.

Leighton, Angela. *Victorian Women Poets: Writing against the Heart*. Charlottesville: U of Virginia P, 1992.

Levin, Susan. *Dorothy Wordsworth and Romanticism*. New Brunswick: Rutgers UP, 1987.

———. "Romantic Prose and Feminine Romanticism." *Prose Studies* 10 (1987): 181–95.

Lindenberger, Herbert. *The History in Literature: On Value, Genre, Institutions*. New York: Columbia UP, 1990.

Lindsay, Lady Anne. *Auld Robin Gray: A Ballad by the Right Honourable Lady Anne Barnard, Born Lady Anne Lindsay of Balcarras*. Ed. Walter Scott. Edinburgh: Bannatyne, 1825.

Linkin, Harriet Kramer. "The Current Canon in British Romantics Studies." *College English* 53 (1991): 548–70.

———. "Romanticism and Mary Tighe's *Psyche*: Peering at the Hem of Her Blue Stockings." *Studies in Romanticism* 35 (1996): 55–72.

———. "Taking Stock of the British Romantics Marketplace: Teaching New Canons through New Editions?" *Nineteenth-Century Contexts* 19 (1995): 111–24.

———. "Women and Romanticism: Reformulating Canons in the Classroom." *CEA Critic* 52 (1990): 45–52.

Lipking, Lawrence. "Aristotle's Sister: A Poetics of Abandonment." *Canons*. Ed. Robert von Hallberg. Chicago: U of Chicago P, 1984. 85–106.

Lives of the Lindsays; or, A Memoir of the Houses of Crawford and Balcarras by Lord Lindsay . . . Together with Personal Narratives by His Brothers . . . and His Sister, Lady Anne Barnard. 3 vols. London: Murray, 1849.

Lockhart, J. G. "Modern English Poetesses." *Quarterly Review* 66 (1840): 374–418.

Lonsdale, Roger, ed. *Eighteenth-Century Women Poets: An Oxford Anthology*. Oxford: Oxford UP, 1989.

Lootens, Tricia. "Hemans and Home: Victorianism, Feminine 'Internal Enemies,' and the Domestication of National Identity." *PMLA* 109 (1994): 238–53.

Lovejoy, Arthur O. "On the Discrimination of Romanticisms." *Essays on the History of Ideas*. Baltimore: Johns Hopkins UP, 1948. 228–53.

Lovell, Terry. *Consuming Fiction*. London: Verso, 1987.

Luther, Susan. "A Stranger Minstrel: Coleridge's Mrs. Robinson." *Studies in Romanticism* 33 (1994): 391–409.

Macaulay, Catharine. "Account of the Life and Writings of Mrs. Catharine Macaulay Graham." *European Magazine and London Review* 4 (1783): 330–34.

———. *The History of England*. 8 vols. London: Nourse, 1764–83.

———. *Letters on Education, with Observations on Religious and Metaphysical Subjects*. London: Dilly, 1790.

Manning, Peter J. "The Nameless Broken Dandy and the Structure of Authorship." *Reading Romantics: Texts and Contexts*. New York: Oxford UP, 1990. 145–62.

Margolis, Joseph. "Genres, Laws, Canons, Principles." *Rules and Conventions*. Ed. Mette Hjort. Baltimore: Johns Hopkins UP, 1992. 130–66.

Maxwell, Caroline. *Feudal Tales*. N.p.: n.p., 1810[?].

McCarthy, William. "'We Hoped the *Woman* Was Going to Appear': Repression, Desire, and Gender in Anna Letitia Barbauld's Early Poems." Feldman and Kelley 113–37.

McCarthy, William, and Elizabeth Kraft, eds. *The Poems of Anna Letitia Barbauld*. Athens: U of Georgia P, 1994.

McFarland, Thomas. *Romanticism and the Forms of Ruin: Wordsworth, Coleridge, and Modalities of Fragmentation*. Princeton: Princeton UP, 1981.

McGann, Jerome J. "Byron and the Lyric of Sensibility." *European Romantic Review* 4 (1993): 71–83.

——— [as Anne Mack, J. J. Rome, and Georg Mannejc]. "Literary History, Romanticism, and Felicia Hemans." *Modern Language Quarterly* 54 (1993): 215–35. Rpt. in Wilson and Haefner 210–27.

———, ed. *The New Oxford Book of Romantic Period Verse*. New York: Oxford UP, 1993.

———. *The Poetics of Sensibility: A Revolution in Literary Style*. New York: Oxford UP, 1996.

———. "Poetry, 1785–1832." *The Columbia History of British Poetry*. Ed. Carl Woodring. New York: Columbia UP, 1994. 353–80.

———. "Rethinking Romanticism." *ELH* 59 (1992): 735–54.

———. *The Romantic Ideology: A Critical Investigation*. Chicago: U of Chicago P, 1983.

McGann, Jerome J., and David Seaman, eds. "British Poetry, 1780–1910: A Hypertext Archive of Scholarly Editions." Available http://etext.lib.virginia.edu/britpo.html.

Mellor, Anne K. "'Am I Not a Woman, and a Sister?': Slavery, Romanticism, and Gender." Richardson and Hofkosh 311–29.

———. "A Criticism of Their Own: Romantic Women Literary Critics." *Questioning Romanticism*. Ed. John Beer. Baltimore: Johns Hopkins UP, 1996. 29–48.

———. "The Female Poet and the Poetess: Two Traditions of British Women's Poetry, 1780–1830." *Studies in Romanticism*, forthcoming.

———. "Joanna Baillie and the Counter-public Sphere." *Studies in Romanticism* 33 (1994): 559–67.

————, ed. *Romanticism and Feminism*. Bloomington: Indiana UP, 1988.

————. *Romanticism and Gender*. New York: Routledge, 1993.

————. "Why Women Didn't Like Romanticism: The Views of Jane Austen and Mary Shelley." Ruoff 274–87.

Mellor, Anne K., and Richard Matlak, eds. *British Literature, 1780–1830*. Fort Worth: Harcourt, 1996.

Miall, David S. *Romanticism: The CD*. CD-ROM. Oxford: Blackwell, 1997.

Michaels, Walter Benn. "Race into Culture: A Critical Genealogy of Cultural Identity." *Critical Inquiry* 18 (1992): 655–85.

Milton, John. *Complete Poems and Major Prose*. Ed. Merritt Y. Hughes. New York: Odyssey, 1957.

Moers, Ellen. *Literary Women: The Great Writers*. 1963. Garden City: Anchor-Doubleday, 1977.

Moody, Elizabeth. *Poetic Trifles*. London: Cadell, 1798.

Moore, Jane. "Plagiarism with a Difference: Subjectivity in 'Kubla Khan' and *Letters Written during a Short Residence in Sweden, Norway, and Denmark*." Copley and Whale 140–59.

Moore, Thomas, ed. *The Works of Lord Byron, with His Letters and Journals, and His Life, by Thomas Moore*. Vols. 1–6. London: Murray, 1832–34. Rpt. of *Letters and Journals of Lord Byron, with Notices of His Life*. 1830.

More, Hannah. *The Complete Works of Hannah More*. 7 vols. New York: n.p., 1855.

————. "A Prefatory Letter to Mrs. Montagu. By a Friend." *Poems on Several Occasions*. London: Cadell, 1786. iii–xii.

————. *Slavery: A Poem*. Breen 10–20.

————. *Strictures on the Modern System of Female Education*. 2 vols. London: Cadell, 1799. Rpt. as vols. 7–8 in *The Works of Hannah More*. London: Cadell, 1818.

Moulthrop, Stuart, and Nancy Kaplan. "They Became What They Beheld: The Futility of Resistance in the Space of Electronic Writing." Selfe and Hilligoss 220–37.

Myers, Mitzi. "Hannah More's Tracts for the Times: Social Fiction and Female Ideology." *Fetter'd or Free? British Women Novelists, 1670–1815*. Ed. Mary Anne Schofield and Cecilia Macheski. Athens: Ohio UP, 1986. 264–84.

————. "Impeccable Governesses, Rational Dames, and Moral Mothers: Mary Wollstonecraft and the Female Tradition in Georgian Children's Books." *Children's Literature* 14 (1986): 31–59.

————. "Little Girls Lost: Rewriting Romantic Childhood, Righting Gender and Genre." *Teaching Children's Literature: Issues, Pedagogy, Resources*. Ed. Glenn Edward Sadler. U. C. Knoepflmacher, consultant ed. New York: MLA, 1992. 131–42.

————, ed. *The Poems of Jane Taylor*. New York: Oxford UP, forthcoming.

————. "Reading Rosamond Reading: Maria Edgeworth's 'Wee-Wee Stories' Interrogate the Canon." *Infant Tongue: The Voice of the Child in Literature*. Ed. Elizabeth Goodenough, Mark A. Heberle, and Naomi Sokoloff. Detroit: Wayne State UP, 1994. 57–79.

————. "Reform or Ruin: 'A Revolution in Female Manners.'" *Studies in Eighteenth-Century Culture* 11 (1982): 199–216.

————. "Sensibility and the 'Walk of Reason': Mary Wollstonecraft's Literary Reviews as Cultural Critique." *Sensibility in Transformation: Creative Resistance to Sentiment from the Augustans to the Romantics.* Ed. Syndy McMillen Conger. Rutherford: Fairleigh Dickinson UP, 1990. 120–44.

Myers, Sylvia Haverstock. *The Bluestocking Circle: Women, Friendship, and the Life of the Mind in Eighteenth-Century England.* Oxford: Oxford UP, 1991.

Nairne, Carolina Oliphant. *Lays from Strathearne, by Carolina, Baroness Nairne.* London: Addison, 1846.

Nangle, Benjamin Christie. *The* Monthly Review, *Second Series, 1790–1818: Indexes of Contributors and Articles.* Oxford: Clarendon, 1955.

Nelson, Theodor H. *Literary Machines.* Sausalito: Mindful, 1980.

Newton, Judith Lowder. *Women, Power, and Subversion: Social Strategies in British Fiction, 1778–1860.* 1981. New York: Methuen, 1985.

Nichols, John Boyer. *Illustrations of the Literary History of the Eighteenth Century: Consisting of Authentic Memoirs and Original Letters of Eminent Persons.* 8 vols. London: Nichols, 1817–58.

————. *Literary Anecdotes of the Eighteenth Century.* 9 vols. London: Nichols, 1812–15.

Ostriker, Alicia. "The Road of Excess: My William Blake." Ruoff 67–88.

————. *Stealing the Language: The Emergence of Women's Poetry in America.* Boston: Beacon, 1986.

Outram, Dorinda. *The Body and the French Revolution: Sex, Class, and Political Culture.* New Haven: Yale UP, 1989.

Pagan, Isabel. *A Collection of Songs and Poems on Several Occasions.* Glasgow: Niven, 1803.

Page, Judith. *Wordsworth and the Cultivation of Women.* Berkeley: U of California P, 1994.

Pascoe, Judith. "Female Botanists and the Poetry of Charlotte Smith." Wilson and Haefner 193–209.

————. "Mary Robinson and the Literary Marketplace." Feldman and Kelley 252–68.

————, ed. *The Poems of Mary Robinson.* New York: Oxford UP, forthcoming.

————. "'The Spectacular Flaneuse': Mary Robinson and the City of London." *Wordsworth Circle* 23 (1992): 165–71.

Paterson, James. *The Contemporaries of Burns, and the More Recent Poets of Ayrshire with Selections from Their Writings.* Edinburgh: Patton; London: Smith, 1840.

PEAL. Available gopher://dept.english.upenn.edu:70/11/E-Text/PEAL.

Perkins, David. *English Romantic Writers.* 2nd ed. Fort Worth: Harcourt, 1994.

————. *Is Literary History Possible?* Baltimore: Johns Hopkins UP, 1992.

Petrarca, Francesco. *Petrarch's Lyric Poems: The* Rime Sparse *and Other Lyrics.* Trans. and ed. Robert M. Durling. Cambridge: Harvard UP, 1976.

Plutarch. *Plutarch's Lives.* Trans. John Langhorne and William Langhorne. Cincinnati: Applegate, 1856.

Poovey, Mary. *The Proper Lady and the Woman Writer: Ideology as Style in the Works of Mary Wollstonecraft, Mary Shelley, and Jane Austen.* Chicago: U Chicago P, 1984.

Price, Lawrence M. *Inkle and Yarico Album*. Berkeley: U of California P, 1937.

Prince, Mary. *The History of Mary Prince, a West Indian Slave, Related by Herself*. Ed. and introd. Moira Ferguson. Preface by Ziggi Alexander. London: Pandora, 1987.

Prior, Mary, ed. *Women in English Society, 1500–1800*. London: Methuen, 1985.

Purinton, Marjean D. *Romantic Ideology Unmasked: The Mentally Constructed Tyrannies in Dramas of William Wordsworth, Lord Byron, Percy Shelley, and Joanna Baillie*. Newark: U of Delaware P, 1994.

Rabine, Leslie. *Reading the Romantic Heroine: Text, History, and Ideology*. Ann Arbor: U of Michigan P, 1985.

Rajan, Tilottama. "Autonarration and Genotext in Mary Hays' *Memoirs of Emma Courtney*." *Studies in Romanticism* 32 (1993): 149–76.

Redpath, Jean, with Abby Newton. *Lady Nairne*. Audiocassette. Scottish Records 168. 1981.

Reiman, Donald H., ed. *Romantic Context: Poetry: Significant Minor Poetry, 1789–1830*. 128 vols. New York: Garland, 1978.

Rice, John. *Bobbed Hair, Bossy Wives, and Women Preachers*. Murfreesboro: Sword of the Lord, 1941.

Richardson, Alan. "Epic Ambivalence: Imperial Politics and Romantic Deflection in Williams' *Peru* and Landor's *Gebir*." Richardson and Hofkosh 265–82.

———. *Literature, Education, and Romanticism: Reading as Social Practice, 1780–1832*. Cambridge: Cambridge UP, 1996.

———. "Romanticism and the Colonization of the Feminine." Mellor, *Romanticism and Feminism* 13–25.

Richardson, Alan, and Sonia Hofkosh, eds. *Romanticism, Race, and Imperial Culture, 1780–1834*. Bloomington: Indiana UP, 1995.

Rieder, John. "Wordsworth and Romanticism in the Academy." Favret and Watson 21–39.

Riga, Frank, and Claude A. Prance, eds. *Index to the* London Magazine. New York: Garland, 1978.

Rivers, Isabel, ed. *Books and Their Readers in Eighteenth-Century England*. Leicester: Leicester UP, 1982.

Robbins, Alan. "The Great Multimedia Debate." *Newsweek* 5 June 1995: 16.

Roberts, William. *Memoirs of the Life and Correspondence of Mrs. Hannah More*. New York: Harper, 1845.

Robertson, Eric S. *English Poetesses: A Series of Critical Biographies, with Illustrative Extracts*. London: Cassell, 1883.

Robinson, Daniel. "Reviving the Sonnet: Women Romantic Poets and the Sonnet Claim." *European Romantic Review* 6 (1995): 98–127.

Robinson, Mary. *Complete Poems*. Providence: Brown U and Natl. Endowment for the Humanities Women Writers Project, 1990.

———. *Lyrical Tales*. London: Longman, 1800.

Rogers, Katharine M., and William McCarthy, eds. *The Meridian Anthology of Early Women Writers: British Literary Women from Aphra Behn to Maria Edgeworth, 1660–1800*. New York: NAL, 1987.

"Romantic   Chronology."   Available   http://humanitas.ucsb.edu/projects/pack/
romchrono/chrono.htm.

Ross, Marlon B. "Configurations of Feminine Reform: The Woman Writer and the Tradition of Dissent." Wilson and Haefner 91–110.

———. *The Contours of Masculine Desire: Romanticism and the Rise of Women's Poetry*. New York: Oxford UP, 1989.

———. "Romantic Quest and Conquest: Troping Masculine Power in the Crisis of Poetic Identity." Mellor, *Romanticism and Feminism* 26–51.

Rossetti, William Michael, ed. *The Poetical Works of Mrs. Felicia Hemans*. London: Ward Lock, 1878.

Rousseau, Jean Jacques. *Emile*. Trans. Barbara Foxley. New York: Dutton, 1969.

Rowton, Frederic. *The Female Poets of Great Britain*. London: Longman, 1850. Ed. Marilyn Williamson. Detroit: Wayne State UP, 1981.

Rubin, Gayle. "The Traffic in Women: Notes on the 'Political Economy' of Sex." *Toward an Anthropology of Women*. Ed. Rayna R. Reiter. New York: Monthly Review, 1975. 157–210.

Ruoff, Gene W., ed. *The Romantics and Us: Essays on Literature and Culture*. New Brunswick: Rutgers UP, 1990.

Scheffler, Judith. "Romantic Women Writing on Imprisonment and Prison Reform." *Wordsworth Circle* 19 (1988): 99–103.

Scott, Joan Wallach. *Gender and the Politics of History*. New York: Columbia UP, 1988.

Scott, Sir Walter. *The Letters of Sir Walter Scott*. Ed. H. J. C. Grierson. 13 vols. London: Constable, 1932–37.

Scrivener, Michael, ed. *Poetry and Reform: Periodical Verse from the English Democratic Press, 1792–1824*. Detroit: Wayne State UP, 1992.

Selfe, Cynthia L., and Susan Hilligoss, eds. *Literacy and Computers: The Complications of Teaching and Learning with Technology*. New York: MLA, 1994.

Seward, Anna. *Letters of Anna Seward, Written between the Years 1784 and 1807*. 6 vols. Edinburgh: Constable, 1811.

———. *Memoir of Erasmus Darwin, Chiefly During His Residence in Lichfield*. Philadelphia: Classic, 1804.

———. *The Poetical Works of Anna Seward*. Ed. Sir Walter Scott. 3 vols. New York: AMS, 1974.

Shattock, Joanne. *The Oxford Guide to British Women Writers*. New York: Oxford UP, 1993.

Shelley, Percy Bysshe. *Shelley's Poetry and Prose*. Ed. Donald H. Reiman and Sharon B. Powers. New York: Norton, 1977.

Shevelow, Kathryn. *Women and Print Culture: The Construction of Femininity in the Early Periodical*. New York: Routledge, 1989.

Showalter, Elaine. *A Literature of Their Own: British Women Novelists from Brontë to Lessing*. Princeton: Princeton UP, 1977.

———. "Women's Time, Women's Space: Writing the History of Feminist Criticism." Benstock 30–44.

Silverman, Kenneth. *A Cultural History of the American Revolution*. New York: Columbia UP, 1976.

Sismondi, Simonde de [J. C. L.]. *Histoire des républiques Italiennes du moyen âge*. 5th ed. 8 vols. Brussels: Société Typographique Belge, Ad. Wahlen, 1858.

Smith, Barbara Herrnstein. *Contingencies of Value: Alternative Perspectives for Critical Theory*. Cambridge: Harvard UP, 1988.

Smith, Catherine F. "Hypertextual Thinking." Selfe and Hilligoss 264–81.

Smith, Charlotte. *Conversations Introducing Poetry: Chiefly on Subjects of Natural History: For the Use of Children and Young Persons*. 2 vols. London: Johnson, 1804.

Smith, Olivia. *The Politics of Language, 1791–1819*. Oxford: Clarendon, 1984.

Smith, R. A., ed. *The Scottish Minstrel: A Selection from the Vocal Melodies of Scotland, Ancient and Modern*. 4 vols. Edinburgh: Purdie, 1822–24.

Smith, Sidonie. *A Poetics of Women's Autobiography: Marginality and the Fictions of Self-Representation*. Bloomington: Indiana UP, 1987.

Southcott, Joanna. *An Answer to Thomas Paine's Third Part of* The Age of Reason, *Published by D. I. Eaton; Likewise to S. Lane, a Calvinist Preacher, at Yeovil, in Somersetshire; and to Hewson Clarke, Editor of* The Scourge, *and Late of Emanuel College, Cambridge*. London: Marchant, 1812.

———. *A Continuation of Prophecies, by Joanna Southcott, from the Year 1792, to the Present Time*. Exeter, 1802.

———. *Joanna Southcott's Answer to Garrett's Book, Entitled* Demonocracy Detected—Visionary Enthusiasm Corrected; *or, Sixpennyworth of Good Advice Selected from the Scriptures of Truth: By the Rev. Jeremiah Learnoult Garrett, Author of* Rays of Everlasting Light. London: n.p., 1805.

———. *The Strange Effects of Faith, Second Part*. Exeter, 1801.

———. *A Word to the Wise; or, A Call to the Nation, That They May Know the Days of Their Visitations from the Prophecies That Are Given to Joanna Southcott, with the Reasons Assigned Why the Spirit of Prophecy Is Given to a Woman; and Which Is Explained from the Scriptures in the Following Pages*. Stourbridge: n.p., 1803.

Spacks, Patricia Meyer. *The Female Imagination*. New York: Knopf, 1975.

Spencer, Jane. *The Rise of the Woman Novelist from Aphra Behn to Jane Austen*. Oxford: Blackwell, 1986.

Spender, Dale. *Mothers of the Novel*. London: Pandora, 1986.

Staël, Germaine de. *Corinne; or, Italy*. Trans. and introd. Avriel Goldberger. New Brunswick: Rutgers UP, 1987.

Stanford, Ann. *The Women Poets in English*. New York: McGraw, 1972.

Stanton, Judith Phillips. "Statistical Profile of Women Writing in English from 1660–1800." *Eighteenth-Century Women and the Arts*. Ed. Frederick M. Keener and Susan E. Lorsch. New York: Greenwood, 1988. 247–54.

Stephenson, Glennis. "Letitia Landon and the Victorian Improvisatrice: The Construction of L. E. L." *Victorian Poetry* 30 (1992): 1–17.

———. *Letitia Landon: The Woman behind L. E. L.* Manchester: Manchester UP, 1995.

————. "Poet Construction: Mrs. Hemans, L. E. L., and the Image of the Nineteenth-Century Woman Poet." *Reimagining Women: Representations of Women in Culture.* Ed. Shirley Neuman and Glennis Stephenson. Toronto: U of Toronto P, 1993. 61–73.

Stone, Lawrence. *The Family, Sex, and Marriage in England, 1500–1800.* New York: Harper, 1979.

Strout, Alan Lang. *A Bibliography of Articles in* Blackwood's Magazine, *Volumes I through XVIII, 1817–1825.* Lib. Bulletin 5. Lubbock: Texas Technological Coll., 1959.

Sullivan, Alvin, ed. *British Literary Magazines.* 4 vols. New York: Greenwood, 1983–86.

Sweet, Nanora. "History, Imperialism, and the Aesthetics of the Beautiful: Hemans and the Post-Napoleonic Moment." Favret and Watson 170–84.

Sypher, Wylie. *Guinea's Captive Kings: British Anti-slavery Literature of the XVIIIth Century.* Chapel Hill: U of North Carolina P, 1942.

Tayler, Irene. *Holy Ghosts: The Male Muses of Emily and Charlotte Brontë.* New York: Columbia UP, 1990.

Tayler, Irene, and Gina Luria. "Gender and Genre: Women in British Romantic Literature." *What Manner of Woman: Essays in English and American Life and Literature.* Ed. Marlene Springer. New York: New York UP, 1977. 98–123.

Taylor, Jane. *Essays in Rhime, on Morals and Manners.* Boston: Wells, 1816.

————. *Writings.* Introd. Isaac Taylor. 5 vols. Boston: Perkins, 1832.

Taylor, Jane, Ann Taylor, Isaac Taylor, Adelaide O'Keeffe, and Bernard Barton. *Original Poems, for Infant Minds.* London: Darton, 1804.

Thompson, E. P. *The Making of the English Working Class.* New York: Random, 1966.

Tighe, Mary. *Psyche; or, The Legend of Love.* Ed. Donald Reiman. London: Carpenter, 1805; New York: Garland, 1978.

————. *Psyche, with Other Poems.* Ed. Jonathan Wordsworth. 1811. Oxford: Woodstock, 1992.

Tompkins, Jane. "Me and My Shadow." *New Literary History* 19 (1987): 169–79.

Todd, Janet, ed. *A Dictionary of British and American Women Writers, 1660–1800.* New York: Rowman, 1984.

————. *A Dictionary of Women Writers.* London: Routledge, 1989.

————. *Sensibility: An Introduction.* London: Methuen, 1986.

————. *The Sign of Angellica: Women, Writing, and Fiction, 1660–1800.* New York: Columbia UP, 1989.

Tristram, Philippa. *Living Space in Fact and Fiction.* London: Routledge, 1989.

Tuchman, Gaye, with Nina Fortin. *Edging Women Out: Victorian Novelists, Publishers, and Social Change.* New Haven: Yale UP, 1989.

Tucker, Herbert R. "House Arrest: The Domestication of English Poetry in the 1820s." *New Literary History* 25 (1994): 521–48.

Turner, Cheryl. *Living by the Pen: Women Writers in the Eighteenth Century.* London: Routledge, 1992.

Turner, John. "Wordsworth and Science." *Critical Survey* 2 (1990): 21–29.

Ty, Eleanor. *Unsex'd Revolutionaries: Five Women Novelists of the 1790s*. Toronto: U of Toronto P, 1993.

Uphaus, Robert W., and Gretchen M. Foster, eds. *The Other Eighteenth Century: English Women of Letters, 1660–1800*. East Lansing: Colleagues, 1991.

Upton, William. The School-Boy *and* The School-Girl. *A Treasury of Illustrated Children's Books: Early Nineteenth-Century Classics from the Osborne Collection*. Ed. Leonard De Vries. New York: Abbeville, 1989. 166–71.

"The Voice of the Shuttle: Web Page for Humanities Research." Available http:// humanitas.ucsb.edu.

Waldron, Mary. "Ann Yearsley and the Clifton Records." *The Age of Johnson: A Scholarly Annual*. Ed. Paul J. Korshin. Vol. 3. New York: AMS, 1990. 301–29.

Walker, Cheryl. *The Nightingale's Burden: Women Poets and American Culture before 1900*. Bloomington: Indiana UP, 1982.

Ward, William S. *Literary Reviews in British Periodicals: A Bibliography*. 4 vols. New York: Garland, 1972–79.

Weitzman, Arthur J. "Confessions of an Eighteenth-Century Editor." *Editor's Notes: Bulletin of the Council of Editors of Learned Journals* 13.1 (1994): 3–6.

Wellek, René. "The Concept of Romanticism in Literary History." *Comparative Literature* 1 (1949): 1–23, 147–72. Rpt. in *Romanticism: Points of View*. Ed. Robert Gleckner and Gerald Enscoe. 2nd ed. Detroit: Wayne State UP, 1970. 181–205.

Wendt, Ingrid. "Dust." *In Her Own Image: Women Working in the Arts*. Ed. Elaine Hedges and Ingrid Wendt. Old Westbury: Feminist, 1980. 130–33.

Whitelaw, Alex, ed. *The Book of Scottish Song: Collected and Illustrated with Historical and Critical Notices, and an Essay on the Songwriters of Scotland*. Glasgow: Blackie, 1848.

Williams, Helen Maria. *Letters from France*. Ed. Janet Todd. 2 vols. Delmar: Scholars' Facsimiles and Reprints, 1975.

Williams, Jane. *The Literary Women of England*. London: Saunders, 1861.

Wilson, Carol Shiner. "Lost Needles, Tangled Threads: Stitchery, Domesticity, and the Artistic Enterprise in Barbauld, Edgeworth, Taylor, and Lamb." Wilson and Haefner 167–92.

Wilson, Carol Shiner, and Joel Haefner, eds. *Re-visioning Romanticism: British Women Writers, 1776–1837*. Philadelphia: U of Pennsylvania P, 1994.

Wilson, James Grant. *The Poets and Poetry of Scotland: From the Earliest to the Present Time, Comprising Characteristic Selections from the Works of the More Noteworthy Scottish Poets; with Biographical and Critical Notices*. 2 vols. London: Blackie, 1876.

Wolfson, Susan J. "'Domestic Affections' and 'the Spear of Minerva': Felicia Hemans and the Dilemma of Gender." Wilson and Haefner 128–66.

———. "Feminizing Keats." *Critical Essays on John Keats*. Ed. Hermione de Almeida. Boston: Hall, 1990. 317–56.

———. "Gendering the Soul." Feldman and Kelley 33–68.

———. "Individual in Community: Dorothy Wordsworth in Conversation with William." Mellor, *Romanticism and Feminism* 139–66.

———. "Keats and the Manhood of the Poet." *European Romantic Review* 6 (1995): 1–37.

———. "Questioning 'the Romantic Ideology': Wordsworth." *Revue International de Philosophie* 3 (1990): 429–47.

Wollstonecraft, Mary. *An Historical and Moral View of the Origin and Progress of the French Revolution.* 1794. Delmar: Scholars' Facsimiles and Reprints, 1975.

———. *Letters Written during a Short Residence in Sweden, Norway, and Denmark.* Lincoln: U of Nebraska P, 1976.

———. *The Love Letters of Mary Wollstonecraft to Gilbert Imlay.* London: Hutchinson, 1908.

———. *Maria; or, The Wrongs of Woman.* Introd. Moira Ferguson. New York: Norton, 1975.

———. *A Vindication of the Rights of Men, in a Letter to the Right Honourable Edmund Burke.* 1790. Gainesville: Scholars' Facsimiles and Reprints, 1960.

———. *A Vindication of the Rights of Woman.* 1792. Harmondsworth: Penguin, 1985.

———. *A Vindication of the Rights of Woman.* Ed. Miriam Brody. 1792. New York: Penguin, 1988.

———. *A Vindication of the Rights of Woman. A Wollstonecraft Anthology.* Ed. Janet Todd. Cambridge: Polity, 1989. 84–114.

Wordsworth, Dorothy. *The Grasmere Journals.* Ed. Pamela Woof. Oxford: Oxford UP, 1993.

Wordsworth, Dorothy, and William Wordsworth. *The Letters of William and Dorothy Wordsworth: The Later Years.* Ed. Ernest de Selincourt. Vol. 2. Oxford: Oxford UP, 1939.

Wordsworth, William. Essay, Supplementary to the Preface. 1815. *Prose Works* 3: 62–84.

———. Explanatory Note to "Stanzas Suggested in a Steam-boat off St. Bees' Heads, on the Coast of Cumberland." 1835/37. *The Poetical Works.* Ed. William Knight. Vol. 7. London: Macmillan, 1896. 351.

———. *Poems.* Ed. John O. Hayden. Vol. 1. London: Penguin, 1977.

———. Preface. *Lyrical Ballads.* 1800. *Prose Works* 1: 118–58.

———. *The Prelude: 1799, 1805, 1850.* Ed. Jonathan Wordsworth et al. New York: Norton, 1979.

———. *The Prose Works.* Ed. W. J. B. Owen and Jane Worthington Smyser. 3 vols. Oxford: Clarendon, 1974.

Wu, Duncan, ed. *Romanticism: An Anthology.* Oxford: Blackwell, 1994.

———, ed. *Romantic Women Poets.* Cambridge: Blackwell, 1997.

Yaeger, Patricia. *Honey-Mad Women: Emancipatory Strategies in Women's Writing.* New York: Columbia UP, 1988.

Yearsley, Ann. *A Poem on the Inhumanity of the Slave-Trade.* M. Ferguson, *First Feminists* 386–96.

———. *Poems on Several Occasions.* London: Cadell, 1786.

———. *Poems on Various Subjects.* London: Robinson, 1787.

Young, Robert J. C. *Colonial Desire: Hybridity in Theory, Culture and Race*. London: Routledge, 1995.

Yudin, Mary. "Joanna Baillie's Introductory Discourse as a Precursor to Wordsworth's Preface to *Lyrical Ballads*." *Compar(a)ison* 1 (1994): 101–12.

Z. "On the Cockney School of Poetry. No. IV." *Blackwood's Edinburgh Magazine* 3 (1818): 519–24.

INDEX

Aaron, Jane, 14, 16
Abrams, Meyer H., 19, 124
Adburgham, Alison, 17
Agress, Lynne, 16
Aikin, Lucy, 41, 67–68, 89, 162
Alexander, Meena, 14–15, 16
Alston, R. C., 11
Altick, Richard, 17
Anderson, John, 14
Apuleius, Lucius, 108
Arac, Jonathan, 18
Armstrong, Isobel, 14, 15, 63
Armstrong, Nancy, 15, 20
Arnold, Matthew, 31
Ashfield, Andrew, 1, 9, 63
Astell, Mary, 90
Auerbach, Nina, 15
Austen, Jane, 87, 90, 101–02, 129

Baillie, Joanna, 3, 10, 16, 56, 71, 85, 89–95,
   106, 129, 135–40, 165
Balleine, G. R., 168
Bannerman, Anne, 29
Barbauld, Anna Letitia, 1, 5, 10, 16, 27, 45,
   48, 52–53, 56, 62, 63, 67–68, 69, 71–74, 75,
   79, 80–83, 85–86, 106, 127, 157, 162–63
Barker-Benfield, G. J., 17
Barrell, John, 86
Bath, Elizabeth, 43
Behrendt, Stephen C., 16, 18
Belenky, Mary Field, 18
Bennett, Betty T., 9, 72
Berry, Mary, 138
Betham, Mary Matilda, 10, 12
Bethune, George, 10, 12
Bewell, Alan, 121
Bible, 64–66, 80, 103, 108, 154, 165–69
Bizzell, Patricia, 166
Blain, Virginia, 12, 19
Blake, William, 3, 28, 52–53, 58, 61–62, 67,
   78–79, 90, 106, 121, 125–27, 157–59,
   161–62, 164
Blamire, Susanna, 9, 36, 157–60
Blanchard, Laman, 20
Bleecker, Ann Eliza, 85
Blessington, Lady Marguerite, 37
Bloomfield, Robert, 58
Bogel, Fredric V., 140
Bolter, Jay David, 46
Bowles, Caroline, 10
Bowles, William Lisle, 60, 122
Boyle, Andrew, 11, 38
Bradley, Marion Zimmer, 108
Brawne, Fanny, 111
Breen, Jennifer, 1, 9
Brewer, William D., 136

Brontë, Emily, 29
Brown, Charles Brockden, 87
Brown, William Hill, 87
Browning, Elizabeth Barrett, 60, 164
Bryan, Mary, 28–29
Buck, Claire, 12
Burke, Edmund, 60–61, 64, 90, 97
Burke, Helen, 166–68
Burns, Robert, 34
Burroughs, Catherine, 93, 95, 135
Bush, Vannevar, 46
Butler, Judith, 62
Butler, Marilyn, 16, 18, 19, 97, 121, 123
Byron, George Gordon, Lord, 3, 36, 44, 58,
   59, 61–62, 85, 87, 101–03, 109, 110–11,
   122, 124, 128, 153

Campbell, Dorothea Primrose, 29
Campbell, Thomas, 26
Candler, Ann, 30, 149, 151
Cantor, Paul, 18
Carhart, Margaret, 12
Carlson, Julie, 19
Carroll, Lewis, 143
Carter, Angela, 108
Case, Sue-Ellen, 138–39
Chambers, Robert, 10, 36
Charlotte Augusta, Princess of Wales, 151
Charney, Davida, 46
Chaucer, Geoffrey, 108
Chodorow, Nancy, 18
Chorley, Henry, 20, 114, 115, 118
Cicero, Marcus Tullius, 104
Cixous, Hélène, 53
Clare, John, 58, 122, 124
Claridge, Laura, 18
Clarke, Norma, 15, 112
Clements, Patricia, 12, 19
Clinchy, Blythe McVicker, 18
Clive, John, 12
Clunie, John, 34
Cobbett, William, 49
Cole, Lucinda, 13
Coleridge, Samuel Taylor, 3, 30, 35, 37, 45, 52,
   56, 60–61, 67, 86, 106, 122, 129, 131, 141,
   157, 159, 161–63
Colley, Linda, 76
Collins, William, 86, 123
Condorcet, Marie-Jean-Antoine-Nicolas Cari-
   tat, Marquis de, 90
Constable, John, 49
Cook, Albert, 52
Cook, James, 76
Cooper, Mrs., 30
Copley, Stephen, 18
Corday, Charlotte, 61

Courtney, Janet E., 12
Cowper, William, 67, 80, 127
Cox, Jeffrey N., 93
Cox, Sarah, 65
Crabbe, George, 58, 158
Cristall, Ann Batten, 28, 49
Croker, John Wilson, 111
Croker, Margaret Sarah, 149, 151
Crosby, Christina, 90
Crosby, Sarah, 65
Curran, Stuart, 1, 2, 9, 13, 14, 19, 20, 41, 47,
    49, 56, 59, 62, 63, 80, 88, 89, 99, 122, 136,
    157, 161

Dabundo, Laura, 12
Dacre, Charlotte, 10, 40
Dante Alighieri, 108
Darwall, Elizabeth, 31
Darwin, Erasmus, 129–30
Davidoff, Leonore, 17, 20, 49, 80
Davidson, Mary, 18
Davis, Gwenn, 11
Day, Thomas, 67
Daye, Eliza, 149, 150
Dekker, George, 15, 20
Deleuze, Gilles, 85
DeQuincey, Thomas, 154
Dickinson, Emily, 29, 41
Dictionary of Literary Biography, 19
Dictionary of National Biography, 19, 24, 109,
    149
Doane, Mary Ann, 62
Donovan, Josephine, 96
Drabble, Margaret, 12
Dunnett, Jane, 40, 44
Dyce, Alexander, 10, 70

Edgeworth, Maria, 16, 36, 79, 91–92, 162–63
Eichner, Hans, 46–47
Eldon, John Scott, Lord, 62
Elinor, Queen, 65
Ellison, Julie, 14, 18, 19, 20, 62
Elwood, Anne Katharine, 12
Erdman, David, 126
Evance, Susan, 43, 44
Ezell, Margaret J. M., 18, 64, 90

Faderman, Lillian, 15
Fanshawe, Catherine Maria, 36
Favret, Mary, 13, 15, 16, 18, 61
Faxon, Frederick W., 11, 38
Feldman, Paula R., 2, 9, 14, 157
Fell, Margaret, 166, 169
Fergus, Jean, 17–18
Ferguson, Frances, 18
Ferguson, Moira, 9, 11, 14, 15, 17, 59, 72–73,
    76–77
Ferriss, Ina, 17

Finch, Anne, 153
Fletcher, Mary Bosanquet, 64–65
Fliegelman, Jay, 61
Fortin, Nina, 17
Foster, Gretchen M., 9
Franklin, Caroline, 10
Freneau, Philip, 86–87
Furniss, Tom, 61
Fussell, Paul, 60

Gainsborough, Thomas, 37
Garnett, Catherine Grace, 31
Garrett, Jeremiah, 168–69
Gaull, Marilyn, 17, 19, 20
Gelpi, Barbara Charlesworth, 17
George, M. Dorothy, 18
Gibbon, Edward, 90
Gilbert, Sandra, 9, 15, 18, 20
Gilligan, Carol, 4, 18
Glaspell, Susan, 81
Godwin, William, 60–62, 90, 150
Goethe, Johann Wolfgang von, 123, 153
Goldberger, Avriel, 103
Goldberger, Nancy Rule, 18
Goldsmith, Oliver, 86, 158
Gorak, Jan, 51–52
Goslee, Nancy Moore, 14
Graff, Gerald, 18
Gray, Thomas, 86, 123
Greer, Germaine, 14
Grier, Roosevelt, 82
Grundy, Isobel, 12, 19
Guattari, Felix, 85
Gubar, Susan, 9, 15, 18, 20
Guest, Harriet, 16

Haefner, Joel, 13, 14
Hale, Sara Josepha, 10, 12
Hall, Catherine, 17, 20, 80
Harding, Anthony John, 14, 155
Hardy, Thomas, 61–62
Harris, James, 65
Hayden, John O., 12
Hayley, William, 125
Hays, Mary, 12, 59, 89, 130
Hazlitt, William, 20, 32–33
Heinzelman, Kurt, 16
Hemans, Felicia, 1, 5, 10, 26, 34, 38, 40, 48,
    52, 56, 60, 62, 63–64, 69–74, 81, 85–88,
    93–95, 101–05, 109, 110–20, 124, 128, 129,
    153–56
Hickok, Kathleen, 5, 15, 20
Hilbish, Florence, 12, 49
Hodgson, John, 56
Hoeveler, Diane Long, 19
Hofkosh, Sonia, 14, 16, 111
Hogg, James, 59
Holcroft, Thomas, 62

Holford, Margaret, 30–31, 41
Homans, Margaret, 2, 15, 16, 20, 88, 106
Homer, 66, 108
Howard, John, 150
Howell, T. B., 61
Howitt, Mary, 89
Hughes, Harriett Mary Browne, 114
Hume, David, 90–91
Hunt, Bishop C., Jr., 122
Hunt, Leigh, 20, 110
Hunt, Lynn, 61
Hunter, Anne, 43

Imlay, Gilbert, 98
Irwin, Joyce, 166

Jackson, J. R. de J., 11
Jacobus, Mary, 88
Jameson, Anna, 89–90
Jewsbury, Maria Jane, 119–20
Johnson, James, 34
Johnson, Joseph, 28
Johnson, Samuel, 65, 85, 129–30
Johnson-Eilola, Johndan, 47
Jones, Ann Rosalind, 18
Jones, Chris, 16
Jones, Vivien, 16, 49
Jordan, Winthrop, 66
Joyce, Beverly A., 11

Kaplan, Cora, 61
Kaplan, Nancy, 46
Kauffman, Linda S., 130
Keats, George, 109
Keats, Georgiana, 109
Keats, John, 3, 25, 42, 54, 59, 61, 101, 109,
    110–11, 116, 122, 124, 128, 137, 141,
    154–56, 157, 159, 162
Kelley, Theresa, 14
Kelly, Gary, 15
Kennedy, Deborah, 14, 16
Klancher, Jon, 17
Knapp, Samuel L., 12
Kohler, C. C., 40
Kohler, Michèle, 40
Kowaleski-Wallace, Elizabeth, 16, 75
Kraft, Elizabeth, 1, 9, 63
Kreissman, Bernard, 40
Kristeva, Julia, 18, 95–96
Krueger, Christine, 64
Kuist, James, 12

LaCassagnere, Christian, 161
Lamb, Charles, 83, 163
Lamb, Mary, 80–84, 163
Landon, Letitia Elizabeth (L. E. L.), 1, 5, 10,
    37, 38, 40, 48, 54, 60, 63–64, 109, 170–74
Landow, George P., 46–48

Landry, Donna, 5, 15, 72, 75, 151
Landseer, Edward, 37
Langbauer, Laurie, 15, 20, 131
Langland, Elizabeth, 18
Lanham, Richard, 48
Laqueur, Thomas, 62
Lawrence, Thomas, 37
Lee, Anna Maria, 12
Leighton, Angela, 15, 63, 112, 117, 155
Levin, Susan, 9, 15, 16, 19
Lewis, Matthew G., 109
Lickbarrow, Isabella, 9, 28–29
Lindenberger, Herbert, 57
Lindsay, Lady Anne, 32–33
Linkin, Harriet Kramer, 14, 18
Lipking, Lawrence, 56–57
Liu, Alan, 10
Lockhart, J. G., 11
Longfellow, Henry Wadsworth, 86–88
Lonsdale, Henry, 36
Lonsdale, Roger, 1, 9, 12, 18, 19, 20, 28, 75,
    157
Lootens, Tricia, 14
Louis XVI, 98
Lovejoy, Arthur O., 57
Lovell, Terry, 5
Lowth, Bishop Robert, 65
Luria, Gina, 13, 20
Luther, Susan, 16

Macaulay, Catherine, 89, 92–94
Mackenzie, Henry, 87
Malthus, Thomas, 90
Mandell, Laura, 10
Manning, Peter, 111
Marat, Jean-Paul, 61
Margolis, Joseph, 52, 57
Marie Antoinette, 60–61
Martin, John, 37
Martineau, Harriet, 89
Marvell, Andrew, 172
Matlak, Richard, 2, 9, 63, 67
Maxwell, Caroline, 40, 43–44
Maxwell, Patrick, 36
Mayhew, Henry, 49
McCarthy, William, 1, 9, 14, 63
McFarland, Thomas, 49
McGann, Jerome J., 1, 9, 10, 13, 17, 18, 45,
    63, 97, 101, 122
Mellor, Anne K., 2, 9, 13, 14, 16, 19, 20, 53,
    62, 63, 67–68, 88, 91, 93, 101, 140, 153, 162
Merry, Robert, 130
Miall, David, 1
Michaels, Walter Benn, 78
Miller, George ("Humanitas"), 150
Milton, John, 103, 108, 111, 123
Mitford, Mary Russell, 40, 49
Moers, Ellen, 15, 117

Montagu, Elizabeth, 30, 142
Moody, Elizabeth, 149, 150
Moore, Jane, 16
Moore, Thomas, 29, 109
More, Hannah, 30, 52, 67, 69, 72–74, 75–78,
    82, 85, 89, 91, 106, 112, 141–43, 145, 162
Morton, Sarah Wentworth, 85
Moulthrop, Stuart, 46
Myers, Mitzi, 9, 16, 82, 163, 164
Myers, Sylvia Haverstock, 15

Nairne, Carolina, Baroness, 33–34
Nangle, Benjamin Christie, 12
Napoleon Bonaparte, 60, 101
Nelson, Theodor, 45–46
Newton, Judith Lowder, 15
Nichols, John Boyer, 12–13

Olds, Sharon, 161
O'Neill, Frances, 29–30
Opie, Amelia, 10, 62, 67–68
Opie, John, 37
Ostriker, Alicia, 43, 162
Outram, Dorinda, 61
Owenson, Sydney, Lady Morgan, 29, 109
Ovid, 102, 164

Pagan, Isabel, 34–35
Page, Judith, 19, 20, 136
Paine, Thomas, 60–61, 90, 127, 169
Pascoe, Judith, 9, 14, 49
Paterson, James, 34, 35
Pawson, Frances, 65
Penn, William, 76
Perkins, David, 2, 9, 18
Petrarch, Francesco, 101, 122
Phillips, Janetta, 42
Pinch, Adela, 86, 88
Piozzi, Hester, 89, 130
Pizarro, Francisco, 67
Plutarch, 102–05
Polwhele, Richard, 74
Poovey, Mary, 15, 19, 20
Pope, Alexander, 42, 85–86, 123, 130, 133
Prance, Claude A., 12
Priestley, Joseph, 45
Prigge, Bill, 48
Prince, Mary, 59, 79
Prior, Mary, 18
Purinton, Marjean, 93

Quigley, Catherine, 29

Rabine, Leslie, 15, 19
Radcliffe, Ann, 71, 72, 87, 131
Rajan, Tilottama, 59
Redpath, Jean, 34
Reiman, Donald, 10

Reynolds, Joshua, 37
Rhys, Jean, 108
Rice, John, 166
Richardson, Alan, 14, 17, 18, 67, 164
Rieder, John, 18
Riga, Frank, 12
Rivers, Isabel, 17
Robertson, Eric S., 12
Robinson, Daniel, 14
Robinson, Henry Crabb, 62
Robinson, Mary, 5, 9, 10, 27, 40, 43, 47, 49,
    58, 62, 68, 71, 80, 106, 129, 130, 165
Rogers, Hester Ann, 65
Rogers, Katharine M., 9
Rogers, Samuel, 26
Roland, Jeanne Manon, Madame, 61
Roscoe, Jane Elizabeth, 31
Roscoe, William, 31
Ross, Marlon, 2, 13, 14, 18, 19, 20, 49, 54, 86,
    88, 94, 101, 136, 153
Rossetti, William Michael, 20
Rousseau, Jean-Jacques, 58, 80–81, 123, 130,
    133
Rowe, Elizabeth Singer, 129
Rowton, Frederic, 10, 11, 70, 74
Rubin, Gayle, 18
Russell, Henry, 170, 172

Sappho, 43, 64, 71
Scheffler, Judith, 16
Scott, Joan Wallach, 96
Scott, Walter, 26, 29, 33, 37, 88
Scrivener, Michael, 72
Seaman, David, 10
Seward, Anna, 5, 9–10, 16, 54–55, 71, 106,
    129–34
Sexton, Ann, 108
Shakespeare, William, 108, 123
Shelley, Mary Wollstonecraft, 37, 60, 89
Shelley, Percy Bysshe, 3, 42, 46, 48, 49, 61, 62,
    88, 101, 103, 105, 109, 128, 129, 141,
    155–56, 157
Shevelow, Kathryn, 17
Showalter, Elaine, 15, 20, 96
Sigourney, Lydia, 64
Silverman, Kenneth, 85
Sismondi, J. C. L. Simonde, de, 103–04
Skarstad, John, 42
Smith, Barbara Herrnstein, 51
Smith, Catherine F., 47
Smith, Charlotte, 1, 5, 10, 25, 27, 40, 43–44,
    48–50, 60, 63, 67–68, 69, 72, 74, 75, 85, 86,
    97–100, 106, 121–28, 131, 163–64
Smith, George, 49
Smith, Olivia, 65–66
Smith, R. A., 33–34
Smith, Sidonie, 165

Southcott, Joanna, 69, 71, 74, 165–69
Southey, Robert, 26, 67, 78
Spacks, Patricia Meyer, 15
Spencer, Jane, 15, 19
Spencer, Mrs. W., 40, 43
Spender, Dale, 5
Spenser, Edmund, 108
Staël, Germaine de, 43, 62, 102, 103–04, 116–20
Stanford, Ann, 9
Stanton, Judith Phillips, 17
Steele, Richard, 85
Stephenson, Glennis, 2, 14, 63
Stone, Lawrence, 17
Strout, Alan, 12
Sullivan, Alvin, 11
Swann, Karen, 88
Swartz, Richard G., 13
Sweet, Nanora, 13, 86, 103, 153
Swift, Jonathan, 86

Tarule, Jill Mattuck, 18
Tayler, Irene, 13, 15, 20
Taylor, Ann, 17, 38, 82–83, 162
Taylor, Jane, 17, 27, 38, 80–83, 157, 162
Tennyson, Alfred, Lord, 37, 114–15
Thaddeus, Janice Farrar, 17–18
Thelwall, John, 61–62
Thompson, Julia, 36
Thomson, James, 86, 123, 125, 158
Tighe, Mary, 10, 40, 70, 85, 106–09, 115, 129
Todd, Janet, 12, 15, 17, 123
Tompkins, Jane, 59
Tooke, John Horne, 61
Tooth, Mary, 65
Trimmer, Sarah, 163
Tristram, Philippa, 136
Tuchman, Gaye, 5, 17
Tucker, Herbert R., 101
Turner, Cheryl, 5, 16
Turner, John, 46
Turner, Joseph Mallord William, 37
Ty, Eleanor, 15–16, 49

Uphaus, Robert W., 9
Upton, William, 162

Vallon, Annette, 98
Vane, Henry, 92, 94

Vergil, 66
von der Wart, Gertrude, 65

Waldron, Mary, 14
Walker, Cheryl, 43, 63
Ward, William S., 11
Warren, Mercy Otis, 85
Warton, Thomas, 123
Watson, Nicola, 13, 18
Watts, Alaric A., 37
Weitzman, Arthur J., 51
Wellek, René, 19
Wendt, Ingrid, 81
Wesley, John, 65
Wesley, Susanna, 65
Whale, John, 18
Whateley, Mary, 31
Wheatley, Phillis, 70–71, 85–86, 166, 168
Whitelaw, Alex, 35
Whitman, Walt, 164
Whittaker, Thomas, 48
Williams, Helen Maria, 5, 10, 40, 60–61, 67–68, 69, 72, 79, 89
Williams, Jane, 12
Williamson, Marilyn, 11
Wilson, Carol Shiner, 13, 14
Wilson, James Grant, 33
Wolfson, Susan J., 13, 16, 18, 88, 95, 103, 111, 162
Wollstonecraft, Mary, 33, 60–62, 66, 80, 82, 83, 87, 89–92, 97–100, 127–28, 130, 162, 164, 166
Women Writers Project, 10, 27, 28, 31, 45
Woodring, Carl, 13
Wordsworth, Dorothy, 5, 53–54, 58–59, 85, 99, 106, 127–28, 144–47, 161
Wordsworth, Jonathan, 9
Wordsworth, William, 3, 25, 28–29, 31, 32, 37, 44, 46–49, 52–56, 58–62, 67, 80–82, 86–87, 97–100, 106, 114, 121–24, 127–28, 129, 131, 133–34, 136, 141–47, 150, 153, 157–59, 161–62
Wu, Duncan, 1, 9, 59–60, 63

Yaeger, Patricia, 15
Yearsley, Ann, 10, 30, 67–68, 71–74, 75–78, 106, 127, 141–47
Young, Edward, 123
Young, Robert J. C., 78
Yudin, Mary, 136

Modern Language Association of America
Approaches to Teaching World Literature
Joseph Gibaldi, series editor

Achebe's Things Fall Apart. Ed. Bernth Lindfors. 1991.

Arthurian Tradition. Ed. Maureen Fries and Jeanie Watson. 1992.

Atwood's The Handmaid's Tale *and Other Works*. Ed. Sharon R. Wilson, Thomas B. Friedman, and Shannon Hengen. 1996.

Austen's Pride and Prejudice. Ed. Marcia McClintock Folsom. 1993.

Beckett's Waiting for Godot. Ed. June Schlueter and Enoch Brater. 1991.

Beowulf. Ed. Jess B. Bessinger, Jr., and Robert F. Yeager. 1984.

Blake's Songs of Innocence and of Experience. Ed. Robert F. Gleckner and Mark L. Greenberg. 1989.

British Women Poets of the Romantic Period. Ed. Stephen C. Behrendt and Harriet Kramer Linkin. 1997.

Brontë's Jane Eyre. Ed. Diane Long Hoeveler and Beth Lau. 1993.

Byron's Poetry. Ed. Frederick W. Shilstone. 1991.

Camus's The Plague. Ed. Steven G. Kellman. 1985.

Cather's My Ántonia. Ed. Susan J. Rosowski. 1989.

Cervantes' Don Quixote. Ed. Richard Bjornson. 1984.

Chaucer's Canterbury Tales. Ed. Joseph Gibaldi. 1980.

Chopin's The Awakening. Ed. Bernard Koloski. 1988.

Coleridge's Poetry and Prose. Ed. Richard E. Matlak. 1991.

Dante's Divine Comedy. Ed. Carole Slade. 1982.

Dickens' David Copperfield. Ed. Richard J. Dunn. 1984.

Dickinson's Poetry. Ed. Robin Riley Fast and Christine Mack Gordon. 1989.

Eliot's Middlemarch. Ed. Kathleen Blake. 1990.

Eliot's Poetry and Plays. Ed. Jewel Spears Brooker. 1988.

Ellison's Invisible Man. Ed. Susan Resneck Parr and Pancho Savery. 1989.

Faulkner's The Sound and the Fury. Ed. Stephen Hahn and Arthur F. Kinney. 1996.

Flaubert's Madame Bovary. Ed. Laurence M. Porter and Eugene F. Gray. 1995.

García Márquez's One Hundred Years of Solitude. Ed. María Elena de Valdés and Mario J. Valdés. 1990.

Goethe's Faust. Ed. Douglas J. McMillan. 1987.

Hebrew Bible as Literature in Translation. Ed. Barry N. Olshen and Yael S. Feldman. 1989.

Homer's Iliad *and* Odyssey. Ed. Kostas Myrsiades. 1987.

Ibsen's A Doll House. Ed. Yvonne Shafer. 1985.

Works of Samuel Johnson. Ed. David R. Anderson and Gwin J. Kolb. 1993.

Joyce's Ulysses. Ed. Kathleen McCormick and Erwin R. Steinberg. 1993.

Kafka's Short Fiction. Ed. Richard T. Gray. 1995.

Keats's Poetry. Ed. Walter H. Evert and Jack W. Rhodes. 1991.

Kingston's The Woman Warrior. Ed. Shirley Geok-lin Lim. 1991.

Lessing's The Golden Notebook. Ed. Carey Kaplan and Ellen Cronan Rose. 1989.

Mann's Death in Venice *and Other Short Fiction*. Ed. Jeffrey B. Berlin. 1992.

Medieval English Drama. Ed. Richard K. Emmerson. 1990.

Melville's Moby-Dick. Ed. Martin Bickman. 1985.

Metaphysical Poets. Ed. Sidney Gottlieb. 1990.

Miller's Death of a Salesman. Ed. Matthew C. Roudané. 1995.

Milton's Paradise Lost. Ed. Galbraith M. Crump. 1986.

Molière's Tartuffe *and Other Plays*. Ed. James F. Gaines and
      Michael S. Koppisch. 1995.

Momaday's The Way to Rainy Mountain. Ed. Kenneth M. Roemer. 1988.

Montaigne's Essays. Ed. Patrick Henry. 1994.

Novels of Toni Morrison. Ed. Nellie Y. McKay and Kathryn Earle. 1997.

Murasaki Shikibu's The Tale of Genji. Ed. Edward Kamens. 1993.

Pope's Poetry. Ed. Wallace Jackson and R. Paul Yoder. 1993.

Shakespeare's King Lear. Ed. Robert H. Ray. 1986.

Shakespeare's The Tempest *and Other Late Romances*. Ed. Maurice Hunt. 1992.

Shelley's Frankenstein. Ed. Stephen C. Behrendt. 1990.

Shelley's Poetry. Ed. Spencer Hall. 1990.

Sir Gawain and the Green Knight. Ed. Miriam Youngerman Miller and
      Jane Chance. 1986.

Spenser's Faerie Queene. Ed. David Lee Miller and Alexander Dunlop. 1994.

Sterne's Tristram Shandy. Ed. Melvyn New. 1989.

Swift's Gulliver's Travels. Ed. Edward J. Rielly. 1988.

Thoreau's Walden *and Other Works*. Ed. Richard J. Schneider. 1996.

Voltaire's Candide. Ed. Renée Waldinger. 1987.

Whitman's Leaves of Grass. Ed. Donald D. Kummings. 1990.

Wordsworth's Poetry. Ed. Spencer Hall, with Jonathan Ramsey. 1986.

Wright's Native Son. Ed. James A. Miller. 1997.